CHARACTER CONSTELLATIONS

REPRESENTATIONS OF SOCIAL GROUPS
IN PRESENT-DAY DUTCH LITERARY FICTION

CHARACTER CONSTELLATIONS

REPRESENTATIONS OF SOCIAL GROUPS IN PRESENT-DAY DUTCH LITERARY FICTION

Roel Smeets

Leuven University Press

Published with the support of
KU Leuven Fund for Fair Open Acces
The Graduate School for the Humanities of the Radboud University
Hendrik Mullerfonds
J. E. Jurriaanse Stichting

Published in 2021 by Leuven University Press / Presses Universitaires de Louvain / Universitaire Pers Leuven. Minderbroedersstraat 4, B-3000 Leuven (Belgium).

© 2021 Roel Smeets

This book is published under a Creative Commons Attribution Non-Commercial Non-Derivative 4.0 Licence.

Further details about Creative Commons licences are available at http://creativecommons.org/licenses/
Attribution should include the following information:
Roel Smeets, *Character Constellations: Representations of Social Groups in Present-Day Dutch Literary Fiction. Leuven 2021, Leuven University Press. (CC BY-NC-ND 4.0)*

ISBN 978 94 6270 295 0 (Paperback)
ISBN 978 94 6166 412 9 (ePDF)
ISBN 978 94 6166 413 6 (ePUB)
https://doi.org/10.11116/9789461664129
D/2021/1869/46
NUR: 617

Layout: Friedemann Vervoort
Cover design: Daniel Benneworth-Gray

CONTENTS

Chapter 1: Introduction — 9

  1.1 Introduction: Character Constellations — 9

    1.1.1 Example: Character Constellations in Joost Zwagerman's *De buitenvrouw* (1994) and Robert Vuijsje's *Alleen maar nette mensen* (2008) — 11

    1.1.2 Delineation of the Study and Research Question — 14

    1.1.3 Character Studies — 18

    1.1.4 Characterization and Character Types — 20

    1.1.5 The One Versus the Many — 24

  1.2. Critique of Representation — 25

    1.2.1 Representation and Ideology — 25

    1.2.2 Critiques of Representation in Dutch Literature — 31

  1.3. Cultural Analytics — 34

    1.3.1 Debates on Distant versus Close Reading — 34

    1.3.2 Modeling in Cultural Analytics — 39

  1.4 Methodological Background — 43

    1.4.1 Tools: Narratology and Network Analysis — 43

    1.4.2 Corpus and Data — 45

    1.4.3 Previous Research on Corpus and Dataset — 47

  1.5 Structure of the Book and Instruction for Reading — 48

Chapter 2: Data — 51

  2.1 Introduction: Descriptive Statistics — 51

  2.2 Information on the Authors — 52

  2.3 Demographic Metadata on the Characters — 52

  2.4 (In)Dependence of Variables — 55

2.5 Relational Information	58
2.6 Interpretation of Descriptive Statistics	59

Chapter 3: Centrality — 63

3.1 Introduction: Narrative Cornerstones	63
3.2 Centrality in Network Theory	64
3.3 Centrality in Narratology	68
3.4 Method for Extracting Character Networks	71
3.4.1 Characters as Nodes	71
3.4.2 Character Relations as Edges	74
3.4.3 Automatic Extraction of Character Networks	75
3.5 Model I: Character Rankings	79
3.5.1 Results Multiple Regression Analysis	79
3.5.2 Close Reading: Centrality, Gender, and Descent in Özcan Akyol's *Eus* (2012)	82
3.6 Conclusion to this Chapter	93

Chapter 4: Community — 97

4.1 Introduction: Narrative Connections	97
4.2 Community in Network Theory	100
4.2.1 Community Detection	101
4.2.2 Homophily	105
4.3 Community in Narratology	108
4.3.1 Syntagmatic and Paradigmatic Collectives	108
4.3.2 Dialogic Interaction and Polyphony	110
4.4 Model I: Community Detection	113
4.4.1 Clauset-Newman-Moore and Girvan-Newman Algorithms	114
4.4.2 Kernighan-Lin Bisection Algorithm	116
4.4.3 Close Reading: Communities in Philip Huff's *Niemand in de stad* (2012)	122
4.5 Model II: Homophily	133
4.5.1 Dyad Assortativity	134
4.5.2 Close Reading: Homophily in Mensje van Keulen's *Liefde heeft geen hersens* (2012)	142
4.6 Conclusion to this Chapter	148

Chapter 5: Conflict — 151
  5.1 Introduction: Narrative Clashes — 151
  5.2 Conflict in Network Theory — 154
  5.3 Conflict in Narratology — 157
  5.4 Model I: Hierarchies in One-on-one Conflicts — 161
    5.4.1 Conflict Scores — 162
    5.4.2 Results of Multiple Linear Regression — 164
    5.4.3 Close Reading: Class Conflicts between Two Characters in Bart Koubaa's *De Brooklynclub* (2012) — 166
  5.5 Model II: Social Balance in Triangular Conflicts — 171
    5.5.1 Automatic Modeling of Social Balance in Enemy/Friend triads — 173
    5.5.2 Social Balance in Leon de Winter's *VSV, of daden van onbaatzuchtigheid* — 176
    5.5.3 Social Imbalance in Tommy Wieringa's *Dit zijn de namen* — 180
  5.6 Conclusion to this Chapter — 187

Chapter 6: Conclusion — 191
  6.1 Findings of the Book — 191
  6.2 Public Debates on Literary Representation — 199
  6.3 Future Research — 202

Appendix A: Statistical tests — 205

Appendix B: Distribution of Relational Roles — 209

Appendix C: Main and Interaction Effects — 219

Appendix D: Pearson Correlations — 221

Notes — 223

References — 239

CHAPTER 1

INTRODUCTION[1]

1.1 INTRODUCTION: CHARACTER CONSTELLATIONS

Like the stars in the sky, the arrangement of fictional characters in literary texts form patterns we might call 'constellations'.[2] Constellations are products of imagination: they are not just there but emerge in the eye of the beholder. Ancient cultures have looked closely at the celestial sphere and discovered images of animals, gods, and mythological creatures in the arrangement of the stars and interpreted those images in light of specific time- and place-related norms, values, and beliefs. In a similar vein, yesterday's, today's, and tomorrow's readers ascribe different meanings to the patterns they discover in the interrelations between characters in narrative fiction. Unlike the stars, however, characters populating books do not change in shape or position. Whereas constellations of stars eventually – although very slowly – transform into different images due to the stars' relative position to planet earth, character constellations remain the same with the passing of time because characters occur in fixed positions in the pages of the book. Unless a story is rewritten, characters will not move an inch from their position in the narrative's linguistic structure. But readers change and so do the images they discover in the relative positions characters occupy in texts.

    This book is about the 'images' of social groups of people that can be discovered in the character constellations in present-day Dutch literary fiction. Through the metaphor of character constellations, it attempts to ground discussions on literary representation in the immovable, fixed positions of characters at the sentence level while leaving room for different interpretations of the images of social groups these characters represent. Just like the ancient people searched for patterns in the stars to gain insight into the world around them, unraveling patterns between fictional characters contributes to a better understanding of the literary representations of people circulating in the world in which these books were written. A deeper insight into depictions of particular groups of people in recent Dutch language fiction may shed light on norms, values, and beliefs associated with the social dichotomies of, for instance, men as opposed to women, people with or without a migration background,[3] the less as opposed to the higher educated, and the young as opposed to the old.

As the literary representation of people with different demographic backgrounds and identities has been subject to heated ideological discussions, the present study ventures into precarious waters. In academia these discussions take place within the critique of literary representation focusing on characters (see section 1.2 of this chapter). Through detailed close readings, this branch of literary criticism has disentangled various representations of people with a particular gender, descent, race, ethnicity, class, age, sexuality, or other identity category in light of Marxist, feminist, postcolonial, or other ideologically oriented theoretical strands. Often, such studies have – more or less convincingly – argued that hierarchies, biases, and inequalities are apparent in the ways in which different social groups are depicted in particular texts. What these discussions have lacked up to the present is a methodology for measuring the relative positions of characters in the narrative similar to the tools astronomers use to measure the relative positions of stars.

This book argues that such a methodology is crucial for a broader and deeper understanding of representations of social groups. One of its premises is that 'images' of social groups arise in the interrelations between characters, just as stars form patterns only in relation to other stars. Building on that idea, it proposes, applies, and evaluates a range of data-driven, statistical models to trace the interrelations between 2,137 identified characters in a sample corpus of 170 Dutch books of literary fiction published in 2012, for which extensive metadata (gender, descent, educational level, age, profession) were gathered (see section 1.4.2 of this chapter for more information). Formalizing the metaphor of character constellations, these models incorporate the tools of network analysis to detect and analyze interrelations between characters. This is done by generating fictional social networks for each of the 170 novels based on co-occurrences of characters on the sentence level, an approach which is described in detail in chapter 3. Each chapter subsequently highlights an aspect of these fictional social networks that affects the representation of social groups: their centrality (which types of characters are important or dominant), their communities (how characters are integrated or segregated into distinct groups), and their conflicts (the clashes between different social groups). Following recent developments within the field of cultural analytics (see section 1.3), these network analytical models are then used in the individual chapters to recursively go back and forth between statistical, pattern-based analysis and qualitative close readings of particular case studies from this corpus. As such, the results generated by the models developed throughout this book showcase what character-based critiques of literary representation gain by integrating data-driven methods into the practice of critical close reading.

By combining the formal methods of social network analysis with the interpretive tools of narratology in these models, this book thus opts for a data-driven critique of literary representation of which both measuring and reading are indispensable parts. The thesis it defends is that the literary representation of social groups is hierarchically structured along the axes of centrality, community, and conflict. This approach yields insights into the representation of social groups in a large body of texts from one sample year of Dutch literary production, and potentially as well into its changing dynamics throughout literary history, paving the way for future longitudinal research to extend the models and their findings presented here.[4] Merging the critique of literary representation as evolving in the Netherlands from the 1990s onwards with more recent developments of data-driven approaches to culture within the field of cultural analytics, it hopes to contribute to a fruitful debate between research traditions and between quantitative and qualitative methodologies. In each of the chapters this is done by confronting the statistical, quantitative patterns with qualitative close readings of selected case studies from the corpus pinpointing which parts of the patterns are reflected or deconstructed.

1.1.1 Example: Character Constellations in Joost Zwagerman's *De buitenvrouw* (1994) and Robert Vuijsje's *Alleen maar nette mensen* (2008)

Discussions on two books of Dutch literary fiction published within a range of 14 years may serve to exemplify the relevance of this book's theoretical and methodological approach. On a thematic level, Joost Zwagerman's *De buitenvrouw* [The mistress] (1994) and Robert Vuijsje's *Alleen maar nette mensen* [Only decent people] (2008) show striking resemblances. Both novels comment on

Dutch multicultural society by staging Dutch-born, male protagonists who have sexual desires for black female characters. Sensitive topics such as racism and colonialism are addressed through Theo Altena's extramarital relation with the Dutch-Surinamese Iris Pompier in *De buitenvrouw* and through David's search for the 'intellectual negress' in *Alleen maar nette mensen*. Although both novels could count on critical acclaim and/or institutional recognition,[5] they received negative criticism for the ways in which black women are depicted. Most notably, public intellectual Anil Ramdas accused Zwagerman of a flat, stereotypical portrayal of his main character's black mistress (1997). 'We know what she smells like (nut oil and dewy woodland)', he writes, 'but not what she thinks'.[6] In response to Vuijsje's novel, gender and ethnicity scholar Gloria Wekker contended that it seems hard for Dutch authors 'to write about black women and to not associate them with sexuality' (Meershoek, 2009).[7] In turn, the ideological objections against Zwagerman's and Vuijsje's literary representation of black women were met with equally fierce arguments emphasizing the autonomous and therefore inviolable position of the literary author (Zwagerman, 1997; Van Aalten, 2009).[8]

Although these discussions show a strong disagreement about the representation of the social group of black women as emerging from these two novels (critics such as Ramdas and Wekker emphasize their offensiveness, while the authors stress that these representations function as part of an autonomous literary-artistic endeavor), all those involved base their interpretations on the same words, sentences, and literary-stylistic configurations present in the texts. While both critics and authors stare at the same sky (novel), they discover different images in the patterns of the stars (characters) and interpret those images in light of their own norms, values, and beliefs. It is, furthermore, fully understandable that the authors and their critics ascribe different meanings to the patterns they see in these novels. As creators of these patterns, authors Zwagerman and Vuijsje might have stronger inclinations to defend the images of black women emerging from their novels as a crucial part of their literary-artistic vision. Conversely, the criticism on the depictions of black women by Ramdas and Wekker can partly be understood in light of their personal background (both were born in Suriname) and their political beliefs (both are known for their outspoken ideas on racial inequality in Dutch society). Without suggesting that one image is more correct than the other, the methodology developed in this book serves to guide such discussions on the representation of social groups by mapping out the concrete coordinates of characters, in order to provide an empirically informed blueprint of the character constellations present in the texts.

The following is what this approach could yield for the narrative worlds presented in Zwagerman's *De buitenvrouw* and Vuijsje's *Alleen maar nette mensen*. A cursory examination of these novels in terms of social networks of characters – or character constellations – helps to pinpoint some basic aspects of their depiction of social groups, of which this book highlights three: centrality, community, and conflict. In terms of centrality or importance, both Dutch-born, male protagonists – Theo (*De buitenvrouw*) and David (*Alleen maar nette mensen*) – are mentioned considerably more often than the black women they desire, and the frequency with which their thoughts and feelings are described stands in sharp contrast with what the readers get to know about the inner lives of the black female characters. The primary focus lies on the perspectives of Theo and David, which makes them the center of attention and makes it *their* stories and less those of Iris and Rowanda. In terms of the groups or communities in which the characters function, the novels are segregated by ethnicity and descent. In *De buitenvrouw*, Iris and Theo are part of the same community of teaching staff at a Dutch high school, but she remains an outsider as she is also part of a community of Surinamese migrants with language and norms exotic to the Dutch-born characters. An even stronger contrast is apparent in the communities in which David and Rowanda in *Alleen maar nette mensen* function: David was born and raised in an elite Amsterdam neighborhood where mostly rich people without a migration background live, whereas Rowanda lives in a black neighborhood full of criminal activity. The protagonists of both books make attempts to become part of these other, exotic communities, but this does not result in an integration between social groups. The segregation between these communities, finally, signals the conflicts and disparities between the Dutch-born, male protagonists on the one hand and the black female characters on the other. Both Iris and Rowanda witness racist remarks of people from the other community, and at the end of the novels they both exclude their Dutch love interests from their own community, resulting in antagonism and polarization between both represented social groups.

Such a blueprint of character constellations can serve as a point of departure for a discussion on the representation of social groups in these novels.[9] In whichever way one might interpret the status of Iris in *De buitenvrouw* and Rowanda in *Alleen maar nette mensen* within the fictional societies depicted in these books, crucial to their centrality, their communities, and their conflicts in the narratives is how often and where they occur, and with whom they interact in which specific way. Although other elements also play a part, aspects of centrality, community, and conflict are co-constitutive of the hierarchical orders underlying the novels' representation of black women as opposed to white men. As literary scholar Philippe Hamon has noted, reading inevitably involves a process of hierarchization in which narrative elements such as characters are placed by the reader in a 'value system', privileging some and downgrading others (1984, p. 54).[10] The claim of this book is that such hierarchies can be studied by both reading and measuring the textual elements these hierarchies are composed of. The literary representation of social groups contains an inevitable quantitative component; counting simple occurrences of characters can already provide a first indication of their status in the text. However, counting is meaningless without reading; it requires the interpretive act associated with it. The status of Iris and Rowanda is not reducible to their occurrences in the narrative; such counts have to be put in the broader thematic and stylistic context of the novel and the world it was produced in. For that reason, the present study goes back and forth between computer-assisted, quantitative analysis on the corpus of 170 novels as a whole and fine-grained, qualitative readings of particular case studies.

1.1.2 Delineation of the Study and Research Question

The contribution of the present study to the field of character-based critiques of literary representation is to develop an empirical, data-driven account of character constellations in the novelistic genre in combination with a narratological evaluation of these accounts. This book inquires into characters populating the Dutch literary field for the simple reason that I was trained in the literature of this language, but it should be possible, with a few language-specific adjustments, to apply its methods to the literature from any other language field. The focus lies on Dutch literature from the present day and age, and more specifically on a corpus of 170 Dutch books of literary fiction from 2012.[11] Although literature from other time periods could also have been the object of focus, the current (Dutch) sociocultural climate provides an argument for studying today's rather than yesterday's literature. The increasing awareness of social, cultural, and economic hierarchies in a variety of societal domains invokes the question of how literature deals with these issues.[12] It simply makes sense to study the representation of social groups in works of literary fiction produced in the same period that fueled attention to the hierarchical societal structures these groups are embedded in.

Case studies from this corpus are selected on the basis of two criteria: 1) Degree of conformation to or deviation from the statistics-based patterns generated by the data-driven models applied to the whole corpus of 170 novels. Novels that seem to fit these models perfectly showcase how the observed statistical patterns are illustrated on the micro-level of individual works, whereas novels that are outliers to the models demonstrate how individual works have the ability to nuance or deconstruct these statistical patterns. 2) Themes related to the topic of the chapter (centrality, community, conflict). Based on cursory examinations of novels that either conform to or deviate from the statistical patterns, works were selected for their depiction of characters from a certain gender, descent, education, or age as more or less central, as more or less belonging to a community, and as more or less engaged in conflict.

In the chapter on centrality, Özcan Akyol's *Eus* (2012) is analyzed because its portrayal of characters with a migration background and female characters simultaneously conforms to and deviates from the model's findings on how central these types of characters are in the corpus as a whole. In the chapter on community, both Philip Huff's *Niemand in de stad* [Nobody in the city] (2012) and Mensje van Keulen's *Liefde heeft geen hersens* [Love has no brains] (2012) demonstrate how the model's findings on segregation and integration between groups is partly reflected and partly deconstructed through particular narrative mechanisms. In the chapter on conflict, the depiction of social class in Bart Koubaa's *De Brooklynclub* [The Brooklyn club] (2012) provides a good example of how one-on-one conflicts between characters take shape within a single narrative and shows how the narrative strategies comment on the found statistical observation regarding such conflicts. Leon de Winter's *VSV, of daden van onbaatzuchtigheid* [VSV, or acts of altruism] (2012) is used in the same chapter to explore how triangular conflicts (between three characters) contribute to a moral privileging of one social group over another, while Tommy Wieringa's *Dit zijn de namen* [These are the names] (2012) deconstructs such a schematic opposition between groups through its narrative conflicts.

The question 'How are social groups represented in present-day Dutch literature?' forms the basis of this book. Underlying this question is the assumption that characters in novels constitute a fictional population that can be studied with the same tools as those used by social science scholars studying real-world populations. This assumption invokes age-old discussions dating back to Plato (*The Republic*, book 10, c. 375 BC) and Aristotle (*Poetics*, 335 BC) on the question of whether fiction is a mimesis, a reflection, of society – and more specifically, whether social structures are mirrored in literary fiction.

Eric Auerbach's *Mimesis: The Representation of Reality in Western Literature* (1946/2003) is commonly regarded as the seminal twentieth-century study on the alleged mimetic power of literature. Roughly, this book follows Auerbach's approach in the sense that it also foregrounds the relation between the artistic dimensions of the literary work and the sociopolitical context it emerged from. In the current study, this 'real-world' context is rather specific: it targets the ways in which concrete social structures are represented in the social networks of characters in the literature of a specific period. There is, however, a radical methodological difference between this book and Auerbach's approach. Whereas Auerbach generalizes about the literary work's represented reality based on single, allegedly exemplary cases, the present study grounds its generalizations in data-driven observations within a larger, representative body of texts and evaluates the resulting statistical patterns through close readings of case studies. By analyzing the characters in the corpus as a fictional population with social networks similar to those of actual populations, this book furthermore explores and assesses the applicability of the sociological methods of network analysis to fictional narratives. In doing so, the book's focus on the person-like qualities of characters, alongside their textual dimensions, also works to break a taboo in literary criticism: treating characters as if they were real people. Recently, Toril Moi traced back the historical roots of this taboo to L. C. Knights' essay *How Many Children Had Lady Macbeth* (1933) and demonstrated that it is 'intertwined with the promotion of a specific understanding of modernist aesthetics and with the belief that formalist analysis is the raison d'être of professional literary criticism' (Moi, 2019, p. 61). Following Moi's argument that this taboo evolved into an untenable dogma, the present study examines *both* the textual and the person-like dimensions of characters in order to enable a full picture of how groups of people are represented in narrative fiction. This study does not, however, make any claims as to answering the million-dollar-question of how narrative fiction reflects societal tendencies.[13] In order to arrive at the contours of an answer to that question within the framework of the present research, a structural comparison between real-world social structures and fictional structures should be made.[14] While applying the analytical tools used for studying real-world populations, this book focuses on the narrative fiction itself. The central research question of how social groups are represented in the fictional character populations in the corpus is examined through three general themes related to the structure of the fictional social networks, each of which forms a sub-question:

Central question: How are social groups represented in present-day Dutch literature?
Sub-question 1: How does the centrality of characters co-shape the representation of the social group(s) characters function in?

Sub-question 2: How do the communities in which characters function co-shape the representation of the social group(s) characters function in?
Sub-question 3: How do conflicts between characters co-shape the representation of the social group(s) characters function in?

Underlying each of the three sub-questions is the hypothesis that the fictional populations are structured according to a hierarchical order (cf. Woloch, 2003). The first question tests this most straightforwardly by exploring the various ways in which characters can be central, important, influential, or dominant in the narrative worlds they inhabit. The second and third questions build more indirectly on this hypothesis. By studying the communities in which characters function, insight can be gained into the degree to which the different social groups are either integrated with other character types in the fictional population or segregated into different clusters – who does and who does not belong to a specific group. Finally, the conflicts between characters illustrate the ways in which clashes between social groups produce hierarchies within the fictional population. The centrality, communities, and conflicts of characters are thus taken to co-constitute an answer to the question of how social groups are depicted in present-day Dutch literary fiction.

'Social group' is a rather broad term used in the social sciences to denote collections of people with similar social, cultural, or economic features. For the sake of clarity, this book focuses on only four of those features: gender, descent, education, and age.[15] Not only are these features the most common variables in studies on actual social networks, they are also defining features of characters, as was first described by Aristotle in his *Rhetoric* (cited in Florack, 2010, p. 479). Subsequently, characters are categorized in the following analyses as functioning in social groups consisting of either male or female characters, characters either with or without a migration background, either higher or lower educated characters, and either older or younger characters.

Literary criticism focusing on such identity categories – the so-called 'critique of representation' – forms one of the two pillars of the theoretical framework underlying the analyses carried out in this book. The other pillar is constituted by the field of cultural analytics, a subfield of digital humanities in which data-driven methods are used to model culture and narrative quantitatively, often from a social or ideological perspective. The remainder of this chapter sketches the contours of the twofold theoretical framework in which the research is situated. Section 1.2 describes how the concepts of representation and ideology have been used in scholarly critiques of literary representation and makes clear how these concepts are defined and operationalized in this book, as well as what the book's place is in the scholarly debate on Dutch literature in particular. In section 1.3, the data-driven aspect of the research is outlined by delineating how it fits within the debates on close and distant reading, particularly with regard to the notion of modeling as operationalized in the field of cultural analytics. The methodological background of the study is described in section 1.4, namely, the tools of narratology and network analysis, the corpus and dataset, and previous studies on the corpus and data. But before the theoretical and methodological frameworks are delineated, some basic questions have to be answered regarding the central analytical unit of this book: characters. What are we talking about when we talk about characters?

1.1.3 Character Studies

Fictional characters in novels are the primary point of focus of this book. Although the concept of character might seem ubiquitous and common sense (don't we simply know what characters are?), the vast number of studies disentangling its complexities suggests otherwise. As the topic has been studied in various disciplines and from a wide variety of theoretical angles, character studies have long been a dispersed area of research (Heidbrink, 2010, p. 67; Jannidis, 2013). Since the 1990s stronger trans- and interdisciplinary accounts of characters started to emerge with the publication of a range of monographs (Culpeper, 2001; Eder, 2008; Florack, 2010; Jannidis, 2004; Koch, 1991; Palmer, 2004; Schneider, 2000), indebted to the earlier theoretical work by scholars such as Uri Margolin (1983) and Shlomith Rimmon-Kenan (1983). From the 1990s onward, these scholars have shaped discussions on character. According to Henriette Heidbrink, these discussions consequently progressed via three lines of inquiry (2010, p. 72):[16]

1. How does the human-likeness of characters relate to the textual, visual, or auditory *material* from which they are made up of? Are characters in literary fiction predominantly linguistic or psychological entities?
2. What is the meaning of characters in terms of their *actions* and *functions*?
3. How does the materiality of characters (words, images, sounds) affect their *reception* by readers?

Whereas the reception of characters (the third question) is not touched upon in this book, both the first and the second questions are addressed. The book's premise is that real-world social groups are represented through characters who are – to a greater or lesser extent – fictionalized linguistic representations of these groups.[17] Men, for instance, are first and foremost represented in novels through male characters. Psychological traits and cultural roles ascribed to men in a particular society might be reflected, criticized, or satirized in the male characters populating the novels written in that society. But there is more to characters than just their psychological, cultural, or social similarities to real people. As characters in novels are linguistic configurations, they are tied to the boundaries of the language from which they are made up of. Because of that, the literary representation of, for instance, men is not just a matter of studying male characters in isolation. The novel's materiality in which these characters are embedded (the second question) is of equal importance: the thematic structure, stylistic devices, metaphors, and symbolism can all co-constitute the ways in which men are depicted. Moreover, gender representation is also shaped by the various ways in which both male and female characters act and function in relation to one another. The representation of Iris Pompier in Zwagerman's *De buitenvrouw* (2008), for instance, is largely determined by her relation to protagonist Theo. Because the actions and functions of fellow characters in the narrative thus co-constitute the representation of a particular type of character, this book takes up a fundamentally relational approach to the study of characters by focusing on the social networks – the character constellations – they function in.

What is a character? Depending on the research question and area of interest, scholars have defined characters in a variety of ways. The ontological status of characters has been subject to philosophical debates: do they, for instance, only exist within or also outside the narrative in which they function (Reicher, 2010)? Or do characters primarily exist as imaginary beings in the minds of the audience (Culpeper, 2000)? Are characters 'pieces of writing' or 'person like entities', or a hybrid of those (Frow, 2014, p. 25)? While being fully aware of the ontological complexities surrounding characters, delving deeply into such questions is outside the scope of this book. Acknowledging both their textual and person-like dimensions, I will use the most common definition of characters as 'fictive persons or fictional analogues to human beings' (Eder et al., 2010, p. 7). As such, the book follows the definition of *The Living Handbook of Narratology*: 'a text- or media-based figure in a storyworld, usually human or human-like' (Jannidis, 2013). A consequence of adopting this definition is that nonanthropomorphic beings, such as animals or inanimate objects, are not taken into account in this study, although present-day novels sometimes – but rarely – feature nonhuman-like characters.[18] Another reason for using this definition stems from the book's focus on the representation of social groups. Although moral rights can be ascribed to wolves, dragons, and flying pancakes, they are usually not considered as social groups in the research disciplines of the social sciences.[19] As this book aligns itself methodologically with the social sciences through its use of social network analysis, it defines social actors in literary texts in strictly anthropomorphic terms. It is, furthermore, hard if not impossible to ascribe demographic labels to nonhuman-like characters (e.g., is the big bad wolf in 'Red Riding Hood' higher or lower educated?).

Characters consist of different properties and dimensions. Prototypical properties distinguishing characters from other types of objects or entities in the narrative relate to their mental interiority; characters possess 'mental states, such as perceptions, thoughts, feelings, and aims' and have 'both an outer appearance and an inner state of the psyche that is not visible from the outside' (Eder et al., 2010, p. 13). Apart from their physical and psychological properties, another property of characters is that they typically perform certain social roles in the narrative (ibid.). All these properties of characters consequently function within different dimensions. In *Reading People, Reading Plots* (1989), James Phelan makes a useful and frequently cited distinction between three dimensions:

1. The synthetic dimension relates to the artificiality of characters and comprises all the narrative elements out of which it is constructed (p. 2).
2. The mimetic dimension denotes the character's relation to recognizable human traits (ibid.).
3. The thematic dimension relates to what a character stands for, what it represents (e.g., a social group) (p. 3).

In each of this book's chapters, the synthetic dimension of characters – the words which they are made up of – is analyzed both quantitatively and qualitatively in order to gain insight into their thematic dimension, that is, how they are representative of one or more social groups. The mimetic dimension is presupposed in the analyses: features of characters relating to the social groups in which they are embedded are implied by both their synthetic and thematic dimensions.

1.1.4 Characterization and Character Types

How to determine to which social groups a character belongs, and how to recognize traits related to these groups? This question relates to the mechanism of characterization and the different character types resulting from specific forms of characterization. Although often the gender, descent, education, and age of characters can be deduced relatively easily from their narrative context, the values associated with these demographic features arise from the specific ways in which characters are characterized. In its broadest sense, characterization can be defined as 'the process of connecting information with a figure in a text so as to provide a character in the fictional world with a certain property, or properties, concerning body, mind, behaviour, or relations to the (social) environment' (Eder et al., 2010, p. 32). Such properties can be ascribed to characters through direct characterization: e.g., 'She – blond hair and blue eyes [body] – was smart and arrogant [mind], and tended to be rude to others [behavior + relations]'. Or through indirect characterization: e.g., 'Her reading of Nietzsche's *Also Sprach Zarathustra* in the local pub might evoke a peculiar kind of awe in the people obsessively staring at her appearance' [mind + behavior + relations + body]. Such processes of characterization shape the social, economic, and cultural features of a character.[20]

The best-known distinction between modes of characterization comes from novelist and critic E. M. Forster, who distinguishes in *Aspects of the Novel* (1927) between round and flat characters. In his view, round characters show more narrative development and are made up of multiple, sometimes changing features, whereas flat characters 'are constructed round a single idea or quality' and 'when there is more than one factor in them, we get the beginning of the curve towards the round' (Forster, 1927, p. 103). How to decide if a character is flat or round?

> The test of a round character is whether it is capable of surprising in a convincing way. If it never surprises, it is flat. If it does not convince, it is a flat pretending to be round. (ibid., p. 118)

As the criterion of 'surprising in a convincing way' is highly vague, it very much remains a matter of interpretation whether or not to categorize a character as either round or flat. There are, however, immediately recognizable instances of both types. An example of a round character in contemporary popular culture is Frodo in *The Lord of the Rings* trilogy. From the quiet peace of the shire to the fires of Mount Doom, the multifaceted hobbit goes through several stages of personal development. A huge gap lies between the first encounter with Frodo in the shire and his destroying of the ring at the end of the trilogy. Frodo undoubtedly witnessed genuine spiritual growth, and his spiritual journey could arguably be labeled as surprising.

An example of a flat character from the same trilogy is the figure of the orc: the 'single idea or quality' (ibid., p. 103) represented by orcs is evil or wickedness. The personal history of orcs is not genuinely articulated, nor do they develop into something differently – they are first and foremost interchangeable evil and wicked creatures. Although flat characters tend to be negatively connotated in contemporary criticism, Forster saw two advantages for a novel writer to stage them: because they stay the same throughout the narrative, they are both easily recognized and remembered by the reader (ibid., p. 105). These negative connotations, however, are due to the fact that flat characters tend also to be caricatures or stereotypes.[21]

Stereotypes are often used as arguments in ideological discussions on representation, which is the case in the discussions on Zwagerman's *De buitenvrouw* and Vuijsje's *Alleen maar nette mensen* (see section 1.1.1 of this chapter). In the qualitative parts of the analyses presented in the subsequent chapters, stereotypes are, furthermore, used as possible indicators of the status of a character in a narrative. What, then, is a stereotype? The present-day usage of the term 'stereotype' as a simplified, reductionist form of characterization of a collection of people or of a set of practices dates back to Walter Lippmann's description of the term in his book *Public Opinion* (1922). Whereas today stereotypes are mostly associated with rather negative, and even offending, figures of speech, he primarily emphasized the usefulness of stereotypes in everyday life. Lippmann describes processes of stereotyping as a natural effect of the way in which human beings perceive the world:

> For the most part we do not first see, and then define, we define first and then see. In the great blooming, buzzing confusion of the outer world we pick out what our culture has already defined for us, and we tend to perceive that which we have picked out in the form stereotyped for us by our culture. (Lippmann, 1922)

Although this definition lacks the strong moral dimension the term has today, Lippmann also sees stereotyping as a simplified, reductionist process, as people, in his view, fall back on 'what our culture has already defined for us'. When people obey a natural tendency to 'define first and then see', they do not have to decide for themselves. Etymologically, the term dates back to premodern printing practices, in which stereotypes referred to printing plates that could be used over and over again.[22] As such, stereotypes made the printing process more time-efficient and cost-effective. Similar to Lippmann's use of the term, this particular historical context foregrounds aspects of non-originality and repetitiveness. In order to make their work easier, printers made use of already available, reusable printing plates instead of using new, original printing plates each time. In Lippmann's view, stereotypes make life easier because people can rely on repetitive images instead of creating new images every time. In a similar vein, Forster values the pragmatic aspects of a flat character as being easily recognizable and remembered (1927, p. 105). There is, in short, a certain convenience, and perhaps even necessity, to stereotypes.

More recent scholarly work on cultural stereotypes also acknowledges their simplified, reductionist, repetitive nature, but it tends to put more stress on the ideological problems related to stereotypical representations (e.g., Florack, 2010; Gymnich, 2010; Schweinitz, 2010).[23] In the seminal article 'The Role of Stereotypes' (1999), Richard Dyer distinguishes between the social type and the stereotype. Both character types are easily recognizable in narratives and thus tend to be rather flat. There is, however, an important difference: social types refer to 'those who "belong" to society', whereas stereotypes refer to 'those who do not belong, who are outside of one's society' (Dyer 1999). Who does and who does not belong is indeed a matter of perspective. In present-day Dutch novels, a character pertaining to, for instance, the *social type* of the Dutch character can be introduced by just a few signals (born in the Netherlands, conforming to certain Dutch customs, norms, and values). But such a social type can be used in the plot 'in a much more open and flexible way than can stereotypes' (ibid.). They can fulfill almost every role in the narrative, which is illustrated by the fact that social types of Dutch characters are prevalent in a wide variety of characters ranging from Gerard Reve's Frits van Egters to Arnon Grunberg's Tirza.

Conversely, the stereotype of, for instance, the Muslim extremist character is bound to a specific set of functions: they are radical, evil, dangerous. In the fourth chapter of this book, on community, the stereotypical representations of Muslim extremist characters in Leon de Winter's *VSV* (2012) illustrate how such stereotypes 'maintain sharp boundary definitions, to define clearly where the pale ends and thus who is clearly within and who clearly beyond it' (ibid). In this definition, stereotyped characters are ideologically restricted to a very specific, one-dimensional depiction that does not do justice to the full complexity of the social group they are representative of. Determining whether a character is a flat or a round character, a social type or a stereotype is thus a convenient way to gain insight into the one- or multidimensionality ascribed to the social group(s) a particular character represents. In the qualitative parts of the analyses in the subsequent chapters, this is done through narratological analyses of the ways in which specific characters are narrated, focalized, and characterized.

1.1.5 The One Versus the Many

In the last decade or so, quantitative and data-driven accounts of characters started to emerge (Bamman, Underwood, & Smith, 2014; Jockers & Kirilloff, 2016; Kraicer & Piper, 2019; Piper, 2018; Underwood, Bamman, & Lee, 2018). Either indirectly, or directly in the case of Piper (2018, p. 219), these studies respond to a central claim of Alex Woloch's book *The One vs. the Many: Minor Characters and the Space of the Protagonist in the Novel* (2003). 'Narrative meaning', Woloch contends, 'takes shape in the dynamic flux of attention and neglect toward the various characters who are locked within the same story but have radically different positions within the narrative' (p. 2). Woloch makes something explicit that might seem quite obvious but has lacked scholarly attention: there is a huge discrepancy in the distribution of attention for characters in a narrative.[24] Most attention is devoted to the protagonist, with only sparse attention left for a wide range of minor characters. These discrepancies raise fundamental questions regarding the hierarchical structure of narrative representation:

> How can many people be contained within a single narrative? How do different narrative forms accommodate the surge of many people into a single story? How do they encapsulate and convey the impact of a human being – of varied human beings – within a coherent literary structure? In these questions we can see the outline of a different, almost inverted, history: a history that would trace not how the literary form, in its intricate coherence, is rendered into a living organism, but how living persons get rendered into literary form. (p. 11)

By formalizing and quantifying the concept of character, the data-driven character studies listed above provide an empirical account of the ways in which 'many people [can] be contained within a single narrative'. Counting characters and their interrelations, in combination with close readings of those character constellations, arguably results in a more complete view on the dominance, subordinance, and hierarchies of characters than a solely qualitative assessment of texts. In line with these quantitative approaches to the study of characters, this book builds forth on the recent attempts to model the relation of 'the many' to the 'one'. By means of computational, data-driven analysis, it broadens the scope from the main character(s) to all identifiable characters in the corpus. Combining quantitative and qualitative analysis in each individual chapter, it aims to gain insight into the ways in which living persons are rendered into literary form while paying special attention in the qualitative parts of the analyses to the different (round/flat, social/stereotypical) character types they are represented through.

1.2. CRITIQUE OF REPRESENTATION

1.2.1 Representation and Ideology

In this book, critique of representation refers to the study of cultural and literary representation as popularized by scholars such as Edward Said, Stuart Hall, and, in the Netherlands, Mieke Bal and Maaike Meijer.[25] The intellectual tradition of this field of inquiry forms the main theoretical background of the analyses carried out in the subsequent chapters. More specifically, the present research builds forth on the ways in which this tradition has conjoined representation and ideology as concepts in the analysis and interpretation of narrative fiction. In the seminal book *Representation* (1997), Stuart Hall systematically explores the notion that 'languages work *through representation*', where language is not narrowly understood as Dutch or English but more broadly as a 'dialogue' between people through which meaning is communicated (p. 4). In a similar vein, Maaike Meijer applies insights from feminist and postcolonial criticism to the study of cultural representation (1996). Central to both of these books is an operationalization of poststructuralist theory and an application of ideas from the ideological strands of Marxist thought, gender studies, and postcolonial studies to the analysis of cultural representation.

What is representation? In the classic accounts of literary theory by Plato and Aristotle, artistic expressions such as literature are viewed as a representation of reality. For Plato, this was a reason to ban literature from his ideal of the perfect state: as a potentially illusory reflection of reality, literature might lead people astray from the path of truth. In modern times, the idea that literature has a reflective – a mimetic – component is still vivid, although scholars have problematized the ways in which the mediation between literature and reality takes shape. Building on the mediating aspect of representation,[26] Maaike Meijer distinguishes 'representation' from the semiotic concept of 'sign', as the first does and the latter does not require a human mediator. Arguing that 'representation is always *of* something or someone, *by* something or someone, *to* someone' (1995, p. 12), W. J. T. Mitchell characterizes representation as a triangular configuration between the represented, the representer, and the audience for whom the representer creates the represented.[27] In its simplest form, the three components of representation in the context of this book are the actual social groups of people as represented objects, the literary representations of these social groups as the representers, and the readers as the targeted audience.

For a critique of representation, each of these components requires a different approach. For instance: the represented social groups can be studied through anthropological analysis, the literary representations of these groups can be studied through text analysis, and a reception analysis of the texts can be carried out with the readers as subjects of study. Without denying the importance of both the actual social groups depicted in the representations and the readers, this book studies the text representations (the representers) largely in isolation from these other two components of representation. Although the literary representation of social groups in the corpus is co-shaped by the features and actions of the respective social groups and its reception by readers, the present text-centric approach aims to foreground the structure and hierarchies within the fictional populations as a starting point for any future analysis considering these other two dimensions of representation. By doing so, the research aligns itself in the first place with formalist approaches to representation deemphasizing both the represented objects (the actual social groups) and the audience (the readers), and stressing the materiality of the literary objects (the literary depictions of the social groups). But while prioritizing the literary object as representer, it does not go as far as to assume that 'literature is about itself' and that 'novels are made out of other novels' (Mitchell, 1995, p. 16). The book's prioritization of the text is not the result of a conviction that the representation of social groups functions in isolation from the actual represented social groups and the readers perceiving these representations, but is due to a methodological choice to narrow down the focus to one of these three dimensions. By means of focusing on this dimension, the study aims to show that blueprints of character constellations at the level of the text – how representations of social groups are rooted in the words on the pages – provide a solid starting point for any discussion on literary representation.

Quite obviously, processes of representation are the objects of critiques of representation. Less obvious, perhaps, is that these critiques tend to be deeply involved with ideological perspectives on these processes. For Mitchell, it is only logical that ideology is a core component of this analytical tradition:

> It should be clear that representation, even purely 'aesthetic' representation of fictional persons and events, can never be completely divorced from political and ideological questions; one might argue, in fact, that representation is precisely the point where the questions are most likely to enter the literary work. If literature is a 'representation of life,' then representation is exactly the place where 'life,' in all its social and subjective complexity, gets into the literary work. (Ibid., p. 15)

With regard to the literary representation of social groups, it is immediately apparent that such 'political and ideological questions' are at play. An author can choose to foreground specific features of characters more than other features: should they stress the physicality, the psychology, the material possessions, the morality, or other dimensions of the respective characters? For instance: an author who – (sub)consciously – chooses to characterize female characters more emphatically by their bodily traits, and to conversely stress the intellectual capabilities of the male characters, is not making a neutral choice. Ideologically, this author creates associations between femininity and physical appearance, and between masculinity and psychological interiority. Based on these associations, further value-laden connections can arise in the narrative, such as those between women and eroticism or sensuality, and between men and rationality. Such textual connections have an ideological component because they co-shape conceptions of the male and the female.

For critiques of representation it thus seems inevitable to inquire into the ideological dimensions of cultural representations. How, then, should ideology be understood as a concept within the framework of this book? Like the concept of representation, ideology is one of the key terms in literary and cultural studies. Since its coinage by the French philosopher Destutt de Tracy in *Éléments d'idéologie* (1827/2015) to propose a new science of ideas, the term has witnessed a complex history.[28] A closer look at the history of the term shows that it has denoted a wide variety of different, often conflicting meanings (Eagleton, 1991, pp. 1–31). This book follows a text-centric definition of ideology as 'the frame of values informing the narrative' as put forward by narratologists Luc Herman and Bart Vervaeck in *The Living Handbook of Narratology* (2013). More specifically, ideology in narrative fiction is considered to '[install] hierarchical relationships between pairs of oppositional terms such as real vs. false, good vs. bad, and beautiful vs. ugly' in the text (ibid.). The above hypothetical example on male-female associations demonstrates that the ideological aspects of representation can foster oppositions such as women as bodies versus men as minds.

Marxist theory has undoubtedly left a major mark on the use of ideology in contemporary literary and cultural criticism.[29] Initially, Marx and Engels used the term to refer to 'a widespread form of epistemological error that a new, more empirically-based – sometimes called "scientific" – mode of thinking could avoid, if not eventually abolish' (Kavanagh, 1995, p. 310). In this definition, ideology is the opposite of truth and pertains to false beliefs about reality. More recent Marxist criticism by Louis Althusser does not equate ideology with false beliefs but rather sees it as the means through which the relation between culture and politics is shaped (1970; 1971). In this view, ideology is an inherent aspect of each cultural product because it functions as a 'system of representation' arising from the 'social process that works on and through every social subject, that, like any other social process, everyone is "in", whether or not they "know" or understand it' (Kavanagh, 1995, p. 311).

Studies of ideology in narrative fiction are divided by Herman and Vervaeck into psychoanalytic, sociological, and discursive approaches (2013). Building on the work of Freud and Lacan, psychoanalytic approaches tend to focus on the way in which the reader creates ideological connections in their mind (e.g., Davis, 1987). From a Marxist perspective, sociological approaches stress the ideological aspects of the social, historical, cultural, and economic contexts in which narratives function (e.g., Williams, 1977). Discursive approaches center on the ideological constellations contained in the literary texts themselves (e.g., Bakhtin 1935/2003; Hamon, 1984). While the psychoanalytic approach is outside the scope of this book, both the sociological and the discursive approach have a place in it. In terms of representation, this study focuses primarily on the literary representations of social groups in the texts themselves and thus aligns itself in the first place with the discursive approach to ideology in narrative fiction. But while it does not study either readers (psychoanalytic approach) or the actual represented social group (sociological approach), it does hinge on the idea that the characters populating the novels can be studied as if they were real people, following Toril Moi's recent proposition to go beyond this taboo in literary criticism (2019, pp. 27–75, see also section 1.2 of this chapter). A study on how fictional characters represent actual groups of people cannot rely on an analysis of the textual components of characters only, but requires one to make a connection between real people and the person-like qualities of characters that are representative of these people. Using the tools of social network analysis, the book thus contextualizes the fictional characters in the texts as representatives of actual social groups. In this specific sense, it hopes to invoke a dialogue between the discursive, text-centered approach and the sociological, contextual approach to ideology in narrative fiction.

While ideology is discussed above in a general sense, critiques of literary representation often focus on specific ideologies, values, or belief systems, building on one or more traditions of criticism, such as gender, postcolonial, queer, disability, or mad studies. Gender and ethnicity have demonstrated to be two of the most widely used identity categories targeted in critiques of representation.[30] Influenced by feminist theorists such as Judith Butler (1990) and postcolonial theorists such as Edward Said (1978), hierarchies between genders, sexes, or sexualities, and between ethnicities, races, or descents have been a central topic in the study of literary and cultural representation. The prevalence of feminist and postcolonial approaches to representation in literary texts is exemplified by the emergence of separate branches of narratology centering on gender and ethnicity. As one of the main proponents of feminist narratology, Susan Lanser contends that the branch's existence is based on 'the shared belief that sex, gender, and sexuality are significant not only to textual interpretation and reader reception but to textual poetics itself and thus to the shapes, structures, representational practices, and communicative contexts of narrative texts' (2013). Similarly, the emergence of postcolonial narratology is motivated by the belief that ethnicity, race, and descent are crucial to how narratives are organized. In Gerald Prince's view, a postcolonial narratology should be 'sensitive to matters commonly, if not uncontroversially, associated with the postcolonial (e.g., hybridity, migrancy, otherness, fragmentation, diversity, power relations)' and should '[envisage] their possible narratological correspondents and [...] [incorporate] them' (2005, p. 373).

Such efforts to develop gender and postcolonial narratologies, among others, exemplify the need for analytical models to specify where and how values on, for instance, gender and race are expressed in texts. The work of scholars such as Susan Suleiman (1983), Philippe Hamon (1984), Liesbeth Korthals Altes (1992), and Vincent Jouve (2001) showcases how ideological dimensions can be traced back to the formal characteristics of texts. While these scholars attribute a greater or lesser importance to the role of the reader in the emergence of ideology in literature, their work provides inspiring examples of how the 'ideology effect' or 'value effect' is rooted in concrete words on the page. An important role is ascribed to characters: which norms and values are imposed by a text can partly be deduced from the actions, utterances, thoughts, feelings, and perceptions of characters. Characters, in this narratological tradition, are often seen as carriers of ideology. How something is narrated or focalized by a character is expressive of the values represented by its point of view. In *Poétique des valeurs* (2001), Vincent Jouve describes the ways in which a text conveys values through characters, as well as through other narrative elements.[31] In his view, values are located in specific points in the text – 'points-valeurs' – and are manifested in characters' thoughts, words, and actions (pp. 35–88). The values characters express through thinking, talking, and acting are subsequently evaluated by the text explicitly (e.g., judgements on a character), through characterization (e.g., which social, cultural, or economic features are ascribed to a character), through modes of narration or focalization (e.g., we might be inclined to empathize more strongly with a first-person narrating character because we are close to their perspective), or through 'mise en texte' (e.g., in which geographic spaces the character functions). Such narrative mechanisms are taken by Jouve to co-shape the 'value effect' of the text or the ideology it imposes on its reader.

A concrete example of how ideology is manifested in the structural features of literary works is provided by Susan Suleiman's *Authoritarian Fictions* (1983). In it, she develops a range of narratological models to study the novelistic genre of the 'roman à thèse', which she defines as 'a novel written in the realistic mode (that is, based on an aesthetic of verisimilitude and representation), which signals itself to the reader as primarily didactic in intent, seeking to demonstrate the validity of a political, philosophical, or religious doctrine' (p. 7). Novels in this genre convey ideology in the form of a particular message, statement, doctrine, belief, norm, or value. As such, the *roman à thèse* 'seeks not only to impose a single meaning, but to propose a system of values' (p. 56). Suleiman analyzes how such novels invoke an ultimately unambiguous and dualistic 'system of values' by dividing narrative elements such as characters, events, and places into a positive and a negative pole. A character-based example: a text can convey a certain message, or ideology, by a positive portrayal of character X voicing this particular message and a negative portrayal of character Y voicing the opposite of this message. Throughout her book, Suleiman describes the defining traits of this genre by breaking down the narratives by means of formal schemata and almost algebraic formulas.[32] In doing so, she anchors the ideological dimension of these texts in the words on the page, an approach followed in the analyses carried out in the subsequent chapters of the present study.

On a more general level, the ideological dimensions of texts, and representations of gender, ethnicity, or any other identity category in particular, are often critiqued by examining how 'the Other' is represented in opposition to the dominant perspective adopted in the text. While it is unclear who coined the term, it can be traced back to Georg Wilhelm Hegel, who ascribes a constitutive role to the Other in the formation of self-consciousness and self-identity in *Phänomenologie des Geistes* (1807/1832). In literary studies, the term is nowadays most notably associated with Edward Said's seminal *Orientalism* (1978),[33] through which it has come to be understood as the process through which entities such as characters are represented as an alterity to the central perspectives, the dominant characters, or the common worldviews as presented in the text.[34] Such processes of othering are closely tied to mechanisms of characterization as described in section 1.1.4 of this chapter; the flatness or roundness of a character tends to influence its position in the narrative. Narratological models such as those of Suleiman (1983) and Jouve (2001) can, furthermore, help to pinpoint where otherness resides in the systems of values imposed by texts. In the qualitative parts of the analyses presented in the subsequent chapters, narratological analysis is used to trace where and how particular represented social groups are depicted as Other or Self, marginal or central, subordinate or dominant, silent or present.

1.2.2 Critiques of Representation in Dutch Literature

Published in 1991, *De canon onder vuur* [The canon under fire], edited by Ernst van Alphen and Maaike Meijer, symbolizes the institutionalization of ideologically oriented critiques of representation within the field of Dutch literary studies. The book's subtitle, 'Reading Dutch literature against the grain',[35] invokes a rather oppositional stance toward the object of inquiry. In order to expose 'the less pleasant smells'[36] of canonical Dutch literary texts, each contribution addresses the – amongst others – sexist and racist dimensions of individual texts operating in 'a realm of sacredness'.[37]

In the decades following this book, a wide range of critiques of representation in its spirit have been published.[38] The following three examples demonstrate how this line of research tends to focus on the narratological units of characters in order to lay bare processes of stereotyping and othering in Dutch literature. Analyzing representations of gender and race in *De stille kracht* [The hidden force] (1900) by Louis Couperus, Pamela Pattynama emphasizes that 'the differences between the colonized and the colonizers [in the novel] are often rendered metaphorically as the unfathomable secrets and dangers that enveloped the Dutch colonial community of the East Indies' (1998, p. 84). In line with the critical scholarship on *Conrad's Heart of Darkness* (see section 1.2.1), Pattynama describes how Couperus depicts the Dutch colony as a mysterious place full of secrets and dangers, and how he portrays the colonized characters as alien forces embodying those secrets and dangers. Such strategies of othering are also the point of focus in Liesbeth Minnaard's analysis of *Blank en geel* [White and yellow] (1894) by Lodewijk van Deyssel. Focusing on the encounter between a young Dutch bourgeois woman and a Chinese merchant, Minnaard shows 'how Van Deyssel's novel tells the story of a dissident, improper desire for an exotic other, and reflects on exotic presence within the Dutch centre' (2010, p. 75). In the eyes of the Dutch character, the Chinese merchant is an 'Oriental prince' and a 'mysterious, almost supernatural being' (p. 71). From a gender perspective, Maaike Meijer analyzes the representation of male and female characters in sex scenes by Jan Wolkers (Meijer, 1996). In her analysis, she observes traces of the Other in the ways the female antagonists in Wolkers's work are presented as naive, sexually compliant, and submissive.

De canon onder vuur and the studies published in its wake mark the transition from a structuralist to a poststructuralist paradigm in Dutch literary studies. As iconic figures of Dutch structuralism, J. J. Oversteegen (1965) and A. L. Sötemann (1966) left their mark on postwar text-centric scholarship on Dutch texts. Especially, Sötemann's dissertation *De structuur van Max Havelaar* [The structure of Max Havelaar] (1966) forms a classic example of a text-centric study dissecting the structural elements of one, highly canonical, novel in order to reconstruct its 'meaning'. In line with Roland Barthes's early structuralist theorizations (Barthes, 2006), Sötemann read Multatuli's novel exclusively in terms of the elements present in the text without paying attention to any contextual information. Adopting the stance of an 'ideal reader', he considered it 'necessary to devote careful attention to the extraordinary qualities of this work' (Sötemann, 1966, p. 5).[39] The premises of the scholarly work carried out in the tradition of Sötemann and those of the critiques of representation kick-started by *De canon onder vuur* could hardly be further apart. Whereas an outright admiration for the structure and meaning of canonical literary works is apparent in the first, the latter adopts a fundamentally resistant stance toward the text.

Resistant reading as practiced in these Dutch critiques of representation is closely related to a poststructuralist, deconstructivist strategy to break open the text in order to illustrate its ambiguity and indeterminacy (cf. Culler, 1983). In the structuralist framework of the likes of Sötemann, such deconstructivist reading strategies conflict with the ways in which the structuralist admiration for canonical texts motivates the reconstruction of structures and meanings instead of demonstrating the openness and multiplicity of texts. The opposition between these two dispositions toward the text is best understood by the terms 'hermeneutics of admiration' and 'hermeneutics of suspicion' as popularized by

Rita Felski in her essay 'After Suspicion' (2009). In it, she builds forth on Paul Ricoeur's observation that recalcitrant thinkers such as Marx, Nietzsche, and Freud have shaped scholarly modes of suspicious interpretation (1970). Signaling the pitfalls and merits of both the hermeneutics of suspicion and the hermeneutics of admiration, Felski proposes a mode of 'reflective reading' moving beyond the suspicion-admiration-dichotomy, which later became known as 'post-critique'.[40]

The present book takes a specific position within the scholarly tradition of critiques of representation on Dutch literature. It is aligned with the deconstructivist, resistant, suspicious readings in the spirit of *De canon onder vuur* as it aims to unravel representations of social groups in present-day Dutch literature by analyzing, among others, narrative mechanisms of othering and stereotyping. Its assumption that such narrative mechanisms are a central part of the literary representations under scrutiny is in line with the work of Maaike Meijer, Pamela Pattynama, and Liesbeth Minnaard as showcased above as examples of this tradition.

Although the book does not in any sense conform to the admiration of canonical works as apparent in the work of structuralists such as Sötemann, its primarily discursive approach to literary representation is indebted to their strong focus on the structure of literary texts. While, other than Sötemann, it does underwrite the belief that the meaning of literature is constituted by more than the text itself, its statistical analyses nevertheless isolate the texts from their institutional contexts and their readers.[41] Focusing on a larger body of texts than the Dutch structuralists did, its aim is to lay bare structural patterns and trends of representation based on primarily textual elements. However, contrary to structuralist attempts to reconstruct a definitive meaning from texts, the narratological evaluations of these statistics-based textual patterns are then used in the qualitative parts of the chapters to point at the ambiguities and indeterminacies of representation. This is especially relevant in light of the rise of digital and empirical methods in literary studies. As Lucas van der Deijl has pointed out, data-driven studies in the humanities tend to rely (implicitly or explicitly) on structuralist notions without reflecting on the hermeneutics of algorithms (2015, p. 49). In a seminal article in which the term 'computational turn' is coined, David Berry highlights the need for such a hermeneutics of algorithms (or code), contending that 'understanding the digital is in some sense also connected to understanding of code through study of the medial changes that it affords, a hermeneutics of code' (2012, p. 6).

Triangulating an ideologically oriented critique of representation, a structural textual analysis, and a hermeneutics of algorithms, the book aims to transcend the opposition between the deconstructivist, resistant accounts of literary representation and structuralist approaches to text analysis. By incorporating data-driven, empirical methods, it shows how text-centric, statistical analyses can help to gain insight into recurring patterns of literary representation. In turn, these structural textual patterns are then deconstructed qualitatively in each chapter by determining the moments at which individual texts conform to or deviate from them. As narratological evaluations of the statistical, text-centric patterns, these close readings thus seek to resist – to be suspicious of – the found structures and the logic of the algorithms developed for this research. The next section dives deeper into the merits and pitfalls of algorithmic approaches to literature.

1.3. CULTURAL ANALYTICS

1.3.1 Debates on Distant versus Close Reading

In the last decade or so, 'digital humanities' have increasingly become a buzzword in academia. Rumor has it that scholars applying for a grant maximize their chances of success by mentioning digital humanities as a component of their future research. The field is witnessing a rapid institutionalizing, as humanities faculties all around the globe have started to incorporate digital humanities courses, minors, specializations, and master programs into their curricula. Such developments might give the impression that digital humanities is the new, popular kid on the block. But in fact, data-driven humanities research has been around for at least 80 years.[42]

Although it seems common sense to juxtapose the 'soft' humanities disciplines with the 'hard' natural sciences, speculative interpretation with factual analysis, words with numbers, intricate historical interrelations exist between the notions of literacy and numeracy. In a contribution to *Defining Digital Humanities* (2013), Edward Vanhoutte offers a detailed account of the history of these interrelations.[43] He sees the birth of the digital humanities symbolized in the person of Ada Lovelace (1815–1852), daughter of the most literate poet Lord Byron and the highly numerate mathematician Anabella Milbanke. In *Notions sur la machine analytique de Charles Babbage* (1842), Lovelace ruminates about using Charles Babbage's (1791–1871) Analytical Engine for more than just mathematical calculations,[44] such as for automatically producing music. From another angle, Jesuit priest Roberto Busa (1913–2011) is commonly regarded as the father of modern data-driven humanities research. In the early 1940s, Busa started working on the *Index Thomisticus*, a searchable database of all the works of Thomas Aquinas.[45] From the 1950s onward, he started cooperating with IBM to automate certain aspects of this database (Vanhoutte, 2013, p. 127). This cooperation between old-school humanist Busa and the IBM technology company is usually regarded as a symbolic stepping-stone toward the practical integration of digital technology into the humanities disciplines.

Since the second half of the twentieth century, a wide variety of terms have circulated emphasizing different aspects of what nowadays goes under the term 'digital humanities'. The term 'humanities computing' was used from the 1950s, and more regularly from the 1980s, to denote 'computing *in* the humanities' as opposed to 'computing *for* the humanities' (p. 140).[46] With its first issue published in 1966, the academic journal *Computers and the Humanities* functioned as platform for research carried out under the header of humanities computing. It was only since the publication of *A Companion to Digital Humanities* in 2004 that 'digital humanities' was commonly accepted as an umbrella term for research combining digital technology with one of the humanities disciplines (Nyhan, Terras, & Vanhoutte, 2013, p. 2). The metaphor of a big tent is often used to explain the broad nature of the term: 'Digital Humanities as a term does not refer to such a specialized activity, but provides a big tent for all digital scholarship in the humanities' (Vanhoutte, 2013, p. 144). As the term is so generic that it obscures rather than elucidates the content of the research, the alternative term 'cultural analytics' will be used to characterize the data-driven component of the research carried out in this book (more on this in section 1.3.2).

In 2011 David Berry signaled the emergence of a computational turn in the humanities. Other than earlier uses of digital technology in humanities research, recent studies appeared questioning 'the "hard core" of the humanities, the unspoken assumptions and ontological foundations which support the "normal" research that humanities scholars undertake on an everyday basis' (p. 4). According to Berry, this new wave of digital humanities did not just use digital technology as an auxiliary to existing practices but 'point[ed] the way in which digital technology highlights the anomalies generated in a humanities research project' and led to 'the questioning of the assumptions implicit in such research, e.g. close reading, canon formation, periodization, liberal humanism, etc.' (ibid). The questioning of these assumptions subsequently led to heated debates on the status of quantity, measurement, objectivity, and replicability in the humanities.[47]

In these debates, the digital humanities are often explicitly framed in opposition with the 'traditional' humanities.

In literary studies, the juxtaposition between the 'new', computer-oriented approach and the 'traditional' approach is most clearly exemplified by the work of Franco Moretti and Matthew Jockers. Coining the terms 'distant reading' (Moretti, 2013) and 'macro analysis' (Jockers, 2013) as alternatives for 'close reading' and 'micro analysis', both scholars quite unfortunately contributed to a polemical, and often unproductive, opposition between methodologies. In his account of the merits and pitfalls of a macro analysis of literature, Jockers asserts that micro analyses are commonly based on what he pejoratively calls 'anecdotal evidence' (2013, p. 5). In a similar vein, Moretti criticizes the inevitable subjectivity of close reading and notoriously contends that data are 'independent of interpretation' (2005, p. 30) – unaffected, in other words, by the scholar's confined subjective outlook.

Quite unsurprisingly, such statements have led to fierce criticism. In a review of Moretti's book *Distant Reading* (2014), Shawna Ross argues that

> when he claims that his grandiose stories are 'resting solidly on facts' [Moretti 2013, 44] or that distant reading yields 'the clarity of the empirical confirmation,' [Moretti 2013, 92] the generalization-spouting bravado by which Moretti skates over impossibly broad terrain finally comes across as glib, revealing one of the primary dangers of digital literary studies to be the adoption of an aggrandized, even hubristic attitude toward literature as so much inert stuff being poked at. (Ross, 2014, p. 5)

Some of the common arguments against distant reading are used by Ross: the positivism in such allegedly facts-based research, the naive belief in generalizations over 'impossibly broad terrain', and the arrogance – 'aggrandized, even hubristic attitude' – implicit in all this 'bravado'. Others, such as computational critic Stephen Ramsay in *Reading Machines* (2011) and philosopher Tom Eyers in *Speculative Formalism* (2017), have also warned against the rise of such neopositivist premises in literary studies.

Two general points of criticism against the digital humanities are relevant here. First, a *problem-solving rhetoric* might overshadow the interpretation and theorization of the findings of data-driven literary studies in the spirit of Jockers and Moretti. When the main issue becomes how to solve a methodological problem (e.g., how to automatically detect characters in literary texts), the theoretical motivations behind such methodological problems tend to become background noise (Scheinfeldt, 2010). Second, a *building-epistemology rhetoric* likewise obscures how data analysis and digital technology might contribute to theoretical issues.[48] According to Natalia Cecire, the widespread focus on the building of algorithms, tools, models, and databases invokes the impression that making technical constructs is the primary aim of data-driven humanities research, which she believes conforms to a neoliberal logic (2011). In the field of Dutch literary studies, these points of criticism are largely reflected in an article by Stephan Besser and Thomas Vaessens on the emergence of the digital humanities in the Netherlands, warning against its alleged scientificity, its uncritical essentialism, and its lack of reflection on theoretical assumptions (2013).[49]

Scientific ideals such as replicability and generalizability as propagated under the headers of distant reading (Moretti) and macro analysis (Jockers) are not, however, new to literary studies. For the Dutch situation, the influential literary journal *Merlyn* (1962–1966), with which the work of J. J. Oversteegen and A. L. Sötemann is frequently associated, embodied the ideal of replicability. In line with structuralist theory, the journal envisioned a fundamental text-centric approach to literature. In their first issue, the editors explicitly mention a 'criterion of replicability' literary analysis should conform to.[50] The ideal of generalizability is explicitly put forward by Suzanne Fagel in her work in the field of Dutch literary stylistics (Fagel, 2015). Arguing for a quantitative approach to literary style, she contends that 'an "introspective" method does not provide a reliable basis for judgements about how often something appears in a text, or how generally shared (generalizable) a certain interpretation is' (Fagel, Stukker, & van Andel, 2012, pp. 180–181).[51]

More generally, the oppositions between close and distant reading, micro and macro analysis, computer-oriented and philologic study, as invoked in these debates, are highly schematic. Although Jockers (2013) and Moretti (2013) adopt a polemical attitude toward 'traditional' forms of literary study, they do not argue for a replacement of micro analysis and close reading but opt for a blended, mixed approach. In fact, it would be hard to find a scholar using digital techniques stating that the human, close, micro element has become obsolete. In the Netherlands, this is exemplified by statements of three professors of literary studies and/or digital humanities. In his inaugural speech, professor of digital humanities Rens Bod proposes that the computational search for patterns (distant) should be combined with critical reflections on those patterns (close) (2013).[52] In her inaugural speech, professor of computational literary studies Karina van Dalen-Oskam emphasizes that both the quantitative, measurable component (distant) and the cultural component (close) of literary phenomena should be taken into account (2012).⁵³ In an article on the gap between close and distant reading, professor of early modern literature Els Stronks contends that both approaches should complement, broaden, and nuance one another (Stronks, 2013, p. 213).

In line with the pleas of Bod, Van Dalen-Oskam, and Stronks for a productive dialogue between methodologies, Paul Fleming (2017) observes that a recent strand of data-driven literary studies has emerged that goes beyond the schematic close-distant reading opposition. Starting from the observation that 'close reading is always exemplary in a double sense: the exemplary reading of exemplary passages' (p. 437), he argues for the importance of a 'recursive relation' between exemplary close reading and computational modelling. After disseminating the fundamental opposition between close and distant reading in Moretti's work (with Moretti as the classic example scholar of distant reading), he encourages us 'to look to other examples in and of digital humanities' (p. 453). These other examples can be found in the 'new wave of scholarship in the digital humanities', exemplified by scholars such as Andrew Piper, Hoyt Long, Richard Jean So, Alan Liu, and Ted Underwood, who '[insist] upon bringing together close and distant reading, computational analysis and exemplary exegesis as inextricable from one another' (p. 439).

The post-Moretti era of distant reading is characterized by a strong emphasis on transcending narrowly defined boundaries of close and distant reading, as well as by a general focus on recursive modelling. Recursively going back and forth between distant and close, macro and micro, data and interpretation, numbers and words, these scholars showcase the importance of creating multidimensional analytical models of literary texts.⁵⁴ Subsequently, this type of research does not easily fall prey to the neopositivist assumptions outlined above. This antipositivist stance is best exemplified by the work of Stephan Ramsay. In *Reading Machines* (2011), he states that 'the scientist is right to say that the plural of anecdote is not data, but in literary criticism an abundance of anecdote is precisely what allows discussion and debate to move forward' (p. 9). Contrary to Jockers's pejorative reference to 'anecdotal evidence' (2013, p. 5) as insufficient means, Ramsay stresses that literary studies, he contends, is not meant to settle these discussions or to solve problems emerging from them. Conversely, Ramsay emphasizes that 'literary criticism operates within a hermeneutical framework in which the specifically scientific meaning of fact, metric, verification, and evidence simply do not apply' (2011, p. 7),⁵⁵ which is in clear opposition to Moretti's claim that computation has the potential to 'falsify existing theoretical explanations' (2005, p. 30).

Following Ramsay, this book does not aim to settle debates on the representation of social groups in present-day Dutch literature once and for all but hopes to open up empirically informed discussions related to the topic. By building, applying, and evaluating recursive models of representation, it does attempt to formulate data-driven generalizations on the topic without denying that these generalizations are the result of specific choices made in the shaping of these models. As explained in the next subsection, the opportunities and dangers of modeling are a central issue within the research associated with cultural analytics.

1.3.2 Modeling in Cultural Analytics

The data-driven critique of representation presented in this book is closely aligned with studies carried out under the header of cultural analytics, a subfield of the digital humanities that studies culture through computation. While originally coined by Lev Manovich in 2005, the term 'cultural analytics' is currently first and foremost associated with the peer-reviewed, open-access *Journal of Cultural Analytics* (2016–present), edited by Andrew Piper. Manovich and Piper opt for relatively similar definitions, but whereas Manovich's definition is slightly more narrowly focused on media theory and visual data analysis, Piper's use of the term encompasses a broader terrain.[56] In the journal's opening article, Piper states that cultural analytics is more than 'computer science applied to culture' as it 'requires a wholesale rethinking of *both* of these categories' (2016):

> Computation forces us to rethink our current disciplinary practices in the humanities from the ground up. What counts as evidence? What is the relationship between theory and practice? How do we account for the technological mediations of our critique? But culture too impinges upon computation. It challenges the universalism and the neutrality implicit in many computational applications. It reminds us that knowledge is always situated, somewhere, at some time, by someone. Putting culture into computation cautions us to remember where we are when we think we know something. (Piper, 2016)

The two-way street between culture and computation as proposed by Piper contains a fundamental recursivity prompting scholars to go back and forth between the practices of cultural study and those of computational analysis. Using computation to study culture forces a rethinking of what David Berry calls the 'hard core' of the humanities (2011, p. 4), for which it is required to make explicit the implicit assumptions about, for instance, the role of evidence and the dynamics between theory and practice. Conversely, cultural study incites computational study to be conscious of its situatedness, its semantics, and its biases and provides it with critical theoretical frameworks. Just as the analysis of cultural products cannot make any claims to neutrality and universalism, neither can writing a set of instructions in the form of an algorithm. Behind both cultural and computational analysis are selective choices that emerged from the perspective adopted.

Such cross-fertilizations between culture and computation highlight the importance of modeling. What, then, is modeling? In *Distant Horizons* (2019), Ted Underwood gives a most straightforward definition of a model as 'a relationship between variables' (p. xii). Reversing the steps of inquiry as proposed by Moretti (2017), Underwood furthermore emphasizes the importance of hypothesis testing: 'Instead of measuring things, finding patterns, and then finally asking what they mean, we need to start with an interpretive hypothesis (a "meaning" to investigate) and invent a way to test it' (2019, p. 17). A simple example: hypothesizing that female authors write longer sentences, the variables 'sentence length' and 'author gender' can be inserted in a model to test whether an author's gender is predictive of the length of their sentences. Applying this model to a corpus of both male- and female-authored texts might result in the claim that female authors indeed write longer sentences, which then should be further tested and interpreted. More metaphorically than Underwood, Piper defines a model as 'a metonymical tool – a miniature that represents a larger whole' (2016). In the example on sentence length and author's gender, the 'miniature' model is applied to a corpus taken to be representative of the 'larger whole' of sentence length in, say, nineteenth-century literature. Importantly, Piper stresses the fact that a model is 'also recursive in that it can be modified in relationship to its "fit," how well it represents this whole' (ibid). Based on the model's performance, there might be reasons to think that the author's gender is not the best predictor for sentence length, in which case the model is a rather poor representation of the 'whole' of sentence length in nineteenth-century literature. The model can then be modified again and again – perhaps other variables such as an author's age or author education should be considered – until there are solid reasons to claim that the model 'fits', within certain statistical bounds of likelihood, the whole it attempts to represent.

Apart from the methodological 'benefits of speed, automation, and scale that computational representations afford' (Ramsay, 2011, p. 8), the importance of modeling shows that there are sound theoretical reasons for using computation to study culture. Modeling does not only provide scholars with 'a science of generalization' (Piper, 2018, p. 9), it also prompts them to think about 'the constructedness of knowledge and the observer's place within it' (ibid). As this book studies the ways in which social groups are *represented* in Dutch literature, it is, furthermore, relevant that models are 'first and foremost *representations*, miniatures that mediate between ourselves and our observations' (ibid., emphasis added). Mediation not only takes place within processes of literary representation (see section 1.2.1), it also has a vital function within the study of these representations as presented in this book. Going back and forth between numbers and words, it aims to make explicit the situatedness of the knowledge resulting from the constructed and reconstructed models presented in the following chapters.

Studies in cultural analytics published in *Journal of Cultural Analytics* regularly take their cue from socially indebted or ideologically oriented perspectives, which is exemplified, among others, by a range of data-driven analyses of gender and race representations in literature.[57] Such topics lend themselves perfectly to recursive modeling: as cultural representations of social reality are always communicated by a human mediator (see section 1.2.1), it seems only fair to make the role of mediation explicit in the study of these representations. As the role of mediation often remains implicit in close reading–based critiques of representation, it tends to be unclear how the findings came about. This is particularly salient in light of Stephan Ramsay's observation that 'the critic who endeavors to put forth a "reading," puts forth not the text, but a new text in which the data has been paraphrased, elaborated, selected, truncated, and transduced' (2011, p. 16). Each – close or distant – reading of a text transforms the original text into something else by selecting parts of it, paraphrasing those parts, elaborating on them, zooming in or zooming out, and so forth. These selections, paraphrases, elaborations, truncations, and transductions are all mediations considered by the scholar to be representative of the original text. Recursive modeling as practiced in this book is an attempt to make these mediating steps explicit.

Within the discussion on symptomatic reading versus surface reading as kick-started by Stephan Best and Sharon Marcus (2009), the recursive models of literary representation as carried out in this book provide an argument for a *data-driven* critique of representation. With the term 'surface reading', Best and Marcus presented an alternative to the dominant, 'symptomatic' form of reading in academia, a mode of reading in which textual elements are considered as symbolic or symptomatic of a deeper lying societal issue.[58]

Whereas symptomatic readings aim to uncover the latent, invisible, silent, or repressed meanings of texts, a surface reading focuses on

> what is evident, perceptible, apprehensible in texts; what is neither hidden nor hiding; what, in the geometrical sense, has length and breadth but no thickness, and therefore covers no depth. A surface is what insists on being looked at rather than what we must train ourselves to see through.' (Best & Marcus, 2009, p. 9)

Critiques of representation in Dutch literature in the tradition of *De canon onder vuur* (see section 1.2.2) are often symptomatic in the sense that they attempt to read between the lines and in the margins of the text, in order to lay bare hidden, and sometimes inconvenient truths about the work under scrutiny. Of course, such analyses do also consider what happens on the surface of the text (e.g., which words are used to characterize a specific character?), but they tend to center on what happens below that surface (e.g., which characterizations of a specific character remain implicit?). Conversely, surface reading is proposed by Best and Marcus as a means to center on what the text says instead of what it does not say. Quite unfortunately, however, Best and Marcus fall prey to the same kind of neopositivism as Jockers and Moretti (see section 1.3.1) when they state that 'digital modes of reading may be the inspiration for the hope that we could bypass the selectivity and evaluative energy that have been considered the hallmarks of good criticism, in order to attain what has almost become taboo in literary studies: objectivity, validity, truth' (p. 17). Despite the flawed, naive positivism ascribed to surface reading by Best and Marcus, their notion of the textual surface does serve as a convenient metaphor to illustrate the relevance of a data-driven, as opposed to a solely qualitative, critique of literary representation. As Terry Eagleton states in *Ideology* (1991): 'To study an ideological formation, then, is among other things to examine the complex set of linkages or mediations between its most articulate and least articulate levels' (p. 50). The ideological formations present in the representations of social groups studied in this book can be broken down in an articulate level (the surface of the text) and a less articulate level (the hidden depth of the text). Recursive modeling is a means to make the 'linkages or mediations' between these two levels explicit. Inserting computation into the study of these representations thus helps to show which textual elements at the surface of the text might lead to statements on the depths of the text.

Best and Marcus do not fail to notice that 'to see more clearly does not require that we plumb hidden depths and that producing accurate accounts of surfaces is not antithetical to critique' (2009, p. 18). The models presented in the following chapters are examples of how this might work in practice. In the data-driven components of these models, hypotheses on the representations of social groups are first tested by 'producing accurate accounts of [the] surfaces' of each of the 170 texts in the corpus. Statistical analysis is used to either reject or confirm the hypotheses. But although these statistical findings are based on what happens on the surfaces of the texts, they might also give a clue as to what happens 'underneath' them. In chapter 3, for instance, the hypothesis is tested that male and migrant characters have lower centrality scores in their co-occurrence networks than female and nonmigrant characters. A predictive statistical model then attempts to arrive at the probability that this is the case solely based on the co-occurrences of characters visible on the textual surfaces. The outcome of this model already *suggests* something about the deeper, hidden meanings related to representation of gender and descent, specifically regarding the dominance of a type of character. But the centrality of characters is, perhaps quite obviously, not fully covered by such a statistical, surface analysis: stylistic, thematic, and other dimensions also contribute to what makes a character important in a narrative. Qualitative assessment – close reading – is then used to evaluate the power of these statistical patterns for specific cases. Whereas the statistical model focuses on textual repetitions at the surface of the novels, the close readings attempt to uncover textual rarity that might possibly provide an argument about how characters in a specific text are central in other than statistical terms.[59]

1.4 METHODOLOGICAL BACKGROUND

1.4.1 Tools: Narratology and Network Analysis

The twofold theoretical framework as described in the previous sections is operationalized in the next chapters by using tools often used in each of the two theoretical strands. In critiques of literary representation, the methodological toolkit of narratology aids in coordinating the qualitative assessment of texts. Studies in cultural analytics can rely on a wide variety of computational or statistical tools, but social network analysis provides the most convenient tool for the study of the relational patterns within the fictional populations of characters in the corpus.

While the term 'narratology' was coined in 1969 by the Bulgarian linguist Tzvetan Todorov, its theoretical origins can be traced back to the early years of formalism at the beginning of the twentieth century (Meister, 2011). Narratology focuses on formal characteristics of texts that are constitutive of the (overall) narrative structure(s). In narratological analysis, interpretations of texts are centered on more or less delineated narratological concepts. One of the concepts that is used throughout each of the following chapters is characterization, as the study of the representation of social groups almost always requires insights into the ways a character is characterized. The narratological concepts of narration and focalization play a central part in chapter 3, 'Centrality'. An important part of the centrality of characters belonging to a social group is the ways in which they (are) narrate(d), as well as how they perceive the narrative world and how they are perceived by other characters. In order to gain insight into the one- or multi-voicedness of the groups in which characters function, chapter 4, 'Community', primarily uses the concept of polyphony as defined by Mikhail Bakhtin. Chapter 5, 'Conflict', makes use of the actantial model as described by A. J. Greimas to grasp the hierarchies in conflicts between characters belonging to a specific social group.

Social network analysis has a range of convenient metrics to dissect the relational structures between characters. A wide range of such metrics is contained in the software library Networkx written for the Python programming language used in most data-driven analyses in this book. Before applying those metrics, it is necessary to create network representations of the fictional populations in the corpus. Chapter 3 first describes a pipeline for extracting social networks of characters from each of the 170 novels, which will be the basis of the data-driven components of each of the chapters. In order to calculate the importance of social groups in statistical terms, this chapter then scrutinizes the social networks through a range of centrality metrics. The one- or multi-voicedness of character communities are studied in chapter 4 by breaking down the 170 networks into subnetworks of characters with a community-detection algorithm, as well as by computing so-called homophily, i.e., the extent to which any two characters share similar features in the networks. Chapter 5 models the dominance or subordination of character types in conflict situations by calculating a 'conflict score' for each character and then more generally models the extent of antagonism or social balance in the networks by analyzing triangular configurations of friends and enemies.

1.4.2 Corpus and Data

The corpus consists of all 170 submissions to one year of the Libris Literatuur Prijs (hereafter: the Libris prize), one of the most prestigious literary prizes in the Dutch language area.[60] As all new novels written in the Dutch language are eligible for the prize, the list of submissions consists of both Dutch and Flemish authors (more on the background of the authors in chapter 2). In this book, 'Dutch literature' thus refers to both Dutch and Flemish literature, as is common in the Dutch language area. The year 2013 is a randomly chosen sample year of the contemporary production of Dutch literary fiction. As the Libris prize targets novels published in the previous year, all novels in the corpus were published in 2012. The prize roughly follows the system used by the Man Booker Prize for Fiction. There is no restriction on the number of novels publishers can annually submit. From the aggregated list of all submitted novels, members of an annually changing professional jury first select a longlist of 18 titles, and then a shortlist of 6 titles. As publishers submit novels that they hope to be possible winners, the full list of submissions reflects what they see as high-quality literary fiction. Since 2010 the prize targets literary novels for adults exclusively. The consequence is that other forms of prose cannot be submitted: the bulk list of submitted novels does not contain young adult novels, children's books, fantasy, or (literary) thrillers.[61] As genre boundaries are obviously fluid, some Libris submissions could, however, to a greater or lesser extent be characterized as something other than literary fiction. Like the BookSpot Literatuurprijs (earlier known as the ECI Literatuurprijs, AKO Literatuurprijs, and Generale Bank Literatuurprijs) and the Fintro Literatuurprijs (earlier known as Gouden Uil), the Libris prize grants a relatively high amount of money to laureates. Each of the six shortlisted authors receives €2500. On top of that, the winner of the prize receives €50.000. Winning or being on the shortlist of the Libris prize thus not only leads to an increase in symbolic capital, it also affects the author's economic capital.

The corpus of 170 novels constitutes a fair share of the production of literary fiction in the sample year 2012. According to the database of the KB, the national library of the Netherlands,[62] 1,475 books with NUR-code 301 (literary fiction) were published in 2012. Subtracting duplicates, reissues, and exclusively online publications from this list results in a total number of 460 works of literary fiction originally published in Dutch. The sample of 170 novels thus represents 36.9 percent of the Dutch books of literary fiction published in this year. Compared to sample sizes in sociological research, the sample size of the current research is highly representative of the 'population' of books published in this genre in this year.[63]

In light of most qualitative, close-reading based scholarship, 170 novels is a rather large sample, but it is relatively small in comparison to other studies in the field of cultural analytics. This is especially true for studies focusing on English language texts, which can rely on extensive databases of texts such as the Hathi-Trust Digital Library, which is for instance used by Ted Underwood in *Distant Horizons* (2019). Andrew Piper uses a corpus of 7,500 English language novels containing 650,000 characters for the analyses presented in his chapter on characterization in *Enumerations* (2018), which is more than 44 times the size of the sample used in this book. The major benefit of the current sample size is that it makes manual annotation of character features possible. Up to the present, it is only possible to automatically detect the gender of characters by using programming pipelines such as BookNLP (Bamman et al., 2014; Piper, 2018; Underwood et al., 2018),[64] but this is done on the basis of predictions and is thus not as accurate as manual annotation.[65] Demographic features such as country of descent, level of education, age, and professional occupation are probably never fully automatically detectable, as they often remain implicit in the text and thus require a fair amount of interpretation. Furthermore, a sample size of 170 also enables a more efficient qualitative evaluation of algorithmic and statistical analyses than would be the case with a larger sample size. It requires less effort to check for, say, 10 percent of the 170 novels if the output of the algorithms match up human intuitions than it would be to do this for 10 percent or even 1 percent of 7,500 novels.

The analyses in the following chapters are based on an extensive collection of metadata – gender, country and place of descent, country and place of residence, age, level of education, profession, or daily activity – on 2,137 characters, as identified by human annotators. The data collection was carried out in several phases roughly between 2014 and 2018.[66] In 2014 a group of annotators contributed to the first phase of data collection, resulting in metadata on 1,176 characters.[67] As the guidelines for annotation were not as precisely defined in the first iteration, the annotation process was repeated twice with more clearly defined guidelines. Most importantly, a formal threshold was introduced to be able to distinguish which entities in a text should or should not be adopted in the database as characters.[68] In the period from 2017 to 2018, two student assistants increased the number of characters to a total of 2,137 characters and complemented some of the missing metadata in the earlier database.[69] Furthermore, these research assistants added relational information between characters (when known) –

friend, enemy, colleague, lover, family – to the database. All collected data and the software created for this book are available via an open-access GitHub repository,[70] which, however, does not contain the digital versions of the 170 texts of the novels due to copyright limitations.[71]

A deliberate reductionism is inherent to the process of data collection. First, not all demographic features are deducible from the narrative worlds. Contrary to most sociological survey data collections, a considerable number of features is unknown for the 2,137 identified characters in the corpus.[72] Second, literary texts have the possibility to (de)construct various definitions of, for instance, gender, as an author can play with notions of femininity and masculinity. In most cases, the annotations of the demographic categories cannot account for such artistic strategies. Third, the annotations are inevitably binary: this either/or logic does obviously not cover the variety of identities within one demographic category. This is not to say that the fluidity of these categories are outside the scope of this book; in the close reading of the case studies, attention is devoted to the ways in which such seemingly fixed categories are commented on.

1.4.3 Previous Research on Corpus and Dataset

The whole and parts of this dataset have been used in studies published earlier. Initially, a study on the first data collected in the period 2014–2015 was published in *Journal of Dutch Literature* in 2016, authored by Lucas van der Deijl, Saskia Pieterse, Marion Prinse, and myself. This article describes and interprets the diversity within the demographic landscape in the novels demonstrating that male, Western, higher educated characters are the dominant voices in the present-day Dutch literature the corpus is considered to be representative of. Although this article was granted the annual academic prize 2018 for best article published in 2016 and 2017 by the Society of Dutch literature (Maatschappij der Nederlandse Letterkunde), it was also met with fierce criticism.[73]

Together with professor of sociology Beate Volker, I coauthored the article 'Imagined Social Structures: Mirrors or Alternatives? A Comparison between Networks of Characters in Contemporary Dutch Literature and Networks of the Population in the Netherlands' in *Poetics* (2019). Based on 1,397 characters of the dataset (the second phase of data collection), this article compares the networks of characters in present-day Dutch literature with the actual networks of the present Dutch population. It argues, among other things, that social networks in Dutch literary fiction are less segregated in terms of descent than actual social networks. Although this comparative line of research between literature and society is not elaborated upon in the remainder of this book, it is a promising perspective on the million-dollar question as to how fiction reflects society.[74] This book is indebted to elements of the theoretical and methodological frameworks of these preliminary studies, and the subsequent chapters build on their findings.

1.5 STRUCTURE OF THE BOOK AND INSTRUCTION FOR READING

The second chapter, 'Data', contains an overview of the data on which the analyses presented in the third, fourth, and fifth chapters are based. It describes some basic statistics of the 2,137 characters populating the 170 novels in the corpus. In chapters 3, 4, and 5, an answer to each of the sub-questions is formulated (see 1.1.2 for an elaboration on the research questions). These chapters are structured in a similar fashion. Following the twofold theoretical framework and the mixed-methods setup presented in this introductory chapter, each of these three chapters starts with an elaboration of how its central concept (centrality, community, conflict) is theorized and operationalized in both network theory (a method used in data-driven research in cultural analytics) and narratology (a method used in qualitative critiques of literary representation). Based on these insights, one or more data-driven models are described and hypotheses are formulated. After the statistical patterns resulting from these models are described, their significance is assessed through one or more close readings of case studies from the corpus. Combining quantitative, network analytical, statistics-based analysis with qualitative, narratological, close-reading based analysis, these chapters demonstrate how centrality, community, and conflict of characters affect the representation of social groups in the corpus. Chapter 3 first describes the book's approach to extract fictional social networks from the texts in the corpus and then presents a model to predict which types of characters are central in terms of network structure. The results are then evaluated in light of a close reading of how certain social groups are depicted as dominant or subordinate in Özcan Akyol's *Eus* (2012).

Chapter 4 presents two models to detect communities of characters. The first model uses community detection algorithms to break down each of the 170 novels into distinct groups in order to test the extent of integration or segregation between genders, descents, classes, and ages. The depiction of communities in

Philip Huff's *Niemand in de stad* (2012) is then read against the background of the pattern generated by the model. In the second model, so-called 'homophily' is computed between every two characters in order to assess how characters of a certain gender, descent, education, and age tend to flock together in the narratives, the results of which are then evaluated through a close reading of how youth, old age, and death are represented in Mensje van Keulen's *Liefde heeft geen hersens* (2012).

Chapter 5 proposes two models of narrative conflict. Based on one-on-one conflicts between characters, the first model is used to test which types of characters are the dominant parties in conflicts between two characters. The resulting statistical pattern is then assessed by narratologically breaking down the conflict between classes in Bart Koubaa's *De Brooklynclub* (2012). The second model tests the extent of social balance in conflicts between three characters. Leon de Winter's *VSV* (2012) and Tommy Wieringa's *Dit zijn de namen* (2012) are then used to qualitatively demonstrate how social balance in such triangular conflicts to a greater or lesser extent results in a (schematic) moral opposition between social groups.

In order to answer the general research question 'How are social groups represented in present-day Dutch literary fiction?', the concluding, sixth chapter brings together the findings of the chapters on centrality, community, and conflict. It furthermore demonstrates the book's theoretical and methodological contribution to the field of cultural analytics and character-based critiques of representation. Finally, it evaluates the study's limitations and strengths and proposes directions for further research on the topic.

Because of the book's interdisciplinary approach, it targets a double audience. Its aim is to interest both scholars working in the qualitative strands of literary and cultural criticism and those experienced in quantitative, statistical, or computational methods. As each of these strands of research has its own academic style and conventions, it is a challenge to conform to prevalent norms in both strands, which I, however, have attempted in this book.

In order to avoid a confusion of tongues between audiences, I have clarified where necessary common narratological concepts and terms as well as the workings of statistical tests and computational techniques. It is, of course, very possible that readers not familiar with these concepts, terms, or techniques still have a hard time following along. If that is the case, there is always the possibility to skip the more technical parts of the book (and take my word for it) and start reading after the statistical results are reported. Likewise, readers who are primarily interested in the computational techniques can of course also focus more on these than on the literary theorizations and the close readings of case studies. Both types of readers can turn to the conclusion to each chapter for the main findings.

CHAPTER 2

DATA

2.1 INTRODUCTION: DESCRIPTIVE STATISTICS

How are social groups represented in present-day Dutch literary fiction? In order to provide an answer to this question, the subsequent third, fourth, and fifth chapters – on centrality, community, and conflict – each break down one aspect of this representation. As each of these chapters is based on the demographic metadata and relational information on 2,137 characters as annotated in several periods of data collection (see section 1.4.2 of the introductory chapter), a description of this dataset is first required. In this chapter, some basic descriptive statistics on the characters populating the 170 novels are presented.[1] A closer look at these descriptives is not only a convenient introduction to the data which the subsequent analyses are based on but also provides a first, general sense of how characters of a certain gender, descent, education, and age are depicted in the corpus.

Information on the authors of the 170 novels in the corpus is provided first. Then, a broad overview on the demographics of the 2,137 characters is reported, and some basic statistical tests are conducted to determine whether the occurrences of characters from a certain gender, descent, education, and age deviate significantly from their hypothesized occurrences. After this, tests are performed to determine whether or not gender, descent, education, and age of characters are statistically (in)dependent of one another. Following the demographic overview and the tests of independence, relational information is provided on how the roles of family, colleague, friend, lover, and enemy are distributed among these characters. Finally, this chapter concludes with a reflection on the reported descriptive statistics.

2.2 INFORMATION ON THE AUTHORS

The 170 novels were all written in the Dutch language. Of these books, 5 novels were written in collaboration, which leads to a total of 175 authors in the database. The gender divide among the authors is almost 70:30; 122 authors are male (69.7%) and 53 female (30.3%). The majority of the authors were born in the Netherlands (76.0%) or Flanders (16.6%).[2] A small portion of 7 authors originated from a non-Western country (4.0%).[3] In terms of education, it proved to be impossible to determine educational level for 14.8% of the male and 15.1% of the female authors. For those whose education could be retrieved, both male and female authors are higher educated (96.2% male, 100% female). Many authors live in Amsterdam (28%),[4] a smaller number lives outside one of the large Dutch cities in the Randstad (17.1%), followed by a share of authors living in a large city in the Randstad other than Amsterdam (10.3%) or one of the large cities of Belgium (8.0%).[5]

2.3 DEMOGRAPHIC METADATA ON THE CHARACTERS

In this book, the 170 novels in the corpus are used as a sample population of present-day Dutch literary fiction,[6] and the characters in those novels are subsequently considered as a sample of the population of fictional characters in present-day Dutch language fiction.[7] This population consists of 2,137 characters of which 59.80% is male and 40.10% is female; for only two characters the gender could not be determined (0.09%). Which gender distribution would we expect? Based on the hypothesis that authors tend to write more about characters of their own gender,[8] the overrepresentation of male authors (69.7%) in the corpus might suggest an overrepresentation of male characters as well. An alternative null hypothesis is that the gender distribution among characters reflects the gender distribution in the society the books were published in. This hypothesis, however, assumes that the fictional population of characters is a reflection of actual demographics, which is a thought-provoking but theoretically problematic assumption.[9] Leaving aside assumptions on the effect of author gender on character gender as well as effects of real-world population demographics, there is no reason to assume that there would not be an equal gender distribution between characters. In order to test if the null hypothesis of an equal gender distribution among characters holds, Pearson's chi-squared goodness of fit test was calculated comparing the occurrence of male and female characters with the hypothesized occurrence of a 50–50 gender distribution.[10] Significant deviation from the hypothesized values was found ($\chi 2$ (1) = 82.030, $p < 0.001$), which means that the gender ratio of, roughly, 60:40 is a statistically significant difference and is thus very unlikely to be due to chance. Male characters are, in other words, significantly more present in present-day Dutch literary fiction.

Figure 1 shows that the great majority of the characters originate from or live in the Netherlands (52.76% and 55.79% respectively), followed by characters originating from or living in Belgium (8.95% and 9.61% respectively), other countries in Europe (10.26% and 10.31% respectively), or non-Western and non-Middle Eastern countries (8.39% and 10.13% respectively; categorized as 'Other'). It is noteworthy that a relatively small portion of countries of descent and residence is unknown. Apparently, these are character features that are made explicit relatively often throughout the novels.

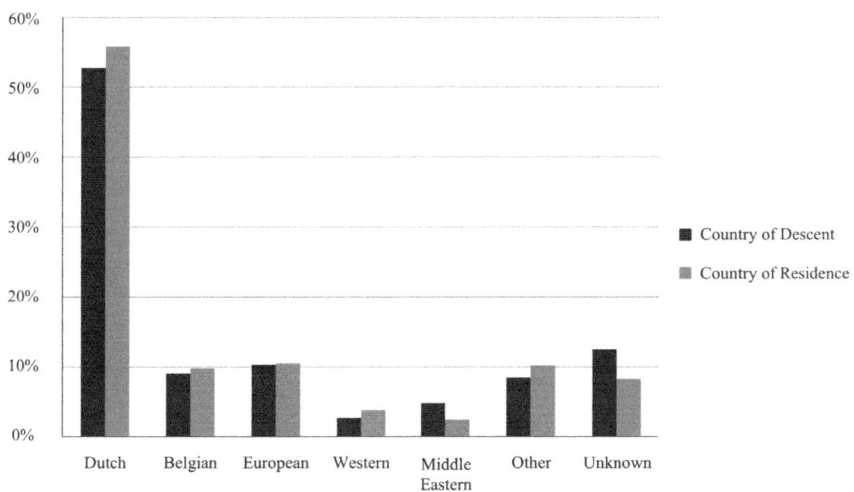

Figure 1. Character distributions for country of descent and country of residence (N = 2,137).

Following the same line of reasoning as for character gender, a reasonable null hypothesis is that distributions among places of origin and places of residence are equal for all categories. Of course, it can be argued that chances are high that Dutch language novels feature Dutch or Belgian characters because of the Dutch or Belgian background of their authors. An equally compelling argument, however, is that literary fiction is not bound to real world demographics, and that we might expect characters of a wide range of places of origin and residence in the Libris corpus. Following that argument, Pearson's chi-squared goodness of fit test was calculated comparing the occurrence of characters with a Dutch, Belgian, European, Western, Middle Eastern, or 'Other' country of descent with the hypothesized occurrence of an equal distribution among those categories. Significant deviation from the hypothesized values was found ($\chi 2\ (5) = 2599.865, p < 0.001$). The same test, with the same hypothesized occurrence, was carried out of for country of residence. This test also demonstrated a significant deviation from the hypothesized values was found ($\chi 2(5) = 2830.463, p < 0.001$). These tests indicate that the unequal distribution among countries of descent and residence is not due to chance, but points at a statistical difference. Given the majority of characters born or living in the Netherlands (52.76% and 55.79% respectively), these tests show that characters in present-day Dutch novels significantly more often originate from or live in the Netherlands than that they originate from, or live in, other countries.

For level of education the portion of unknown takes up 40.39% (see Figure 2). This suggests that education is a relatively less articulated or significant aspect of characters. This also applies to age (see Figure 3): for the largest part of the characters this is an unknown demographic feature (37.02%).

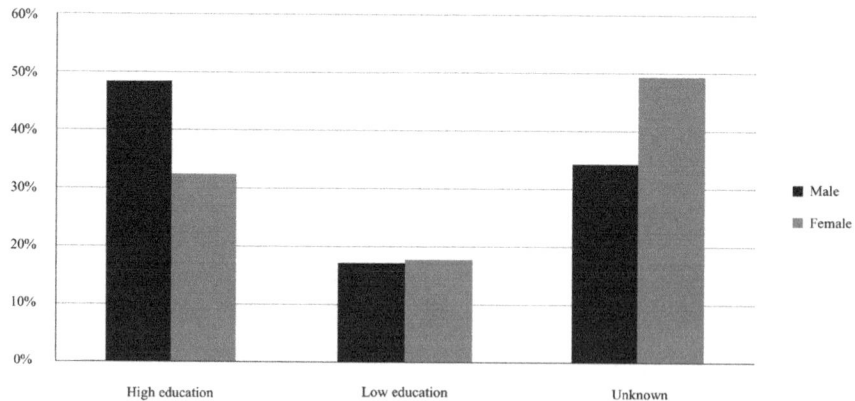

Figure 2. Character distributions for level of education, divided by gender (N = 2,137).

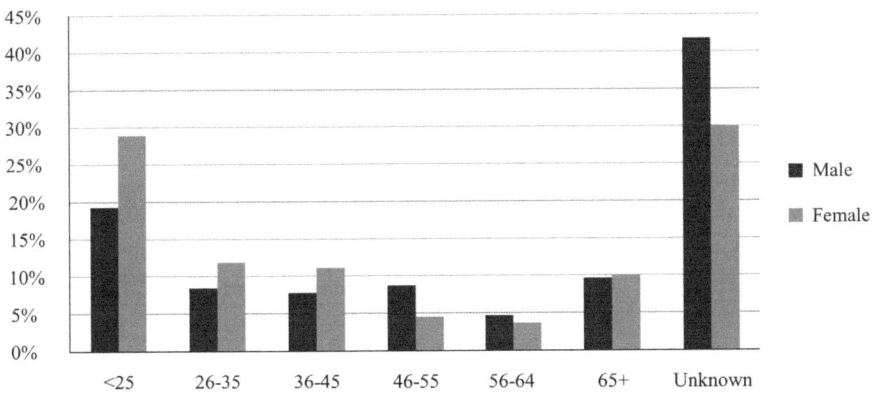

Figure 3. Character distributions for age, divided by gender (N = 2,137).

Again, there is no reason to assume that education or age would be unequally distributed among the characters. A chi-squared goodness of fit test was calculated comparing the occurrence of characters in age categories <25, 26–35, 36–45, 46–55, 56–64, 65+ with the hypothesized occurrence of an equal distribution among those categories. A significant deviation from the hypothesized values was found ($\chi2$ (6) = 1218.344, p < 0.001). For education, the same chi-squared goodness of fit test was calculated comparing the occurrence of characters with a high and a low level of education with the hypothesized occurrence of an equal distribution among those categories. Again, a significant deviation from the hypothesized values was found ($\chi2$ (2) = 247.890, p < 0.001). The results of these two tests indicate that the earlier found patterns of young and higher educated characters being overrepresented are thus significant.

2.4 (IN)DEPENDENCE OF VARIABLES

In order to determine whether or not two variables are (in)dependent on one another (e.g., gender on age or descent on education), Pearson's chi-squared tests of independence were conducted for a range of combinations of two variables.[11] The outcomes of these tests give a general insight in the intersections between demographic features and identity categories. For each of the four targeted categories in the analyses presented in the subsequent chapters (gender, country of descent, education, age), chi-squared tests of independence were computed for a range of combinations of the variables gender, education, age, and country of descent.[12]

For gender, associations between the variables education and age were tested. It would be interesting to see if gender is dependent on educational status, as well as to see if gender is dependent on youthfulness or maturity. There appears to be a significant association between character gender and character age ($\chi2\ (6) = 64.724, p < 0.001$), as well as between character gender and character education ($\chi2\ (2) = 60.579, p < 0.001$). This means that a character's gender and a character's age, as well as a character's gender and a character's education are not independent from one another but are significantly associated. These findings, however, only pertain to the general dependence of gender on respectively age and education, but do not reveal whether or not, for instance, female characters are more often higher educated and older than male characters. Below, the statistical significance of such differences is reported.

Looking at education and age from this binary gender perspective, some basic trends stand out. In general, the characters are higher educated (42.08%). Interestingly, level of education is more unknown for female than for male characters (see Figure 2), which is also a statistically significant difference (see Appendix A). Apparently, education is less mentioned or made less often explicit for female characters than for male characters. The opposite holds true for age (see Figure 3). In general, most characters are in age group <25 (23.01%) and the smallest portion of characters is represented in age group 56–64 (4.26%). More specifically, age is considerably more unknown for male characters (41.60%) than for female characters (29.94%), which appears to be a statistically significant difference (see Appendix A). These statistically significant differences demonstrate that age is more often mentioned for female than for male characters. Furthermore, female characters are on average younger than male characters, which is best visible in the overrepresentation of female characters in age categories <25, 26–35 and 36–45 (all differences are statistically significant, see Appendix A).

Besides interdependencies of gender on the one hand and education and age on the other, it is insightful to see how education and descent are statistically associated with one another. One hypothesis is that class, as indicated by education, is dependent on place of birth. A significant association between character education and character country of descent was found ($\chi2\ (10) = 99.562, p < 0.001$), as well as between character education and character city of descent ($\chi2\ (22) = 81.039, p < 0.001$). A character's education and a character's country of descent, as well as a character's education and a character's city of descent, are thus not independent of one another but are significantly associated.

Breaking down these associations between education and descent, Figure 4 shows that 45.3% of Dutch characters is higher educated. This is a statistically significant difference from the 29.8% of Belgian and 29% of Middle Eastern and 'Other'-descent characters who are higher educated (see Appendix A).

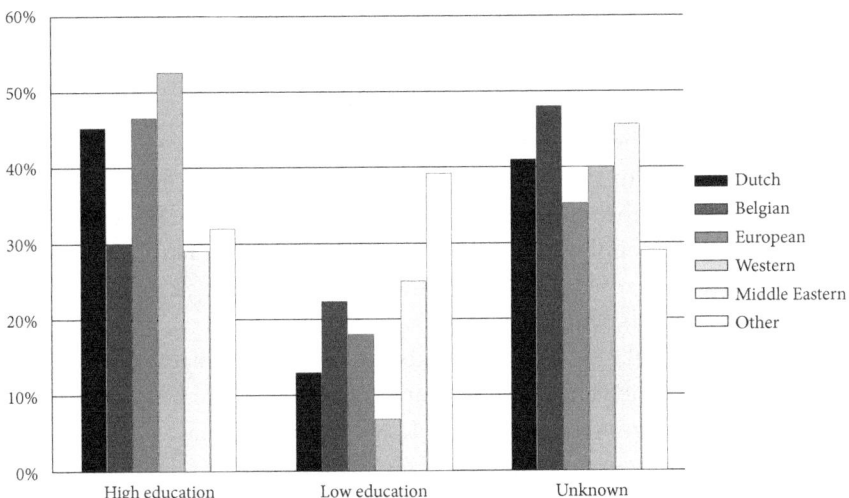

Figure 4. Character distributions for education, divided by country of descent (N =2,137).

The differences between European characters with a higher education (46.6%), Western characters with a higher education (52.6%), and Dutch characters is not statistically significant, indicating that for those characters a higher education is an equally mentioned character feature. A similar pattern holds for lower educated Dutch (13.3%), European (17.8%), and Western (7%) characters; those differences are again not statistically significant. Similar to higher education, the amount of lower educated Dutch characters (13.3%) differs significantly from lower educated Belgian (22.5%), Middle Eastern (25%), and 'Other' (39.1%) characters. Apparently, characters with Belgian, Middle Eastern, and 'Other' roots are significantly more likely to be lower educated than characters with Dutch roots.

The demographic landscape thus far presents an image that is complementary to the findings from earlier, preliminary research on the same corpus (Van der Deijl et al., 2016), which was based on a less extensive dataset.[13] The reported descriptive statistics on the present dataset do not dispute the general trends which were reported earlier: present-day Dutch literary fiction is predominantly populated by male, higher educated, Dutch characters (39). In this preliminary study, no Pearson chi-squared tests were conducted. These current tests statistically confirm the patterns that were observed earlier on a larger scale.

2.5 RELATIONAL INFORMATION

The added value of the present dataset not only lies in the larger number of characters, but also in the appended relational labels between characters. Appendix B contains the total distributions among the relational roles colleague, friend, lover, enemy, family. This general overview shows that family is the most prevailing relational role (42.39%), followed by colleague (25.49%), friend (16.56%), lover (9.7%), and enemy (5.86%).[14]

Breaking these relational data down by gender, a remarkable trend stands out. The gender distributions among characters sharing the above-mentioned relational roles are represented in Table 1. As opposed to male-male relations (38.57%) and opposite-sex relations (43.27%), female-female relations take up a minor part in these types of character relations (17.77%).

Relation type	*Frequency distribution*	*By male authors*	*By female authors*
male-male	38.57%	47.54%	19.72%
male-female / female-male	43.27%	41.60%	46.00%
female-female	17.77%	10.49%	33.79%

Table 1. Distribution of gender-gender character relations (N = 2,137), divided by gender author (N = 175).

These results bring to mind the famous Bechdel test for testing female presence in artworks, which is used to validate whether or not a story features a scene in which two women speak about something other than a man. The namesake of the test, cartoonist Alison Bechdel[15], was inspired by the feminist writings of Virginia Woolf, whose quote from *A Room of One's Own* first sparked the idea on which the Bechdel-test is based:

> All these relationships between women, I thought, rapidly recalling the splendid gallery of fictitious women, are too simple. [...] And I tried to remember any case in the course of my reading where two women are represented as friends. They are now and then mothers and daughters. *But almost without exception they are shown in their relation to men*. It was strange to think that all the great women of fiction were, until Jane Austen's day, not only seen by the other sex, but seen only in relation to the other sex. And how small a part of a woman's life is that [...] (Woolf, 1929, chapter 5; my emphasis)

Woolf signals that female characters in literary fiction are often primarily defined in their relation to male characters. Although Woolf had no dataset to back up her statements, the notion that the importance of women in fiction is relative to the male perspective has become common sense, of which the Bechdel test is a clear illustration. For the present dataset, this notion is supported by the relational data between male and female characters. Although Woolf's statement that female characters are 'almost without exception [...] shown in their relation to men' does not hold completely for this dataset, it is the case that relations between female characters are underrepresented in relation to male-male and opposite-sex relations.[16]

Filtered out by author gender, Table 1 also shows that male authors tend to write more about male-male (47.54%) or opposite sex relations (41.60%), and that female authors write more often about female-female (33.79%) or opposite sex relations (46.00%). Both male and female authors write sparsely about relations between two characters of the other gender.

In the subsequent chapters, the backgrounds of authors will not be a main focus in the analyses. In line with this book's text-centric focus,[17] the presented models will primarily target representations of social groups on the level of the text. The findings presented in Table 1, however, do suggest that at least author gender has an effect on these representations.

2.6 INTERPRETATION OF DESCRIPTIVE STATISTICS

The reported descriptive statistics provide a first, general image of the representation of social groups in present-day Dutch literary fiction. Anticipating the following chapter on centrality, the frequency distributions of the demographic categories are, in a broad sense, indicative of the dominance of certain character types over others. The 60:40 gender distribution indicates that male characters are more present, more visible, and thus possibly more central, than female characters. Another indication is given by the distributions within the categories of country of descent and country of residence: there is a significant overpopulation of Dutch characters as opposed to characters from other countries of descent and residence. These findings, however, only relate to frequency of occurrence. Male and Dutch characters are relatively central in terms of their frequency of occurrence in the corpus as a whole, but this does obviously not shed light on how male and Dutch characters in individual novels are represented.

The frequency distributions also suggest patterns that pertain to stereotypes or biases related to gender, class, and cultural background. This is particularly demonstrated by the amount of unknown or missing data with regard to education and age. From a gender perspective, these missing data invoke the bias that age is a more important demographic category for women than for men, which is also strengthened by the relatively large number of young female characters. In a similar vein, the discrepancy in unknown age between male and female characters relates to the bias that class, as expressed by educational status, is a more relevant demographic category for men than for women. Furthermore, the overrepresentation of higher educated Dutch, European, and Western characters as opposed to the underrepresentation of lower educated Middle Eastern and 'Other' characters reproduces existing class hierarchies between people of 'Western' and 'non-Western' descent. Belgian characters form an interesting exception to this pattern: they are in the same position as Middle Eastern and 'Other' character with regard to educational status but are clearly not part of the 'non-Western' category.

Descriptive statistics regarding the relational data indicate that family is the most central relational role which characters perform. This finding alludes to the commonplace of the family being the cornerstone of a society, which is described by former American president Lyndon B. Johnson in the following terms:

> The family is the cornerstone of our society. More than any other force it shapes the attitude, the hopes, the ambitions, and the values of the child. And when the family collapses it is the children that are usually damaged. When it happens on a massive scale the community itself is crippled. (Johnson, 1965)

In this view, the social structure of the family is crucial for a society's well-being; removing this cornerstone would lead to society gradually falling apart. For characters in present-day Dutch literary fiction, this also seems to hold: removing the family roles between the 2,137 characters in the 170 novels would lead to the decline of almost 40% of the relational roles in the corpus, and arguably to less connected, more fragmented fictional populations.

The overrepresentation of the colleague role as opposed to the friend and lover roles might be indicative of the dominance of work-related social roles. This ties in to another commonplace: the separation of professional and personal life. These findings suggest that the societies depicted in the corpus tend to be more focused on the former than the latter.

While some broad patterns regarding the hierarchies of depicted social groups in present-day Dutch literary fiction can be deduced from the descriptive statistics reported in this chapter, a network analytic approach is required to specify the nature of the relations between these groups. Whereas a first insight into the relational dimension is already hinted upon by the distribution of relational roles, it is still unclear how and to what extent characters with certain demographic backgrounds interact with one another on the level of the text. The subsequent chapter on centrality presents an approach to extracting social networks of characters from each of the texts in the corpus and proposes and evaluates a model to compute the centrality of characters based on the structure of these fictional social networks.

CHAPTER 3

CENTRALITY[1]

3.1 INTRODUCTION: NARRATIVE CORNERSTONES

How does the centrality of characters co-shape the representation of the social group(s) characters function in? In this chapter, the literary representation of social groups will be studied through the concept of centrality. Centrality will be used as an umbrella term to refer to abstract notions such as importance, dominance, influence, and power. A central character is important, dominant, influential, or powerful in one way or another. The term centrality will be operationalized through both a narratological and a network theoretical approach. By interconnecting these two seemingly distinct methodological traditions, a model is developed to pinpoint what it means for a character to be central in a narrative structure. As such, this chapter aims to show how the cross-fertilization between the methodological toolkits of narratology and social network analysis contributes to a better understanding of the centrality of characters belonging to a certain social group in present-day Dutch language fiction.

First, it will be discussed how centrality is commonly defined and operationalized in both network theory and narratology. On the basis of that discussion, a method is developed to extract fictional social networks of characters from each of the 170 texts in the corpus. Building on the descriptive statistics of the population of 2,137 characters in the dataset as reported in chapter 2, a hypothesis is formulated as to which types of characters occupy central positions in each of the extracted fictional social networks. A data-driven, statistical model is then developed to rank characters in each individual novel according to five common centrality metrics. Then, a multiple regression analysis is carried out to test which demographic categories predict a character's place in the rankings. Finally, the statistical pattern resulting from this regression analysis is discussed in light of a close reading of Özcan Akyol's *Eus* (2012), which is qualitatively assessed to determine how its depiction of female and migrant characters relates to the centrality of these types of characters in the corpus as a whole.

3.2 CENTRALITY IN NETWORK THEORY

The Russian-American mathematician and psychologist Anatol Rapoport is commonly regarded as one of the pioneers of social network analysis. In the 1950s, he voiced one of its central premises by pointing at the 'well-known fact that the likely contacts of two individuals who are closely acquainted tend to be more overlapping than those of two arbitrarily selected individuals' (Rapoport, 1954, as cited in Leinhardt, 1977, p. 75). Individuals, in other words, function in social networks in which some individuals are more closely related than others.

What is a network? Most generally, it can be defined as 'a pattern of interconnections among a set of things' (Easley & Kleinberg, 2010, p. 1). In network theory, those 'things' are commonly called 'nodes' and can consist of virtually anything: people of flesh and blood, molecules, trains, computers, Facebook profiles, commercial products, academic articles, cities, and fictional characters in literature or film. The term 'edges' is used to refer to the 'interconnections' between the nodes and can denote a variety of relations: cooperation, co-occurrence, affiliation, et cetera.

One of the founding articles of social network theory is 'The Strength of Weak Ties' (1973) by the American sociologist Mark Granovetter.[2] Its influence is demonstrated by its citation score on Google Scholar: in a period of 25 years, it has been cited 47,761 times.[3] By stressing the difference between strong and weak connections between individuals, Granovetter laid the foundation for viewing network relations in terms of their strength. Whereas it might seem obvious that strong relations between family or friends are important for individuals, Granovetter has emphasized that weak relations (e.g., between acquaintances) can have a significant influence on social cohesion as well (Granovetter, 1973). Of similar importance for the development of social network theory is Milgram's small-world experiment, in which the average distance between all inhabitants of the United States was shown to be only five or six (Milgram, 1967). Although Milgram never used the term 'six degrees of separation',[4] this led to the now common knowledge that everyone is connected with everyone else through a maximum of six steps, which suggests that the social world is extremely connected.

One of the core assumptions of network theory is that the relations between actors in a network affect the relative importance of those actors. Network theory has therefore been occupied with the question of how to measure the centrality of nodes in a network. The centrality of a node can be measured in a number of ways to consider different aspects of the network structure. In 1978 the American sociologist Linton Freeman observed that there is 'certainly no unanimity on exactly what centrality is or on its conceptual foundations, and there is very little agreement on the proper procedure for its measurement' (Freeman, 1978, p. 217). He conceptualized three basic centrality measures – degree, betweenness, and closeness – which are still being used today, albeit frequently in revised form, and which are thought to 'cover the intuitive range of the concept of centrality' (p. 237). It is worth mentioning that Freeman's intent was not 'to "lock in" to any sort of ultimate centrality measure' (p. 217), as centrality is a rather abstract concept and therefore hard to pinpoint statistically. Existing measures as those proposed by Freeman at best help to clarify what might be understood as central, but they do not necessarily give any definitive answers on which actors are most important in a network.

Before Freeman's innovation, centrality was mainly viewed in terms of degree. In Figure 1, node A has an advantage over B, C, D, and E because it has more relations to others in the network: A has a degree of 4, B, C, D, and E have a degree of 1. The main limitation of *degree centrality*, however, is that it does not consider the overall structure of the network. A node can be related to many other nodes but located in the periphery of the network, which results in a situation where the node is far removed from the opposite side of the network.

As an alternative to degree centrality, *closeness centrality* is defined as the sum of distances to all other nodes in the network. An advantage of closeness is that it accounts for the relative access that a node has to other nodes in the network. In Figure 1, node A has a higher closeness than B, C, D, and E, as it is directly connected with its neighbors, whereas B, C, D, and E need to cross through A to reach a node other than A. The disadvantage of closeness centrality, however, is that it cannot properly be applied to networks that are not fully connected. By definition, nodes in two disconnected components of a network are unable to reach one another, and therefore closeness cannot be computed for the overall structure of a network with disconnected components.[5]

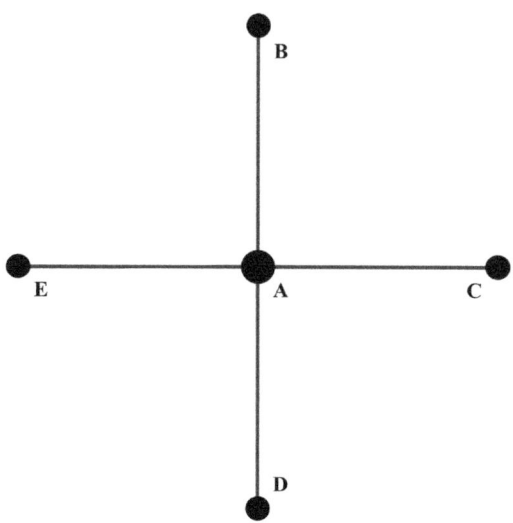

Figure 1. A star network with 5 nodes and 4 edges. The size of the nodes corresponds to the nodes' degrees. Adapted from Freeman (1978) and Opsahl, Agneessens, & Skvoretz (2010).

Freeman was the first to propose *betweenness centrality*, which computes the extent to which a node lies on the shortest path between two other nodes. In Figure 1, node A has a high betweenness centrality because it connects all four nodes with each other. As it is applicable to networks with disconnected components, betweenness has an advantage over closeness. However, as a metric, it is limited because nodes are often not located on the shortest path between any two other nodes. Because of that, B, C, D, and E in Figure 1 all have a betweenness centrality of 0.

In some networks, edges between nodes have the same status. For instance, networks of Facebook friends, in which the nodes are people on Facebook who are connected by virtue of being Facebook friends, features binary edges: a Facebook profile either is or is not befriended with another Facebook profile. This is essential rather than gradual: such edges have a weight of 1 as there is no spectrum on which the relation can be positioned. Compared to real-world friendships, this is of course a highly reductive representation of affairs. In a circle of friends, not every person is befriended with everyone else in exactly the same way. Jan might have a closer bond with Piet than with Marie, whereas Piet and Marie can share childhood memories that strongly connect the two of them together. Viewing such a circle of friends as if it were a Facebook network distorts this gradual spectrum on which the relational structures exist. Specific weights have to be added between every two nodes: a weight of, say, 5 might be ascribed to the relation between Jan and Piet (their connection is moderately strong), the relation between Marie and Piet might have a weight of 10 (because of their childhood connection), and the relation between Jan and Marie a weight of 2 (they only see each other at Piet's birthday parties).

In order to account for this, network theory makes a distinction between unweighted and weighted graphs. In a weighted graph, the edges represent the intensity with which two nodes are connected. As the basic centrality measures of degree, closeness, and betweenness are devised for application to unweighted, binary networks, alternative metrics have been proposed. Degree centrality has been redefined for weighted graphs by focusing not on the number of relations but on the sum of the weights of those relations (Barrat, Barthélemy, Pastor-Satorras, & Vespignani, 2004). Dijkstra's algorithm (Dijkstra, 1959), named after the Dutch computer scientist Edsger W. Dijkstra, has been used to redefine closeness and betweenness centrality by looking at the shortest paths in terms of distances (Brandes, 2001; Newman, 2001). As these new proposed metrics target primarily the weights and are less reliant on the number of relations, a second redefinition was needed to take into account both weight and number of relations (Opsahl et al., 2010).

Every network thus demands a specific approach; there is no general method that applies to every network. The first question is which elements constitute the network, the second how those elements are related. Then, it should be decided if the network is binary and unweighted, or if the elements are gradually related to one another. The appropriate centrality metrics should be derived from the specific nature of the network (weighted/unweighted, unipartite/ bipartite[6]) and the question through which it is approached, as not every centrality metric is relevant in all possible instances. There are cases in which degree centrality is most insightful, such as in the earlier mentioned binary, unweighted Facebook network. The Facebook profile with the most connections to other Facebook profiles is arguably a highly central actor in the overall Facebook network – the more connections, the more access to information on Facebook.[7]

Conversely, in a weighted, real-world network of friends, degree might actually not be a good indication of someone's importance in a circle of friends. Marie is connected to 35 other people, but the intensity of the larger part of those connections is very low (with a weight of only 1 or 2); only with Piet does Marie have an intense relation (with a weight of 10). Furthermore, the 35 people Marie is connected to all live in the same village, which makes her circle of friends geographically restricted. Piet, on the other hand, is befriended with only 10 people, but he has very strong connections with all of them, and they all live in different cities. For that reason, Piet's circle of friends is both very strongly connected and geographically widely distributed. Degree centrality is in this case a less suitable indication of centrality, as it only focuses on the number of relations but not on the exact position in the network. Betweenness centrality might be more suitable in this case, as it is able to differentiate between nodes that are able to bridge different, dislocated parts of the overall network. Having a variety of friends in different cities, Piet is a so-called 'broker': he functions as a mediator, a bridge, between remote circles of friends in different places.

Whereas network theory provides tools to compute the centrality of nodes in a network based on statistical metrics, narratology offers insights into the ways in which characters occupy more or less central positions in a narrative structure, which is described in the section below.

3.3 CENTRALITY IN NARRATOLOGY

Narratology offers different instruments to analyze the centrality of characters in narrative fiction, of which this section will mention two of the most straightforward. A character's position in the storyworld is already predetermined by some basic structural features of a literary text. The mode of narration is commonly a first indicator of how important a character is in the storyline. Handbooks of literature train first-year students to be aware of the embeddedness of certain narrative situations. Illustrative is the following introduction to the analysis of narrative texts from a frequently used handbook in Dutch literature departments:

> Epic or narrative texts are characterized by an embedded language situation. They mainly pivot on spokesmen that enter into a dialogue with one another, just as in drama. These are the characters. But this dialogical situation is embedded in a textual frame that is produced by a narrating instance. This instance produces text that is not perceived by the characters. Therefore, *the narrating instance is located on a higher textual level.* He can tell something about the characters; he can represent their words directly by creating dialogues; he can also

summarize their conversations; he can even represent their thoughts, directly or indirectly. *The narrating instance is thus above the world of the characters*, he has insights into the world of the characters and he reports information on that world in the text.[8] (Van Boven & Dorleijn, 2013, p. 33, my emphasis)

Although terms such as centrality, importance, or power are not explicitly mentioned, a hierarchical relation is posited between the narrating instance and the characters: the first 'is located on a higher textual level' and is 'above the world of the characters'. The idea that a narrating instance is located at the top of hierarchically embedded narrative layers is an axiom of narratology. From a network theoretical perspective, this makes sense: the narrator is the one who controls the flow of information in a narrative and therefore occupies a key role in the depiction of events and description of characters. The main insight is that narrating characters are not on an equal footing with non-narrating characters. Mode of narration can therefore be taken as a point of departure for the study of the centrality of characters.

Another concept suited for the study of character centrality is focalization, which was coined by the French structuralist Gerard Genette to distinguish between who narrates and who perceives in a text (1980). Others have suggested revisions of the concept (e.g. Bal, 1977; Jahn, 1996; Nelles, 1990); the revision that has become most popular is that of the Dutch scholar Mieke Bal. She defines focalization as 'the relation between the vision and that which is "seen", perceived' (Bal, 2009, pp. 145–146). An important difference with Genette's use of the term is that Bal's definition is able to discriminate between a focalizing subject (the one who perceives) and a focalized object (the one who is perceived). In this definition, focalization makes it possible to discern hierarchical relations between characters who occupy active focalizing roles and characters who are mainly in a passive position in which they are being focalized by other characters. The extent to which a character features in active focalizing roles is thus another indicator of its place in the character hierarchy.

Similar to the relation between the narrator and the narrated, the focalizer is in a hierarchical relation with the focalized:

> If the focalizer coincides with the character, that character will have an advantage over the other characters. The reader watches with the character's eyes and will, in principle, be inclined to accept the vision presented by that character. (Bal, 2009, pp. 149–150)

Even more than with the narrating instance, the focalizing instance has a major influence on the reader's perception of the narrative. A character's perception of an event or of another character usually goes hand in hand with a value judgment (cf. Jouve, 2001). The vision that is presented is not neutral but colored by a character's disposition toward an event or fellow character. More importantly, the character who is being perceived is not in a position to put forward his or her own vision on the state of affairs. As such, the perceived instance, the focalized object, is subjected to a process of objectification. There is, therefore, an inherent power imbalance between the focalizer and the focalized, which is of particular relevance for a qualitative assessment of which social groups are depicted as more or less central in literary texts.

It is noteworthy that narrators and focalizer sometimes coincide in texts. This is typically the case for novels that are narrated from a first-person perspective. In such novels, the first-person narrator is usually part of the world of characters. Often, the first-person narrating character is the main focalizing instance in the story: the chain of events is presented through his or her vision, while the vision of other characters is mostly presented indirectly. In third-person narratives, the narrating instance is usually anonymous and not part of the world of characters. Although such anonymous narrators are sometimes also focalizing other characters, it does not make much sense to frame this as a power imbalance between the anonymous narrator and the characters. This is because the narrator is only connected to the characters on a meta level but is not part of the fictional social network of characters as such. As a concept for the analysis of character centrality in third-person narrated novels, focalization is thus primarily suited to analyze characters that are part of the fictional social network.

As the basic features of mode of narration and focalization affect the position of characters in the narrative, they are taken into account in this book's method for extracting fictional social networks of characters from the 170 texts in the corpus. The corpus is divided into three sub-corpora based on their mode of narration and/or focalization: first-person narrated novels (63), third-person narrated novels (73), and multi-perspective novels (34). The next section describes in detail the method developed for each sub-corpus individually.

3.4 METHOD FOR EXTRACTING CHARACTER NETWORKS

In this section, a method is described to extract fictional social networks of characters from each of the 170 texts in the corpus.

3.4.1 Characters as Nodes

Each novel in the corpus can be regarded as a network with characters as nodes and relations between those characters as edges. In character studies, multiple definitions of the concept of characters circulate (see the introductory chapter, section 1.1.3). This book follows the most straightforward definition of *The Living Handbook of Narratology* as 'a text- or media-based figure in a storyworld, usually human or human-like' (Jannidis, 2013). In order to automatically extract character networks from the novels, characters first have to be detected in the texts, which requires a formalization of the concept of character. Following Van Boven and Dorleijn's definition of characters as 'people or creatures which to a greater or lesser extent are presented as human, existing of not more than a few linguistic features' (2013, p. 335), the challenge is to define which linguistic features are essential characteristics of characters. The most eye-catching linguistic feature of a character is commonly its name,[9] although not every character bears one. But a character is usually referred to not exclusively through their name but also through pronouns ('he', 'she', 'I') and coreferents ('the man in the alley', 'the one who has been chosen', 'the mother of the child'). To this date, coreference resolution is an unresolved problem in Natural Language Processing (e.g. Clark & Manning, 2016).[10] Previous studies (Vala, Jurgens, Piper, & Ruths, 2015) have shown that automatic detection of characters is difficult due to the poor performance of existing coreference resolution techniques.[11] Because of this poor performance, the present study does not aim for full coreference resolution but instead uses a semi-automatic method that builds on a predefined set of characters. Building on Van Boven and Dorleijn's formal definition (2013, p. 335), characters are defined here as *people or creatures which to a greater or lesser extent are presented as human, existing of not more than a few linguistic features including one or more names*.[12]

For each novel, a list of names is generated with Named Entity Recognition (NER);[13] characters whose name frequency is above a normalized threshold value (based on the number of words of the text) will be regarded as characters. With this most viable approximation of a character's presence in a text, the detection of characters in the present study is thus restricted to occurrences of name variants of each character. Lists of all variants of a character's name are generated and stored in a database called NAMES, which corresponds to the databases NODES, EDGES, and BOOKS (see Figure 2). BOOKS contains all relevant metadata of the novels, such as title, the name, gender, and age of the author, the publisher, and the filename of the digital version of the novel. NODES contains all relevant metadata of the characters, such as name, gender, country of descent, city of descent, country of residency, city of residency, education, and profession. EDGES contains all relevant metadata on the character relations, such as the specific nature of the relation (friend, family, enemy, lover, professional). NAMES contains all variants of a character's name. All databases are linked to one another through a unique book id. NAMES, NODES, and EDGES are also connected through a unique character id. Based on these interlinked databases, the character networks are computed through an Object-Oriented model written in the Python programming language, consisting of three main classes: Book, Character, and Network (Smeets & Sanders, 2018).[14]

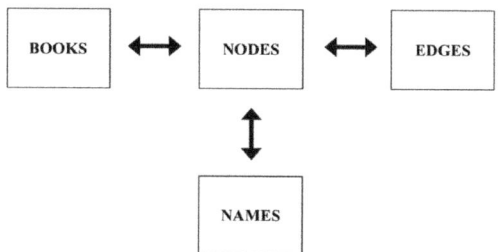

Figure 2. Visualization of database linkage.

Each book in the corpus has a unique id ranging from 1 to 170. Every character in the corpus has a unique id that corresponds to this book id stored in database BOOKS. For instance, *De lichtekooi van Loven* by Ineke van der Aa is represented by the book id 1. In database NODES, character 'Louise' is represented by this same book id followed by character id 1 and her name (1_1_Louise). In database NAMES, this same unique identifier is followed by every name variant of the character. The name variants for this character are 'Louise', 'Louisje' and 'Louiseke', which is represented in NAMES as 1_1_Louise_Louise, 1_1_Louise_Louisje and 1_1_Louise_Louiseke. Each novel's text is then automatically searched for every of these name variants, after which these variants are replaced by the unique character identifier.[15] Figure 3 shows a piece of text from *De lichtekooi van Loven*, in which name variants 'Lili' and 'Louisje' occur. Figures 3 and 4 show how these aliases are replaced by a unique character identifier.

As such, each text is marked with character identifiers representing the occurrences of each character. These markers are then used to map interactions between characters.

```
's Nachts werd het stiller, maar nooit helemaal. Als de kinderen
eindelijk zwegen, begon de trillende stem van mijn vader: 'Lili
…' maar Lili kwam hem nooit troosten. Alleen ik lag daar,
ineengekruld op mijn matras. Om hem niet te horen, trok ik mijn
deken over mijn hoofd. Als ik goed luisterde, hoorde ik de
kakkerlakken en vlooien krioelen onder mijn gewicht.

Elke nacht, voordat ik de slaap kon vatten, kwam mijn moeder ons
huisje binnen. Ze werd omringd door wit licht zoals de Madonna
van Sint-Pieter, maar zij droeg een witte robe à la française[2]
met kanten boordjes. Haar blonde haar krulde tot op haar heupen
en ze had een blik die vertelde dat alles goed was. Ze boog zich
over mijn vader en legde haar armen om hem heen terwijl ze een
slaaplied zong. Het suste hem en hij werd stil.

'Droom zacht, Louisje', fluisterde ze tegen mij en ze legde een
warme hand op mijn hoofd. Als in een betovering viel ik in
slaap, en zag haar in mijn dromen weer.
```

Figure 3. Original text snippet from De lichtekooi van Loven by Ineke van der Aa.

```
's Nachts werd het stiller, maar nooit helemaal. Als de kinderen
eindelijk zwegen, begon de trillende stem van mijn vader:
'1_12_L|i|l|i|a|n|n|e_L|i|l|i …' maar
1_12_L|i|l|i|a|n|n|e_L|i|l|i kwam hem nooit troosten. Alleen ik
lag daar, ineengekruld op mijn matras. Om hem niet te horen,
trok ik mijn deken over mijn hoofd. Als ik goed luisterde,
hoorde ik de kakkerlakken en vlooien krioelen onder mijn gewicht.

Elke nacht, voordat ik de slaap kon vatten, kwam mijn moeder ons
huisje binnen. Ze werd omringd door wit licht zoals de Madonna
van Sint-Pieter, maar zij droeg een witte robe à la française[2]
met kanten boordjes. Haar blonde haar krulde tot op haar heupen
en ze had een blik die vertelde dat alles goed was. Ze boog zich
over mijn vader en legde haar armen om hem heen terwijl ze een
slaaplied zong. Het suste hem en hij werd stil.

'Droom zacht, 1_1_L|o|u|i|s|e_L|o|u|i|s|j|e', fluisterde ze
tegen mij en ze legde een warme hand op mijn hoofd. Als in een
betovering viel ik in slaap, en zag haar in mijn dromen weer.
```

Figure 4. Text snippet from De lichtekooi van Loven by Ineke van der Aa, in which name variants are automatically replaced by unique character identifiers.

3.4.2 Character Relations as Edges

In networks consisting of fictional characters, nodes are perhaps quite obviously represented by the characters in the text, but it is less obvious how edges between these nodes are constituted. Earlier research on character networks differed in their approaches. One of the most used definitions of character relations frames connections between characters in terms of conversations or dialogues (Elson, Dames, & McKeown, 2010; Jayannavar, Agarwal, Ju, & Rambow, 2015; Lee & Yeung, 2012; Lee & Wong, 2016; Moretti, 2013; Stiller et al., 2003). The quantifiable unit of the conversation is, however, not the best indication for character interactions, as there are plenty of characters that do not enter into a conversation but are related to one another in some other way. For instance, two characters with family ties might never speak to each other, but such a relation should definitely be regarded as a character relation. Another way to define relational ties is in terms of co-occurrence in the same window of N words, sentences, paragraphs, or chapters (Alberich, Miro-Julia, & Rossello, 2002; Grayson, Wade, Meaney, & Greene, 2016). Defining character relations in terms of adjacency in the text will be able to capture more instances of character interaction than when it is defined in conversational terms. This is the most bottom-up definition of character relations, as characters do not have to communicate in a literal sense (as is the case in conversation networks) to be considered as having a form of interaction. Character relations are defined here as *co-occurrences of character name variants in a window of N tokens*.

This definition is based on the assumption that the strength of a character relation increases when a character occurs more often near another character. Nearness is defined here as characters occurring in the same reach, referred to as a window consisting of a specific amount (= N) of for instance words, sentences, paragraphs, or chapters (= tokens). Experiments were conducted with different window units and sizes for different types of novels to find the 'sweet spot' where not too many and not too few character interactions are detected (cf. Grayson et al., 2016). However, such a sweet spot is different for every novel. In order to be able to compare the novels, the same window unit and window size for every novel was used. As sentences are the smallest linguistic structures which are semantically meaningful in themselves (cf. Mann, William & Thompson, Sandra, 1988), sentences were as the window unit, which were tokenized using the Ucto software.[16] The window size was set to two sentences, as semantic relations are known to extend over two sentences through connectives (cf. Blühdorn, 2010).[17] A customized co-occurrence approach for each mode of narration was developed (first-person, third-person, multi-perspective), which is described in detail in section 3.4.3.

However, character co-occurrence does not capture any thematic relations such as family or friend. For that reason, the dataset was manually enriched by two student assistants who gathered extensive relational information.[18] Among all 2,137 characters identified in the corpus, the following thematic roles were annotated: friend, lover, colleague, enemy, family (specified through all possible subcategories such as mother, son, brother, grandmother, et cetera). 8,732 of these roles were stored in the EDGES database. As it was not always evident which labels apply for a relation between two characters, interpretive deduction was therefore sometimes unavoidable. In general, the roles were defined as narrowly as possible. Colleague, for instance, was used for every two characters who had a professional relation of some kind, whereas enemy was used for characters who were clearly hostile to one another. Note that 'professional' and 'hostile' are not objective categories but require interpretation. Changing relations between characters were also accounted for. In those cases double labels were assigned, such as Colleague_Enemy. Double labels were also assigned when the nature of the relation changed over time, such as friends becoming enemies.

3.4.3 Automatic Extraction of Character Networks

For each sub-corpus (first-person, third-person, multi-perspective) a slightly different co-occurrence approach was developed based on the specific mode of narration. Third-person novels are narrated by an anonymous narrator who follows one main character. First-person novels are narrated by an I-narrator. Multi-perspective novels are narrated by multiple narrators, either in third or first-person. For all novels, irrespective of their mode of narration, relations between characters are preestablished when they are annotated with one of the relational labels that are stored in EDGES (friend, family, lover, enemy, colleague). In all cases, the procedure below is used to establish the weight of the relations.[19]

1. Third-person narrated novels [63 novels]
   For every character in the novel, a sliding window approach is used in which co-occurrences of two characters are mapped in a window of two sentences. Whenever two characters occur in the range of the same two sentences, a relation between those characters is established. The more often such a co-occurrence takes place, the stronger their relation becomes.

2. First-person narrated novels [73 novels]
    a. As the first-person narrator has a priori high centrality in narratological terms, the relation of the first-person narrator with all other characters are simply defined by counting every occurrence in the novel of characters other than the first-person narrator. As every character is embedded in the narration of the first-person narrator, it can be argued that every character occurrence represents a relational tie with the first-person narrator. The more often a character occurs in the novel, the stronger its relation with the first-person narrator is.
    b. For every character other than the first-person narrator, a sliding window approach is used in which co-occurrences of two characters are mapped in a window of two sentences. Whenever two characters occur in the range of the same two sentences, a relation between those characters is established. The more often such a co-occurrence takes place, the stronger their relation becomes. Note that this approach will in most cases rightfully lead to relatively strong relations between the first-person narrator and all other characters, whereas this is not the case for the relations between and among all other characters.
3. Multiple perspective novels [34 novels]
    A student assistant annotated for each of these novels where a character perspective begins and ends in the text.[20] These annotations also contain information on the narrative mode and focalization: a first-person or third-person narration was annotated as such, and for third-person narration the main focalizer was annotated. On the basis of those annotations, each novel was divided in separate sections. For sections narrated respectively from first- or third-person, the first- or third-person method was applied. After that, the co-occurrence counts between characters were aggregated for all the separate sections.

All these relations are symmetrical and thus undirected. This means that the character relations are not regarded in terms of directionality, which is a logical consequence of the co-occurrence approach, as adjacency is an a priori symmetrical issue. Furthermore, the resulting networks, with characters as nodes and character relations as edges, are both undirected and weighted. Not every relation between any two characters will have the same status as the strength of a relation is increased when two characters occur more often in the same window.

Of major importance is the definition of 'window' that is used in the sliding window approach. The goal is to automatically compartmentalize the narrative in order to detect character interaction in a precisely delineated context. This delineation can be done on the basis of three quantifiable linguistic units, from small to large:

1. characters (i.e., the letters of the alphabet and symbols, and not in the sense of 'fictional characters')
2. words
3. sentences

Which of these linguistic units is most suited for mapping character interaction depends on linguistic-semantical considerations. The smallest building blocks of a text are characters, the symbols that represent a number or a letter. These are not semantically meaningful in themselves but gain their significance only when formed into words, which are the second smallest building blocks of the text. Words carry meaning in different ways: function words ('the', 'a') only perform a grammatical function in a text, whereas content words ('animal', 'person') carry meaning in themselves.

One can argue that words only become meaningful in relation to the syntactical structure in which they are embedded. A sentence is commonly regarded as the smallest syntactical structure that is meaningful as a closed-off system in itself (cf. Mann et al., 1988). Furthermore, as well as the linguistic units used, the size of this window (of characters, words, or sentences) will greatly influence the results (Grayson et al., 2016; Wade & Grayson, 2016; Zadeh & Handschuh, 2014). A window size too small will capture too few character interactions, whereas a window size too large will capture too many. The smallest possible window size would be 1 (character, word, or sentence). Essentially no interaction takes places in a window size of 1 based on characters or words. When the unit of a window is a sentence, interaction is possible: two characters can occur in one sentence. The biggest window size would be as big as the total number of units (characters, words, or sentences) in the novel. A window this big would lead to nonsensical results as every character will be connected to every other character as often as they occur in the novel. Therefore, it is essential to find a so called 'sweet spot': a window size of N tokens (characters, words, or sentences) that leads to a network that is not too small or too large, but reasonably reflects the intensity of interaction between any two characters.

Although this methodological problem could have been approached in a bottom-up, data-driven way,[21] it was tackled top-down by taking into account linguistic theoretical considerations. As mentioned above, sentences are the smallest syntactical structures in which the linguistic elements are semantically related to another (cf. Blühdorn, 2010). Whenever two characters occur in the same sentence, one can therefore be sure that they are somehow related to one another. This is not necessarily the case for two characters appearing in the same window of N characters or words, as those characters or words are not always part of an overarching semantic framework. For this reason, the window unit was set to sentences. All novels from the corpus are thus split into sentences by tokenizing the texts with the Ucto software.[22]

Furthermore, linguists have shown that semantic connections in language are formed not only in a sentence but also between two adjacent sentences (cf. Blühdorn, 2010), for instance through connectives in the form of conjunctions (as, and, but, if, or), prepositions (at, by, in, to), relative pronouns (who, which, what, that), conjunctive or relative adverbs (hence, when, whence, where, why). It can therefore be argued that characters occurring in the same two sentences have a relational tie. Because of these considerations the window size was set to two sentences. Interestingly, windows defined in this way come close to the window size used by Grayson et al. (2016). Although they use words instead of sentences, the sizes are similar. Grayson et al. (2016) use varying window size that are not much smaller or bigger than around 50 words, which approximates the number of words in two sentences, considering that the average sentence has around 15–20 words.

Figure 5 shows an example window of two sentences in which two characters, represented by their unique identifier, occur. Whenever the algorithm finds co-occurrences of two characters in this context, the weighted relation between characters X and Y is incremented by 1. The generated weights are subsequently used to compute the degree, betweenness, closeness, and other centrality metrics for each character in the corpus.

```
Misschien keek ik nog ' te hard ' , zoals 1_3_G|e|r|t|r|u|d|e_T|r|u|d|i het noemde , dus keek ik naar de grond en liet
ik mijn schouders wat hangen , zoals ik bij een hond zou doen die zich bedreigd voelt .
1_12_L|i|l|i|a|n|n|e_L|i|l|l|i|a|n|n|e wendde op haar beurt haar hoofd af en gebaarde met trillende handen naar de
fauteuil .
```

Figure 5. A window of two sentences in De lichtekooi van Loven by Ineke van der Aa.

In order to determine the extent to which this approach to character network extraction matches up human intuitions, a sample of extracted character networks was qualitatively assessed. For each of these cases, the extracted character networks were compared with a reading of the novel. In all instances, the characters that seemed central units in the narrative also ended up as central characters in the character networks, while the side characters ended up in more peripheral positions. This cursory validation suggests that the presented approach to character network extraction at least conforms to common sense perceptions about protagonists, main characters, and side characters.

3.5 MODEL I: CHARACTER RANKINGS

For each of the 170 novels in the corpus a unipartite, undirected, weighted network is thus extracted based on the method explained in the previous section. With Python's software package networkx,[23] the resulting networks for each individual novel are used to rank the characters on the basis of five centrality metrics (see section 3.2 of this chapter for an overview of centrality metrics). These rankings provide a view on how central a certain character in the corpus is according to one of the centrality metrics. Among those metrics are the above-described degree, betweenness and closeness centrality, as well as eigenvector and Katz centrality, two metrics on which Google's PageRank algorithm is based. PageRank is used by Google's search engine to rank web pages by relevance. PageRank, eigenvector, and Katz are all based on the same, seemingly circular assumption that a node in a network becomes more important when it is connected to other important nodes (Page, Brin, Motwani, & Winograd, 1999). Unlike eigenvector centrality, Katz centrality tends to be more useful for networks that are not strongly connected. For Katz centrality, the default options were used as free parameters. The computation of all these metrics is based on the weighted edges.

3.5.1 Results Multiple Regression Analysis

A regression analysis was carried out to determine the extent to which the demographic variables (gender, descent, age, education) predict a character's place in the rankings.[24]

Because of the exploratory nature of the present study and the absence of prior research on this topic, there were no strong suggestions for a hypothesis about which demographic factors would possibly determine a character's place in the rankings. However, it was preferable to not just enter all possible variables into the regression equation as this would possibly obscure the results of the analysis. Therefore, a nonformal hypothesis was formulated based on qualitative, nonstatistical research in the critique of literary representation. Several studies suggest that female characters and/ or characters of mainly non-Western descent are often represented in a stereotypical manner and are therefore likely to be featured in less central, more marginal positions in literary texts (e.g. Meijer, 1996a, 1996b, 2011; Minnaard, 2010; Pattynama, 1994, 1998). Gender and descent are therefore possible predictors of a character's position in the rankings. Based on descriptive statistics on the dataset (see chapter 2 'Data'), it can be suspected that male and nonmigrant characters will end up as more central,[25] since these types of characters are simply more present in the dataset (see Figure 6).[26] More precisely, it is hypothesized that both male characters and nonmigrant characters will score higher on the centrality metrics than female characters and characters with a migration background.

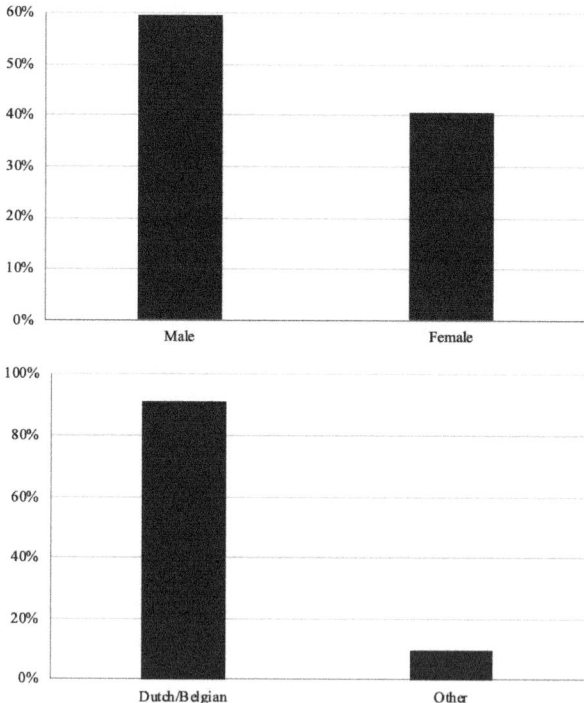

Figure 6. Gender and descent distributions among characters in the corpus (N=2,137). The numbers are based on types, not on tokens. Missing data are not displayed in this figure.

For each of the five centrality metrics (degree, betweenness, closeness, eigenvector, Katz), a multiple linear regression was conducted to predict characters' centrality scores based on their gender and descent. Gender is coded as 0 for male and 1 for female. Descent is coded as 0 for nonmigrant and 1 for migrant. As the aim was to generalize over all novels, the division between sub-corpora (third-person, first-person, multi-perspective) is not included in the statistical model. This division was only used for the computation of the extraction of networks and does not need to be accounted for in the outcome of the regression model.

No significant results were found for betweenness, closeness, and eigenvector centrality. Gender and ethnicity are thus no predictors for characters' scores on betweenness, closeness, and eigen-vector centrality.

However, significant results were found for degree and Katz centrality. First, for degree centrality, a significant regression equation was found ($F(2, 2128) = 6.424$, $p < 0.01$), with an R^2 of 0.006. Characters' predicted degree centrality is equal to a B value of 0.428 + 0.024 (GENDER) + 0.059 (DESCENT) (see Table 1). This means that, on degree centrality (on a scale from 0 to 1), female characters scored 0.024 higher than male characters, and migrant characters scored 0.059 higher than nonmigrant characters.

Model		Unstandardized coefficient		Standardised coefficient	
		B	Std. Error	Beta	Sig.
1	(Constant)	0.438	0.006		0.000
	Descent revised	0.058	0.019	0.065	0.003
2	(Constant)	0.428	0.008		0.000
	Descent revised	0.059	0.019	0.066	0.002
	Gender	0.024	0.012	0.043	0.048

Table 1. Linear model of predictors of degree centrality.

Secondly, for Katz centrality a significant regression equation was found ($F(2.2128) = 6.124$, $p < 0.01$), with an R^2 of 0.006. Characters' predicted Katz centrality is equal to a B value of 0.272 + 0.009 (DESCENT) + 0.007 (GENDER) (see Table 2). This means that, on Katz centrality (on a scale from 0 to 1), migrant characters scored 0.009 higher than nonmigrant characters, and female characters scored 0.007 higher than male characters.

		Unstandardized coefficient		Standardised coefficient	
Model		B	Std. Error	Beta	Sig.
1	(Constant)	0.273	0.002		0.000
	Gender	0.007	0.003	0.061	0.005
2	(Constant)	0.272	0.002		0.000
	Gender	0.007	0.003	0.062	0.004
	Descent revised	0.009	0.004	0.045	0.038

Table 2. Linear model of predictors of Katz centrality.

These findings suggest that the initial hypothesis, based on qualitative critiques of literary representation, should be rejected. Contrary to what was expected, female characters and migrant characters scored higher, at least on two of the five centrality metrics used in the analysis. Based on these results, it can be argued that a higher frequency distribution of a character type does not necessarily lead to a more central position in a character network, as the results of the regression analysis have shown. Although male and migrant characters are more present in the corpus, they do not end up as more central in network analytic terms.

These results invoke questions with regard to the notion of centrality in narrative fiction. While the frequency of occurrence of certain types of characters impacts their presence, their visibility, in narrative fiction, characters who occur relatively less frequently (and thus are less present, less visible) can still occupy central positions in their social networks. Does this mean that authors ascribe more central roles to social groups that are less present? In order to better understand what this finding means for centrality of characters in narrative fiction, the pattern is qualitatively assessed in the next section by close reading one novel from the corpus.

3.5.2 Close Reading: Centrality, Gender, and Descent in Özcan Akyol's *Eus* (2012)

As it is unclear what the significance of the quantitative representational patterns generated by the regression model is for the critique of literary representation, a narratological evaluation of these patterns is warranted to pinpoint what these patterns mean at the level of the individual text. In concrete terms, the finding for degree centrality is that female and migrant characters have significantly more relations than male and nonmigrant characters. More specifically, women and characters with a migration background often co-occur with a wider range of fellow characters in the novels. The higher scores of female and migrant characters on Katz centrality indicate that they often co-occur with characters who also have relatively high Katz centrality. In sum, female and migrant characters have both *more* relations in general and more relations with *important* characters.

In order to make sense of this pattern, a narratological exploration of character centrality in one novel from the corpus was conducted and confronted with the results of the statistical analysis. The data-driven model presented in the previous section generated a statistical baseline: the finding that female and migrant characters occupy relatively central positions in fictional social networks. Individual works can be compared to this baseline in order to determine the extent to which they conform to or deviate from it. This statistical baseline thus functions as a norm of representation in light of which this section's case study was qualitatively assessed. As there is a field of tension between the usage of 'centrality' or 'importance' in network theory and its usage in narratology, special attention was paid to the various meanings of these terms in both disciplines and the potential conflicts between them.

As a case study, a novel was used in which both gender and descent are thematized, as these were also used as variables in the regression analysis. For the sake of clarity, only the two earlier mentioned basic concepts of narration and focalization were used as points of departure. Note that there is a wide variety of other narratological concepts and perspectives that might potentially lead to alternative insights. How do narration and focalization shape the centrality of female and migrant characters in this particular narrative? And how does the relative importance of these types of characters in this novel relate to the statistical baseline that female and migrant characters are relatively central in the corpus as a whole?

Eus (2012) by Özcan Akyol is a semi-autobiographical first-person narrated novel, in which the reader follows the life of first-person narrator Eus. The novel clearly conforms to certain conventions of the (Dutch) picaresque novel ('schelmenroman') in the tradition of Jan Cremer's *Ik, Jan Cremer* (1964): Eus is a sly social outcast with loose sexual morals who gets involved in criminal activities. Unlike most novels in this genre, however, the migration background of Eus's family plays a crucial role in his story. He is the son of Turkish migrants living in Deventer, a small city in the Netherlands. Because of his criminal activities he ends up in jail, where he starts a writing career. This plotline thus foregrounds the theme of upward social mobility: a character with a migration background from the lower social classes, who initially has a hard time finding his way in Dutch society, eventually finds his creative ambition and becomes a successful author.

Oppositions between people with either Dutch or non-Dutch cultural backgrounds are thematized by Eus's emphasizing of the socioeconomic hierarchies that exist between these social groups. At the beginning of the novel, Eus states that he and his friends 'didn't dare to go to the better neighborhoods', although they 'knew that they existed' (Akyol, 2012, p. 24).[27] An implicit opposition is thus postulated between 'better neighborhoods' populated by Dutch, higher class people and Eus's own, apparently lesser neighborhood inhabited by a wide range of people with a migration background. Later on in the novel, his characterization of the 'indigenous youth, rich kids' as 'white scum' (p. 120) explicitly shows that *Eus* expresses a negative disposition towards people in these 'better neighborhoods'.

Another less prevalent, but latently present theme in the novel is the way in which men (with a migration background) engage with (Dutch) women. Throughout the novel, women are treated with little respect by Eus and his friends. Female characters are either object of sexual desire or considered a man's possession. They are repeatedly referred to as 'whore' (pp. 36, 58, 85, 145) and variants on the term 'slut' (pp. 43, 57, 62, 86, 145, 157, 176, 253). The male characters seem mostly interested in whether or not a woman is 'fuckable' (p. 163). More generally, women tend to be sexualized by the men in this novel, of which the following quote is a clear illustration:

> Sometimes I stared out of the window for hours, in search of the hottest girls in school, about whom I then started fantasizing. How beautiful they were! Nice tits! Nice ass! (p. 50)

On the basis of such thematic cues, one could argue that at least two binary oppositions take shape in the narrative: between characters with and without a migration background, and between male and female characters. The first binary opposition is anchored in the premise of the book: a street-smart boy from a family with a migration background fights his way up in the social hierarchy of Dutch society. The second binary opposition emerges from the sexualization and objectification of female bodies by *Eus* and his male friends. The binary oppositions between these social groups – characters with versus characters without a migration background, male versus female characters – will be taken as a point of departure in the analysis below. How to assess which of these social groups are represented as more or less central in this novel?

As was described in the introductory chapter (section 1.2.1 'Representation and ideology'), scholars such as Susan Suleiman (1983), Philippe Hamon (1984), Liesbeth Korthals Altes (1992), and Vincent Jouve (2001) have devised narratological models to trace the 'ideology-effect' or 'value-effect' in texts. Such models can help to pinpoint which characters are more central than others in the normative hierarchy of each single narrative structure. In *Authoritarian Fictions* (1983), Susan Suleiman grounds her analysis of the ideological dimensions of texts on a model that represents the different constituents and levels of narrative texts (pp. 156–157). This model breaks down the narrative text at the 'Level of Story' and the 'Level of Discourse'. The first level of story relates to the components of the narrative content and contains *events* as experienced by *characters* in a specific *context*. The second level of discourse refers to how this narrative content is put into discourse (i.e., 'the way in which the story is presented to the reader or listener' (p. 156)), which is done through *narration, focalization*, and *temporal organization*.

For the present analysis, the processes of narration and focalization are particularly useful to determine which types of characters occupy more central positions than others in the narrative of *Eus*. A closer insight into its narration ('who is telling the story, to whom, under what circumstances?' (ibid.) and focalization ('from whose perspective(s) is the story "seen" or experienced?'(ibid.)) helps to pinpoint the relative position of the characters in the hierarchy of values that the text communicates. More specifically, it helps to assess how central characters with a certain gender and descent are in this particular narrative.

First of all, the novel is narrated by Eus, which means that he controls the flow of information in the narrative. It is a logical consequence of the first-person narration that Eus decides which events to either report or leave out. When he, for instance, reports that 'I was born and raised in Koekstad, a small town by the IJssel, exactly on the border of two eastern provinces' (p. 13), he chooses to use an alias ('Koekstad') for a town which the reader might know as Deventer. As an I-narrator, Eus is thus able to manipulate the narrative at will. Furthermore, his specific position in the narrative structure enables Eus to perform one of the various functions Suleiman ascribes to narrators, which is the 'interpretive function': 'to analyze, interpret, formulate judgements about characters, events, or contexts' (p. 157). Unlike all of the other non-narrating characters in the narrative, Eus has the opportunity to evaluate and judge his fellow characters directly through his first-person narration.

Furthermore, he is also the main focalizer: the narrative events are filtered through his perceptions. This means that the description of events are not neutral but colored by the vision and judgement of Eus, which is exemplified by the following quote:

> The coming four years I went to the Hegius school, amidst the beautiful, posh girls who followed the highest level of education. According to the rumors, these girls were above average interested in foreign boys because they never saw those types of boys. (p. 37)

Lumping together a group of girls, Eus ascribes the features 'beautiful' and 'posh' to these other non-narrating characters. By foregrounding their physical appearance and their alleged poshness, Eus suggests that they are spoiled rich kids, whose most interesting features are their looks. While the clause 'According to the rumors' suggests that the statement made in the next sentence should be taken with a grain of salt, Eus chooses to foreground the rumor that these girls are sexually interested in boys with a migration background. These two sentences contain an extremely colored representation of a specific type of character (in this case: female, higher educated). They ascribe features to characters that are not verifiable within the context of the first-person narration; readers can either take his word for it or adopt a critical stance toward Eus's description of events and other characters. Either way, such descriptions of other characters say more about Eus than about them. As such, the quote is a manifestation of what Suleiman calls the 'interpretive function' of narrators (1983, p. 157): Eus's descriptions of women denote *his* values and *his* judgements about other characters.

These basic narratological observations are key to the interpretation of character centrality in the novel. As first-person narrator and main focalizer, *Eus* is part of both the social group of people with a migration background and the social group of men. These simple observations suggest that the non-Dutch and (heterosexual) male perspectives are a priori more dominant than the Dutch and female perspectives. Taking into account that most of *Eus*'s friends and fellow criminals (Kosta, Ata, Meltem, Mahir) are also both male and from a non-Dutch descent, one could argue that the center of gravity lies with both male characters and characters with a migration background.

However, a closer look at 'the interpretive function' (Suleiman, 1983, p. 157) of Eus as a narrator complicates this preliminary conclusion. While Eus seems to embody the perspective of people with a migration background, the values which he communicates do not tend to coincide with the values he ascribes to other characters with a migration background. More specifically, his judgments on characters with a Turkish descent are often outspokenly negative. This is most notably exemplified by his descriptions of his father Turis, a first-generation Turkish migrant, who is characterized by Eus as a drunken 'tyrant' (Akyol, 2012, p. 12) and a work-shy social parasite who is 'Rather lazy than tired' (p. 13). Through such judgements on people with whom he shares his cultural roots, Eus adopts a critical stance toward their values. Moreover, Eus does not seem to identify with Turkish people more generally. This is illustrated by his friendship with his Dutch friend Kareltje, with whom he joins a football club consisting of 'fifteen gypsies' (p. 87). Although most Turkish boys play football at the 'club for all Turks in the city' (p. 88), Eus would never think of joining that club:

> I would never play football there. I had nothing in common with those people. They didn't even serve beer in the cantine. Only tea.

Such negative judgements on the values of Turkish people make Eus a very atypical Turk. While the fact remains that he has a Turkish background, he does therefore not automatically represent the typical Turkish perspective. According to Eus, he even has 'nothing in common with those people' as he feels more strongly connected to the group of Dutch gypsies: '[t]hey did not see me as a migrant. I was one of them'.

Despite his adversarial attitude toward people with a Turkish background and his connections with Dutch gypsies, Eus cannot avoid being stigmatized as belonging to the social group of people with a migration background. This is best exemplified by the ways in which he is treated in the Dutch school system. Despite his excellent performance in primary school, his teacher did not allow him to follow the highest educational level because of his Turkish background ('She said that I would have had a very hard time as a Turk' [p. 36]). This stigmatization continues in high school when his math teacher pejoratively calls him and his friend Metin 'de Hasans' (p. 42). While Eus's judgements on the social group of migrants give the impression that he does not identify with this group, the actions and words of other characters make painfully clear that he cannot escape this social identity. From a narratological perspective, however, it still is the question whether or not the first-person narration of *Eus* therefore ascribes a more central role to characters with a migration background. As a narrator and main focalizer, Eus represents a complex sociocultural identity that resists being part of binary categories such as the Dutch or the non-Dutch. Based on his dominance as a narrator, it is clear that *his* perspective is most central to the narrative. However, his resistance toward a fixed sociocultural identity makes it problematic to claim that therefore the center of gravity lies with the migrant perspective.

Things are less ambiguous with regard to gender. Almost without exception, Eus's first-person narration and dominant focalization communicates an extremely masculine, heterosexual worldview. Throughout the novel, he and his friends encounter a variety of girls whose sole function is to fulfill their sexual desires. In high school, Eus and his friend Metin arrange a double date with Eef and Levine. The conversation they have prior to this date serves as a clear example of the dominance of the male, heterosexual perspective:

> In the afternoon Metin and I had discussed the terms and conditions of our meeting with the girls. We agreed that he would take Eef and I would take Levine. For him, double dates were a routine job. 'The one with the big tits is more compliant,' he said, 'I can immediately tell. She won't be making a fuss. You can take the other one. You like serious girls.' (p. 59)

Because of the first-person narration, the novel is structured in such a way that only sparse attention is dedicated to the female perspective represented by girls such as Eef and Levine. Most information on the female characters is indirect, for instance through conversations between Eus and his friends such as this one. These conversations tend to follow a similar routine: a self-confident bravado, machismo, an objectification and sexualization of female bodies, lack of respect, lack of interest for anything other than bodily traits or sexual performance, et cetera. There is simply no female counterview present in the novel to nuance, criticize, or reverse the images of women as 'whores' (pp. 36, 58, 85, 145), 'sluts' (pp. 43, 57, 62, 86, 145, 157, 176, 253), or 'preys' (p. 60) as represented by the first-person narration of *Eus* and the focalization of the main character and his male friends.

But how seriously should the reader take all this macho bravado? *Eus* is clearly inspired by Jan Cremer's *Ik, Jan Cremer* (1964), one of the classics of Dutch picaresque novels. Not only does it have an intertextual relation with this novel through its thematization of being a social outcast, it also imitates the repetitive descriptions of sexual intercourse with attractive women. Although it can be argued that the sexualization and objectification of women in *Eus* is simply a convention of the genre of the picaresque novel, it nonetheless expresses an extremely masculine, heterosexual worldview. While the reader can choose to read the sexual escapades of the womanizing protagonist as an ironic allusion to the genre of the picaresque novel ('*Eus*, the biggest player of the East. See how he rolls!' [p. 62]), this does not change the fact that the female perspective is subordinate to the male perspective. Moreover, there is a wide range of scenes with female characters in which irony is hard to find. When Eus, for instance, finds out that Levine had had sexual intercourse with another man, his double moral standards regarding men and women are unambiguously expressed. While Eus has a variety of sexual contacts, Levine is not supposed to do so. In his eyes, she is 'a whore, a piece of filth' (p. 85), and 'a slut who has loose sexual morals' (p. 86). Such scenes show how the 'interpretive function' (Suleiman, 1983, p. 157) of narrators co-shapes the masculine worldview presented in the narrative by expressing judgements on other characters. Narratologically, it thus seems safe to say that the male perspective occupies a more central, important, dominant, influential, and powerful position in the narrative than the female perspective.

How do these narratological observations relate to the statistical baseline that female characters and characters with a migration background are relatively central in the corpus as a whole? First of all, it is insightful to determine to what extent *Eus* conforms to or deviates from this pattern in a statistical sense. Does it live up to the pattern or does it form an exception to the rule? An answer to that question can help to contextualize the narratological analysis of centrality based on narration and focalization in light of the statistical baseline. Table 3 shows the characters in the novel ranked by their scores on degree centrality. The character ranking in this table demonstrates that the particular narrative of *Eus* conforms to the general pattern as observed in the multiple linear regression (see section 3.5.1 of this chapter) only with regard to descent. Of the 21 identified characters, 12 have a migration background, and they are higher in the rankings than the Dutch characters, which is in line with the general pattern according to which characters with a migration background have a significantly higher degree of centrality.

However, with regard to gender, the novel deviates from the pattern. Of the 21 identified characters, 14 are male, and they occupy higher positions in the rankings on degree centrality, indicating that the male characters in *Eus* have *more* relations than the female characters.

For Katz centrality, a similar pattern emerges. Table 4 lists the characters in the novel ranked by their scores on Katz centrality. Here, too, both characters with a migration background as well as male characters occupy higher positions in the rankings than nonmigrant characters and female characters. The first types of characters are thus connected to *more important* characters than the latter.

	Name	*Gender*	*Descent*	*Degree*
1	Kosta	male	immigrant	0.65
2	Kareltje	male	non-immigrant	0.55
3	Eus	male	immigrant	0.50
4	Turis	male	immigrant	0.40
5	Meltem	male	immigrant	0.40
6	Ata	male	immigrant	0.40
7	Mahir	male	immigrant	0.35
8	Selma	female	immigrant	0.30
9	Metin	male	immigrant	0.30
10	Haakneus	female	immigrant	0.30
11	Levine	female	non-immigrant	0.30
12	Theo	male	non-immigrant	0.15
13	Nathan	male	non-immigrant	0.15
14	Eef	female	non-immigrant	0.15
15	Inez	female	non-immigrant	0.1
16	Ömer	male	immigrant	0.1
17	Angelo	male	non-immigrant	0.1
18	Vinny	male	non-immigrant	0.1
19	Osman	male	immigrant	0.05
20	Daphne	female	non-immigrant	0.05
21	Moeder Eus	female	immigrant	0.00

Table 3. Characters in Eus (2012) ranked by degree centrality score.

	Name	Gender	Descent	Katz
1	Kosta	male	immigrant	0.218218982823223
2	Mahir	male	immigrant	0.21821840342212764
3	Eus	male	immigrant	0.2182184034212662
4	Kareltje	male	nonimmigrant	0.2182182875401764
5	Turis	male	immigrant	0.21821822960063142
6	Ata	male	immigrant	0.218218113719957
7	Meltem	male	immigrant	0.2182179398985992
8	Selma	female	immigrant	0.21821782401818632
9	Haakneus	female	immigrant	0.218217824018094
10	Levine	female	non-immigrant	0.21821782401787862
11	Metin	male	immigrant	0.2182178240177709
12	Theo	male	non-immigrant	0.2182177660783798
13	Nathan	male	non-immigrant	0.21821770813789643
14	Eef	female	non-immigrant	0.21821765019709
15	Inez	female	non-immigrant	0.21821759225711432
16	Angelo	male	non-immigrant	0.218217592257022
17	Vinny	male	non-immigrant	0.218217592257022
18	Ömer	male	immigrant	0.21821759225692972
19	Daphne	female	non-immigrant	0.21821753431670787
20	Osman	male	immigrant	0.21821753431661559
21	Moeder Eus	female	immigrant	0.21821747637639374

Table 4. Characters in Eus (2012) ranked by Katz centrality score.

Statistically speaking, *Eus* thus conforms to the baseline only with regard to descent and not with regard to gender. As is the case in the corpus as whole, characters who are categorized as having a migration background occupy relatively central positions in the fictional network of this novel. Novels such as *Eus* arguably contribute to the relatively central network position of characters with a migration background in the corpus as a whole. *Eus*, however, is an outlier with regard to gender: while female characters tend to be relatively central in the corpus as a whole, they are statistically less central in the fictional network of this novel.

How does the statistical analysis of network centrality in *Eus* relate to the qualitative, narratological analysis of centrality, gender, and descent in the novel? Interestingly, the rankings of characters as presented in Table 3 and 4 are partly in line with the narratological analysis. This is most clearly exemplified for character centrality with regard to gender. While the narratological analysis has made the case that the narration and focalization in the novel co-constitute an extremely dominant male perspective, male characters also occupy more central positions in the fictional network of this novel. Furthermore, the fact that *Eus* deviates from the overall finding that female characters are more central in the fictional social networks in the corpus as a whole – i.e., the baseline – ascribes even more significance to the narratological finding that the female perspective is subordinated to the male perspective in the novel. Statistically speaking, *Eus* is a peculiar case with respect to how central female and male characters are as it deviates from the statistical baseline. As such, the qualitative, narratological assessment of the extremely masculine worldview is backed up by the quantitative, statistical finding that male characters have higher scores on degree and Katz centrality. The dominance of the male perspective in the novel, as reported by the narratological analysis, thus deviates from a statistical norm, and is therefore even more salient. It suggests that *Eus* does not just follow a norm of representation (i.e., female characters occupy relatively central network positions), but forms an exception to the rule. In light of its deviation from this norm, this baseline, the qualitative observation of this dominant masculine view stands out more than it would have without a comparison against this norm.

While the findings of the statistical analysis and the narratological analysis are complementary with regard to gender, they are less so with regard to descent. Statistically, *Eus* ascribes relatively central positions to characters with a migration background, which is in line with the baseline that was generated for the corpus as a whole. Narratologically, the centrality of the sociocultural identity of 'the migrant' is more complex. Although the qualitative assessment of narration and focalization in *Eus* demonstrate that Eus as a first-person narrator is in any case the most central actor in the narrative, it has also underscored how Eus resists being part of a social group of either 'the Dutch' or 'the migrants'. As such, the narratological analysis highlights a fundamental challenge of statistics-based approaches to literary representation. While a statistical analysis requires clear categorizations, literary texts have the potential to disrupt, criticize, or deconstruct such seemingly fixed boundaries. Although the migration background of Eus is indeed part of his identity, the novel more generally thematizes the nuances and complexities of categorizing people in binary categories, such as migrants and nonmigrants.

In sum, this narratological evaluation of the statistical baseline highlights two important points with regard to the interpretability of a statistical analysis of literary representation in general and the centrality of characters specifically. 1) A qualitative, narratological analysis of an individual text can provide a more nuanced backup of a statistical argument. Mode of narration and focalization in *Eus* illustrate the dominance of the male perspective, which is supported by the character rankings for the novel. In light of the statistical finding that *female* characters occupy more central network positions in the corpus as a whole, the deviation of this particular narrative from this pattern underscores the abnormality of the narratological finding that the novel communicates an extremely masculine worldview. 2) However, narratological observations might also nuance or conflict with statistical findings, which is the case with regard to the centrality of characters with a migration background. Characters with a migration background score higher than Dutch characters in the novel in terms of network centrality, which is in line with the statistical baseline. But despite the novel's seemingly conformation to this overall pattern, the very notion of a fixed sociocultural identity is problematized in *Eus*. As such, the narratological analysis highlights that individual narratives have the potential to challenge statistics-based patterns of representation. More generally, this insight emphasizes the various, sometimes conflicting meanings that 'centrality' or 'importance' can have in qualitative narratology as opposed to quantitative network theory.

3.6 CONCLUSION TO THIS CHAPTER

This chapter aimed to find an answer to the question of how the centrality of characters co-shapes the representation of the groups in which they function.

Informed by insights from both network theory and narratology, a method was developed to extract fictional social networks of characters from the 170 novels in the research corpus. Based on these fictional social networks, a model was proposed to rank characters according to five centrality metrics. In order to determine which groups of characters tend to end up high in these rankings, and thus are central in statistical terms, a regression analysis was conducted to test which demographic features of characters predict their places in the rankings. The output of this data-driven, statistical model on the whole corpus, combined with the close reading of centrality, gender, and descent in the case study of Özcan Akyol's *Eus*, indicates that centrality co-constitutes the representation of social groups in present-day Dutch literary fiction in at least these two ways.

First, the frequency of distributions of characters belonging to a certain social group such as reported in the previous chapter are not sufficient for analyzing how central men as opposed to women, migrants as opposed to nonmigrants, the higher as opposed to lower educated, and the young as opposed to the old are in narrative fiction. Although female and migrant characters are less present in the corpus, statistically speaking, they take up a more central position in the social networks of present-day Dutch literary fiction than nonmigrant and male characters. This remarkable outcome requires an explanation, particularly in light of the highly imbalanced frequency distribution of migrant and nonmigrant characters in the corpus. For those characters in the corpus whose descent is known, almost 90% do not have a migration background (i.e., a Dutch or Belgian background), but the regression model suggests that migrants are more central in the networks than nonmigrants. These higher centrality scores might be explained by the probability that novels that thematize descent, and stage a higher number of migrants, also ascribe more central roles to them, which was demonstrated in the close reading of *Eus*. Overall, the corpus contains fewer migrant characters (only around 10% of all characters have a migration background), but these migrants score higher on degree and Katz centrality. Something similar holds for female characters: there are fewer female characters than male characters in the corpus (almost a 40–60 ratio), but they have relatively high centrality values. In order for migrant or female characters to be central in network theoretical terms, a high frequency of occurrence is not a necessary prerequisite as long as they interact with a high number of other (central) characters.

Whereas frequency of occurrence of characters belonging to a certain social group is the most straightforward indication of their centrality in the text (how present they are), the model developed in this chapter proposes an additional, more sophisticated measure of centrality. Other than simply counting frequency of occurrences of characters with a certain demographic profile, the network analytic approach developed in this chapter views centrality in a fundamentally relational sense. As result of this, centrality of characters is defined in relation to their interactions with other characters. While a certain social group (male, without a migration background) occurs more often in the corpus, they occupy fewer central positions in the social networks of their fictional worlds. This is not to say that their frequency of occurrence does not affect their centrality. How often a certain social group is depicted definitively affects its visibility (and thus centrality) in literary fiction, but equally important is the position characters from these groups have in the social structure relative to the position of other types of characters.

Second, the close reading of case study *Eus* has demonstrated how centrality in quantitative, statistical terms (frequency of occurrence, position in the network) relates to, and sometimes conflicts with, centrality in qualitative, narratological terms (thematic structure, mode of narration, focalization). Whereas the high number of characters with a migration background in *Eus* is not representative of the corpus, the centrality of these types of characters in the novel's social network probably explains why migrant characters in the corpus take up relatively central positions in the networks. The novel thematizes descent, and ascribes a central role to the migrant perspective through its mode of narration and focalization, although it also challenges the notion of a fixed socio-cultural identity. As a consequence of this, migrant characters in this novel not only occupy more central roles in the network structure, statistically speaking, but arguably also leave their mark more profoundly on the narrative structure. As the novel's first-person narrator represents the perspective of the social group of migrants, his perception of the events and the other characters in the novel is colored by this specific migration background. Because of this, the centrality of the first-person narrator in a narratological sense (through his narration and focalization) reinforces his centrality in the social network. However, the narratological analysis also shows that the narrator is resistant toward being categorized in a binary category such as 'migrant' or 'nonmigrant,' which highlights the potential of individual texts to disrupt, distort, nuance, or criticize inevitably reductive statistical patterns.

Qualitative assessment of an individual novel does, therefore, also show how individual narratives can not only support the statistics-based patterns found for the corpus as a whole but also have the potential to escape or transcend these patterns. Whereas statistical trends might indicate general patterns of literary representation in large collections of texts, they can subsequently serve as an analytic backdrop for the individual analysis of particular novels. Using such statistical patterns as a baseline for comparison, the extent to which a single novel either conforms to or deviates from them can be used to determine the particularity of a certain aspect of representation. Contrasting the narratological analysis of centrality in *Eus* with the pattern that migrant and female characters occupy relatively central positions in each of the 170 networks, helps to pinpoint how peculiar or deviant this particular narrative is in this respect.

CHAPTER 4

COMMUNITY

4.1 INTRODUCTION: NARRATIVE CONNECTIONS

How do the communities in which characters function affect the representation of the social group(s) these characters are part of? The representation of social groups in present-day Dutch literature will be studied in this chapter through the lens of community. The concept will be used as an umbrella term denoting a variety of interrelated terms. It refers to a range of relational notions such as 'clustering', 'coexistence', 'collective', and 'connectivity', although each of these notions stresses a slightly different aspect of community. Whereas the next chapter on conflict focuses on the ways in which negative affiliations co-constitute the representation of social groups in literature, this chapter aims to understand how such representations are co-shaped through the bonds that characters form. While social groups are defined in terms of shared demographic characteristics (e.g., gender, descent, age, education), communities do not necessarily consist of individuals belonging to the same social group (e.g., a community can consist of both male and female characters, both migrant and nonmigrant characters, both older and younger characters, both lower and higher educated characters). The homo- or heterogeneity of communities of characters in narrative fiction can shed light on the extent to which social groups are either integrated or segregated into different communities.

What is a community? Classical social theorists such as Ferdinand Tönnies, Émile Durkheim, and Georg Simmel have been occupied with the question of why people unite in group-like structures. Tönnies famously made a distinction between *Gemeinschaft* (commonly translated as community) and *Gesellschaft* (commonly translated as society). In his view, premodern social structures were typified by communities in the form of families and neighborhoods that were held together by a sense of belonging and a moral obligation to one another. Modernity witnessed the decay of these premodern communities and a transition to societies in which companies and states became the essential social structures (Tönnies, 1887/2005). To his regret, Tönnies observed that this transition also embodied a shift from intrinsic, morally connoted motivations for being together to social structures that merely serve as instruments to achieve joint goals.

An alternative view on the shift from premodern to modern modes of living is proposed by Émile Durkheim in *The Division of Labour and Society* (1893/2013). Whereas Tönnies ascribes rather positive features to his idea of the premodern *Gemeinschaft*, Durkheim has a more negative conception of such primitive social structures. These early communities are built upon what Durkheim calls mechanical solidarity. As there is little division of labor (people are mostly carrying out similar tasks), such communities subsequently share similar values and are conjoined in what he calls a 'collective conscience'. Katherine Giuffre characterizes Durkheim's idea of primitive community as 'an entity that is more than the sum of its parts' because 'the moral force of the collective conscience acts on the members of the community to create the feeling of a shared identity' (Giuffre, 2013, p. 22). In order to ensure that this collective conscience does not fall apart, repressive law is installed to sustain their shared identity and to prevent a divergence into distinct, individual identities. Individuality, in other words, is a threat to the very existence of the community.

Durkheim is more positive about modern, capitalist societies in which organic instead of mechanical solidarity is the binding mechanism. The labor in such societies is highly differentiated, a result of which is that there is great heterogeneity among its members. In contrast to primitive communities, individuality is not a threat but a driving force behind these advanced societies. Law is not repressive but restitutive, the point of which is 'not to punish transgressions against the collective conscience – which has been weakened by the division of labor to the point where it can no longer provide a source of community cohesion – but to ensure the orderly functioning of the various differentiated "organs" of the community' (p. 24). The strong collective conscience of primitive communities brings about a shared identity; the downside is that it needs repressive laws to smother individuality and heterogeneity. Modern societies have a weak collective conscience, but individuality can thrive for the greater good. For Durkheim, it is not sameness but difference that binds people in modern societies.

A fundamentally different take on communities can be found in the formal sociology of Georg Simmel. Whereas Tönnies and Durkheim utilize abstract notions such as moral belonging and shared identity, Simmel emphasizes the concrete pathways through which a community member's individuality takes shape. A dual interplay between individual and social group lies at the heart of the theory that he developed in *Group Expansion and the Development of Individuality* (1908/1971): an individual is defined by the social groups it belongs to, a social group is defined by its individual members. 'The uniqueness of the individual,' Giuffre summarizes, 'is based on her or his position at this nexus of a unique set of circles' (Giuffre, 2013, p. 28). For Simmel, communities are equal to the sum of their elements; they are not entities on their own as is the case for Tönnies and Durkheim. Simmel's approach is fundamentally relational, which is why he is commonly regarded as a forerunner of social network analysis. In network theory, communities are not defined through metaphorical notions such as 'collective conscience' but through the concrete relational ties between nodes. By adopting such a relational approach, a collection of nodes can be broken down into subgroups of nodes that are more densely connected with one another than they are with others.

This chapter takes up a Simmelian, network analytic approach to community combined with a narratological perspective. Most importantly, this approach enables a better measurability and quantifiability of the bonds between characters than the theories of Tönnies or Durkheim would. This does, however, not mean that Durkheim's and Tönnies's more metaphorical conceptions of community are not relevant for the purposes of this chapter. In thinking about the representation of groups of people in literature, it is unavoidable to refer to, for instance, the notion of a shared identity. Metaphors are, moreover, an indispensable part of literary fiction; and characters can comment on their social worlds through many different figures of speech. In general, there are fruitful analytic angles to be found in literary theory taking such literary-stylistic mechanisms into account. Because of their reliance on literature's metaphorical and symbolic abilities, these theories are usually miles apart from the formal network analytical approach to communities as represented by Simmelian sociology. As the raw material of literary texts is language, most of these angles depend upon a particular idea of how literary language works. Such is the case in the writings of scholars associated with the Bakhtin circle that will be used in one of the subsequent sections.

In accordance with the twofold theoretical setup of this book, the empirically oriented approach of network theory will be put in dialogue with a more top-down perspective from literary theory. These theoretical frameworks will be used to gain a closer understanding of how character communities play a part in shaping the literary work's depiction of social groups. This is particularly relevant in light of the observation that the notion of community can gain insight into the extent to which social groups are either integrated or segregated (Blau, 1977). Which characters do and which characters do not belong to specific groups? Two models will be presented to assess the degree to which social groups in the present corpus are integrated or segregated. The first model uses community detection algorithms to trace which groups of characters cluster more strongly together than others. The second model computes how strongly characters with the same demographic profile tend to interact. Following Bakhtin, the results of both of these models are used to assess how homo- or heterogeneous – 'polyphonic' or 'dialogic' – the novels are in terms of their differentiation into different communities of characters (see paragraph 3.2). Combining these two statistical models with a Bakhtinian framework allows for an interpretation of the overall cohesion or fragmentation in the fictional populations of present-day Dutch literary fiction. Is there a con- or divergence of represented identities in the corpus? In order to assess the meaning of the statistical patterns generated by each model, the observed general trends are evaluated through close readings of Philip Huff's *Niemand in de stad* [Nobody in the city] (2012) and Mensje van Keulen's *Liefde heeft geen hersens* [Love has no brains] (2012).

4.2 COMMUNITY IN NETWORK THEORY

One of the seminal articles of social network analysis, Granovetter's 'The Strength of Weak Ties' (1973), hypothesizes that strong edges exist within communities and weak edges between communities.

> Linkage of micro and macro levels is thus no luxury but of central importance to the development of sociological theory. Such linkage generates paradoxes: weak ties, often denounced as generative of alienation [Wirth, 1938] are here seen as indispensable to individuals' opportunities and to their integration into communities; strong ties, breeding local cohesion, lead to overall fragmentation. (Granovetter, 1973, p. 1378)

This idea is both intuitively clear and counterintuitive. It seems obvious that strong ties between members of a community are a *conditio sine qua non*, as otherwise it would be hard to speak of a community at all. A logical consequence of this observation is that such strong ties between subgroups are detrimental to the overall cohesion of networks. Paradoxically, strong ties lead to less cohesion. The storyworld of *Lord of the Rings*, for instance, consists of one large fictional population in which groups of elves, dwarves, wizards, men, and orcs are (in) directly connected through positive or negative associations. There are arguably stronger ties between the members within each of these groups, resulting in communities, than there are between, for example, groups of elves and dwarves. These relatively strong connections within each of these groups, however, do not lead to a cohesive and densely connected overall network. Quite the contrary: the *Lord of the Rings* network is fragmented into relatively separated communities consisting of groups of elves, dwarves, wizards, men, and orcs. Among these individual, fragmented communities of characters, a few elves, dwarves, wizards, and men – the fellowship of the ring – join forces to fight evil (orcs, Saruman, Sauron). In order to establish cohesion in an utterly fragmented world, they are obliged to transcend the boundaries of their individual communities. Fellowships (or communities) consisting of people from a wide variety of groups are, however, not the norm not in the fictional Middle Earth in *Lord of the Rings*, nor are they in real-world societies, regions, and countries. Most social worlds contain distinct, densely connected communities, which subsequently leads to fragmentation in the social world as a whole. It is, however, not at all an obvious task to draw lines between communities. What counts as relatively strong ties? What do 'densely connected' and 'cohesive' mean? One of the major challenges of network theory is how to assess the boundaries between different subgroups within a network.

4.2.1 Community Detection

Community detection is the header under which this methodological challenge is carried out. Confusingly, a variety of terms is used to refer to the objects of detection. *Community* is the most metaphorical of the terms, having different associations depending on the theory one adopts (e.g. Tönnies, Durkheim, or Simmel). (Cohesive) *subgroup* and *cluster* are more formal but also rather general terms denoting different things in different contexts as well. Clique is perhaps the most precisely defined among these terms, referring to a fully interconnected subset of nodes in a network. It was first coined by Luce and Perry in 1949 and represents the most stringent definition of group-like network structures.

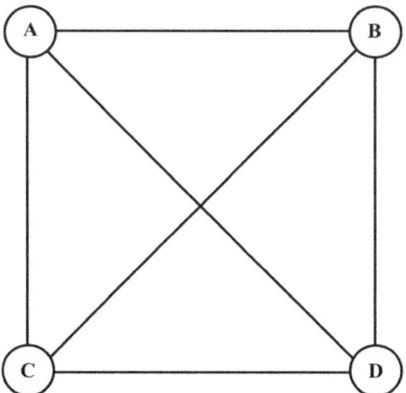

Figure 1. Example of a clique. A, B, C, and D are all directly connected.

Figure 1 shows an example of a clique. A, B, C, and D all have direct links to all other nodes. While some definitions relax the criteria for cliques, the strictest definition ascribes that A-B-C-D ceases to be a clique when, for instance, edge A-D falls away.

The tight interconnectedness of A, B, C, and D does not mean, however, that A-B-C-D is fully isolated from other nodes. A construction such as shown in Figure 2 is quite possible.

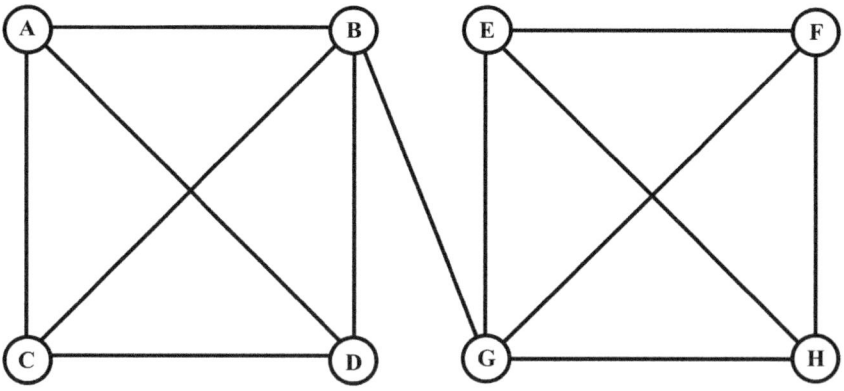

Figure 2. Example of two cliques. Both A-B-C-D and E-F-G-H are fully connected. B and G form a bridge between the two cliques

In the example of *The Lord of the Rings*, A-B-C-D might represent a clique of dwarves and E-F-G-H a clique of elves. Although both of these cliques share more dense connections with their own group than with the other group, there are no isolated entities within the overall *Lord of the Rings*. For instance, B may represent the dwarf Gimli and G may represents the elf Legolas; two characters connected through their co-participation in the fellowship of the ring.

It is debatable whether a stricter or looser definition of cliques should be adopted and whether linkages such as those between B and G should be taken into account. In order to avoid associations with the most stringent definition of clique, the looser term community will be used throughout the rest of this chapter to refer to any densely connected subset of characters within the overall character network in the novel. Not only is it a widely used term in different fields of inquiry, its metaphorical associations will prove to be useful in the interpretive parts of the chapter.

Thus, a community is generally defined here as 'a cohesive group of nodes that are connected "more densely" to each other than to the nodes in other communities' (Porter, Onnela, & Mucha, 2019, p. 1086). What 'more densely' entails is dependent on the method adopted for identifying communities of characters in literary texts. Ever since the first analyses of community structure (e.g. Homans, 1950; Rice, 1927; Weiss & Jacobson, 1955), different detection methods have been proposed in different fields of inquiry. Up to the present there is no generally accepted solution to the problem. Especially since the seminal paper by Girvan and Newman (2002), who first applied large-scale data handling and powerful computational tools to detect communities, the development and advancement of methods have been on the agenda of people working in applied mathematics and physics. Community detection gradually became 'hip' (Porter et al., 2009, p. 1083).

Community detection methods can be divided into agglomerative and divisive techniques. Agglomerative techniques start from the level of the individual node and gradually connect nodes into larger sub-communities of the full network. An example of an agglomerative method is linkage clustering (e.g. Johnson, 1967), in which 'nodes are conjoined sequentially into larger clusters starting with the [most strongly connected pair]'. Conjoining the nodes into larger clusters is done stepwise by 'recomput[ing] the similarities between the new cluster and each of the old clusters and [joining] the two maximally similar clusters, [continuing] iteratively until all clusters with nonzero similarity are connected' (Porter et al., 2009, p. 1087). Conversely, a divisive technique starts 'with the full graph and breaks it up to find communities' (ibid.) instead of starting from individual nodes.

One of the most popular community detection methods is optimizing so-called modularity (Prokhorenkova, Pralat, & Raigorodskii, 2016), which can be done either bottom-up by starting from individual nodes (agglomerative) or top-down by decomposing the overall network (divisive). Networks with high modularity have dense connections within communities and sparser connections between communities. The aim of modularity optimization algorithms is to '[seek] an arrangement in which the difference between the number of within-community relationships and the number anticipated in a randomly structured network is as large as possible' (Marsden, 2011, p. 599). Such algorithms thus hinge on a comparison between the network as it is and a hypothetical network in which the nodes are randomly connected. For weighted networks (networks in which a particular weight is ascribed to edges), such methods '[measure] when a particular division of the network has more edge weight within groups than one would expect by chance' (Porter et al., 2009, p. 1089). A disadvantage of using modularity optimization algorithms is that they have an inherent resolution limit (Fortunato & Barthélemy, 2007), the result of which is that 'it misses communities that are smaller than a certain threshold size that depends on the size of the network and the extent of interconnectedness of its communities' (Porter et al., 2009, p. 1091). Several algorithms therefore allow one to adjust a resolution parameter specific to the network size.

Approaching communities from a modularity perspective opens up interesting possibilities with regard to node attributes such as gender, descent, age, and education. The concept of modularity is often associated with assortativity, the notion that nodes/edges sharing features are more likely to be connected than nodes/edges that do not have these features in common. For the purposes of this chapter, assortativity relating to node attributes is especially relevant. Node attributes relating to, for instance, descent, can be used to determine the extent to which characters from the same descent are part of the same communities. Subsequently, this might be an indication of how fragmented the network is:

> Fragmentation results when a network's elements are clearly partitioned into subgroups, with few between-cluster relationships. If the network's activities require little coordination among elements in its different parts, such loose coupling can allow clusters to function in appropriately autonomous and efficient ways. Fragmentation can compromise a network's capacity to pursue joint tasks, however, especially when it

is polarized, with between-community antagonism alongside within-cluster solidarity. (Marsden, 2011, p. 600)

Networks with high modularity have dense connections within communities but sparse connections between members of different communities. In order to find an answer to this chapter's question on how community-formation affects the representation of social group(s), it is worthwhile to assess how fragmented the fictional networks are in terms of gender, descent, education, and age. The extent of fragmentation, then, is an indication of how these fictional populations are depicted as being either integrated into a densely connected whole or as being segregated into distinct clusters – whether there is a convergence or divergence of identities. Quantitative, statistical analysis may be informative about the general nature of this fragmentation, but insight into phenomena such as polarization or 'between-community antagonism' can only be gained through qualitative close readings. In section 4.4.3, such a qualitative assessment of narrative communities will be conducted for Philip Huff's *Niemand in de stad*.

4.2.2 Homophily

Communities tend to consist of members with a similar background (Marsden, 2011, p. 599). In network theory this mechanism is studied through the concept of homophily, 'a principle of social organizing defined as people sharing similarities tending to have more social interaction' (Seidel, 2011, p. 382). Often it is characterized through the proverbial expression 'birds of a feather flock together' coined by Lazarsfeld and Merton in 1954. Ideologically, homophily is an interesting sociocultural mechanism as 'limited homophilous networks may serve as a structural barrier for minorities' (Seidel, 2011, p. 383). Groups of similar members tend to exclude people who are not similar to them. Studying homophily in literature can thus be a means to gain insight into structural inequalities and hierarchies between characters with different demographic profiles.

The first written records associated with the notion of homophily date back to Aristotle and Plato, both of whom suggested that similarity binds people together.[1] From the 1920s onward, systematic studies have been conducted that to a greater or lesser extent confirm the idea that similarity leads to stronger associations. Initially, studies focused on small groups such as friend circles at schools and colleges (e.g. Bott, 1928). Later, research on the topic witnessed a growth in scale because of the use of sample surveys that could be applied to societies as a whole (e.g. Marsden, 1987). More recently, even larger-scale homophily studies have been conducted on online networks such as those of Facebook or Goodreads users (e.g., Bucur, 2019). There is one study that explores the idea of gender homophily in networks of characters in English-language fiction in depth (Kraicer & Piper, 2019), which is closest in nature to the analyses carried out in this chapter. Preparatory work for the present research was done in Volker and Smeets (2019),[2] in which the Libris dataset was compared with actual personal networks of Dutch people through the framework of homophily. In this comparative analysis, we found that the character networks in the Libris corpus are less homophilous in terms of descent, education, and age than actual networks in Dutch society. The Libris dataset used in this analysis, however, only contained 1,292 characters. Currently, the Libris dataset has been augmented to a total of 2,137 characters and thus covers a larger portion of character interactions in the books, taking into account a fair number of less visible side characters as well. Moreover, the methodical setup of the present chapter differs from the research in Volker and Smeets (2019). The results reported in this chapter broadly confirm the findings reported in this previous study.

There are two categorical distinctions that are generally made within this field of inquiry. The first divides homophily into a *baseline* and an *inbreeding* category. Whereas baseline homophily refers to the opportunities that people have to engage in contact with similar others, inbreeding homophily denotes the internal motivation people have to interact with similar others. The baseline category is linked to the statistical chances of a network member to have the opportunity to interact with similar others. Being born in a particular situation, one might have a certain a priori chance to interact with similar people. Conversely, inbreeding refers to the interaction with similar others beyond this a priori chance. Regardless of the statistical possibility that someone connects with similar others, similarity of (for instance) race, gender, or social class might attract someone to find contacts outside of this opportunity structure.

The second categorical distinction is between *status* and *value* homophily (Lazarsfeld & Merton, 1954). Status homophily refers to similarity based on sociodemographic status. This status can either be ascribed, relating to characteristics such as gender, descent, race, ethnicity, or age, or this status can be acquired, relating to characteristics such as education, profession, or religion. Value homophily applies to network members who have similar thoughts, values, beliefs, and motivations regardless of their social status. One of the first observed examples of value homophily is a study reporting that people with similar intelligence levels are likely to get in contact (Almack, 1922). Political orientation is another feature that tends to fuel homophilous associations

(Verbrugge, 1977). For pragmatic reasons, this chapter only focuses on status homophily. Although forms of value homophily such as intelligence or political orientation are interesting from an ideological perspective, such characteristics are commonly features of characters that are not articulated, which makes it practically impossible to determine what every character's level of intelligence or political orientation is. The present dataset contains metadata on the characters on the basis of which either ascribed (gender, descent, age) or acquired (education, profession) status homophily can be studied.

As in the previous chapters, the four demographic categories of descent, gender, age, and education will be the point of focus in the following analysis. The categories of race and ethnicity are the cause of the largest divides in contemporary societies. Strong baseline and inbreeding homophily on these features have often been reported (e.g., Marsden, 1987, 1988). Gender forms a considerably less large divide in societies. Although studies reported that, for example, schoolchildren tend to form gender homophilous circles of friends at an early age (Maccoby, 1998), no strong baseline or inbreeding homophily is found in contemporary societies such as is the case with race and ethnicity (Marsden, 1988). Homophily related to age differs per nature of the network but it is generally high in marriages and in networks of school children (McPherson et al., 2001, pp. 424–425). Education homophily has been reported to be high (Marsden, 1987; Verbrugge, 1977) and has a strong inbreeding component (Marsden, 1988).

What are the causes of such homophilous associations? There are at least two causes of why people engage in relationships with people that are like themselves. The main cause is geographic space. Although we live in a globalized world, our main relationships are structured locally in households, neighborhoods, and schools (Gans, 1968). Such functional local spaces foster meeting opportunities with people from similar backgrounds. For the social worlds depicted in novels, this raises questions about the role of narrative space: does the fact that two characters co-occur often in the narrative increase the chance of them being demographically similar? Another cause for homophily is family structure. Although family networks are rather non-homophilous with regard to gender (because of the dominance of heterosexual relations and the equal chance of having either sons or daughters), they tend to produce race, ethnicity, and religion homophily (Smits, Ultee, & Lammers, 2000). In light of the fact that family ties constitute the majority of the type of relations in the corpus (see chapter 2, 'Data'), a possible hypothesis is that the unit of the family also fosters segregation in character networks. In the close reading of Mensje van Keulen's *Liefde heeft geen hersens* in section 4.5.2, it will be assessed how geographic space and family structure form a breeding ground for the homophilous associations related to age in the novel.

4.3 COMMUNITY IN NARRATOLOGY

Modern Western literature is arguably less about community than it is about the self. In *The Political Unconscious* (1981, pp. 137–171), Fredric Jameson emphasizes the role of the novel in 'the emergence of the ego or centered subject' in late capitalist societies (p. 140).[3] On a concrete level, this is exemplified by the observation that most present-day novels center on the thoughts and feelings of particular subjects in the form of characters. One might even suggest, as Sandra Zagarell does in a contribution to *Signs* (1988), that such a focus on the subjective experiences of protagonists rather than on the shared experiences of groups, collectives, or communities fuels a sense of ego in contemporary culture.

There is, however, a literary tradition in which community rather than the self prevails. 'Narrative of community' is the term Zagarell uses to refer to this tradition. Novels in this tradition 'take as their subject the life of a community (life in "its *everyday* aspects",) and portray the minute and quite ordinary processes through which the community maintains itself as an entity' (Zagarell, 1988, p. 499, emphasis in original quote). Obviously, the self is not fully absent network of the community rather than as an individualistic unit' (ibid.). Historically, this genre grew in response to processes of modernization, urbanization, and industrialization that were detrimental to premodern ways of living characterized by a stronger sense of community (see Durkheim, 1983/2013 and Tönnies, 1887/2005, and the introductory paragraph of this chapter). With its roots in the nineteenth century,[4] traces of this literary tradition are arguably still visible in literary fiction today.[5] The following two subsections explore in more depth narratological terms and theories applicable to the study of narrative representations of communities.

4.3.1 Syntagmatic and Paradigmatic Collectives

Whereas network theory has a wide range of concepts and tools to study communities in networks, narratology lacks obvious instruments for studying narrative communities. This is exemplified by the absence of the lemma 'Community' in Greimas and Courtés's analytic dictionary of semiotics (1979).

The lemma 'Collective', however, describes elements that are indirectly relatable to representations of communities in literary texts. As always, the definition of the authors is rather dense: 'An actant is called collective when he, being part of a collection of individual actors, is provided with a modal capacity and/or actions that are shared with all actors that he arranges' (Greimas & Courtés, 1979, pp. 54–55).[6] In the context of this chapter's focus on the representation of social groups, the collective actant in this sentence can be considered as representing a group of characters and the individual actors as representing single characters. The 'modal capacity' can be viewed as a shared feature of characters belonging to a group; an all-female group of characters, for instance, share the modal capacity of being female. Thus, a collective of characters comes into being when characters have something in common. Indeed, this can be everything ranging from the same gender, country of descent, educational level, or age group, to shared histories, political beliefs, or religious views. Importantly, Greimas and Courtés make a distinction between two kinds of collectives. They define the 'syntagmatic collective actant' as 'the actant in which the single actors, added up as ordinal numbers, alternate in the performance of one [narrative] programme (similar to the joint effort of single workers when building a house)' (p. 55). Characters in a syntagmatic collective, then, are on an equal footing as they jointly operate in a shared effort. The authors describe the notion of the 'paradigmatic collective actant' as the hierarchical counterpart of the syntagmatic collective. This paradigmatic collective actant is 'a more extensive and hierarchically higher distribution defined by classes'. Characters in a paradigmatic collective cluster together in different classes, such as characters with a high, middle, and low education. In most cases, a novel represents a paradigmatic collective as it contains hierarchies between characters belonging to a certain category. The population of characters in a novel can, for instance, be divided in different subpopulations of higher educated, middle educated, and lower educated characters. But specific syntagmatic collectives exist amidst the paradigmatic collective of the novel as a whole, which are represented by these different subpopulations. All members of a collective of higher educated characters are equal with respect to their education; a hierarchical ordering with respect to education only becomes apparent in relation to communities of characters with a different educational level.

Thus, the novel as a whole represents a paradigmatic, hierarchically ordered collection of collectives, in which each individual collective has a syntagmatic, nonhierarchical structure. At least, in this example. If an individual collective features characters with, for instance, both higher, middle, and lower educated characters, than there is a paradigmatic, hierarchical ordering within that collective as well. The distinction between syntagmatic and paradigmatic collective will be used as a general conceptual framework in the close readings of the case studies in sections 4.4.3 and 4.5.2 of this chapter.

4.3.2 Dialogic Interaction and Polyphony

More generally, the ideas of Russian scholars associated with the Bakhtin circle cater to a conceptualization of communities in the novelistic genre. This is especially true for the early twentieth-century work of Valentin Nikolaevich Voloshinov and Mikhail Mikhailovich Bakhtin himself. Although they do not explicitly focus on the community concept, their ideas about the assets and mechanisms of literary language provide a fruitful analytic angle for the study of narrative communities.

In *Marxism and the Philosophy of Language* (1929/2003), Voloshinov philosophizes about the workings of language in general. Voloshinov's main point, and the theoretical point of departure for most of those of the Bakhtin circle, is that all utterances are inherently a form of dialogic interaction:

> Utterance, as we know, is constructed between two socially organized persons, and in the absence of a real addressee, an addressee is presupposed in the person, so to speak, of a normal representative of the social group to which the speaker belongs. The *word is oriented towards an addressee, toward who that addressee* might be: a fellow-member or not of the same social group, of higher or lower standing (the addressee's hierarchical status), someone connected with the speaker by close social ties (father, brother, husband, and so on) or not. There can be no such thing as an abstract addressee, a man unto himself, so to speak. With such a person, we would indeed have no language in common, literally and figuratively. Even though we sometimes have pretentions to experiencing and saying this *urbi et orbi*, actually, of course, we envision this 'world at large' through the prism of the concrete social milieu surrounding us. In the majority of cases, we presuppose a certain typical and stabilized *social purview* toward which the ideological creativity of our own social group and time is oriented, i.e., we assume as our addressee a contemporary of our literature, our science, our moral and legal codes. (Voloshinov, 1929/2003, p. 58; emphasis in the original text)

The fundamental idea here is that utterances between people only make sense 'through the prism of the concrete social milieu'. This served as an important framework for the more ideologically oriented strands of literary criticism from the 1960s onwards, which foregrounded the specific social lenses through which literature can be approached.[7] A word is a bridge thrown between myself and another' (ibid.): language is a fundamentally dialogic, interconnective, interactive, and interrelational mechanism of communication. Language has therefore the potential to connect people, identities, and cultures. This insight forms the conceptual backdrop for a series of essays by Bakhtin on the nature of the novelistic genre.

In the essay 'Discourse in the Novel' (1935/2003b),[8] Bakhtin coins the concept of heteroglossia to refer to the stratification of language into multiple social discourses, of which each represents a specific ideological system of beliefs. He distinguishes between the *centripetal* forces of unitary language striving to verbal *unification* and *centralization*, and the *centrifugal* forces of heteroglossia striving to verbal *deunification* and *decentralization*. Whenever Bakhtin writes about the centripetal and centrifugal forces of language, he is not so much referring to a (de)unification and (de)centralization of language in a purely linguistic sense, as he is first and foremost describing the ideological mechanisms underlying linguistic utterances. According to Bakhtin, literary language is one of the so-called 'heteroglot' languages striving for verbal and thus ideological deunification and decentralization and is itself also stratified into different heteroglossia. For instance: although most of the novels from the Libris corpus are written in the same standard Dutch, each novel is made up of language that does not represent one specific – unified and centralized – ideological position but rather represents a variety of different, possibly conflicting ideological messages. From the standpoint of Bakhtin's theory, each of those novels has the potential to escape the ideological constraints of unification and centralization to which other, nonliterary, linguistic utterances are subjected to.

What this exactly entails for the study of literature becomes most clear in Bakhtin's analysis of Dostoevsky in *Problems of Dostoevsky's Poetics* (1929/2003a). In this essay he makes a widely recognized distinction between monologic novels such as those of Tolstoy and dialogic novels such as those of Dostoevsky. In the monologic novel, character voices are subordinated objects of the standpoint of the author, whereas the dialogic novel features character voices that exist alongside the authorial point of view. Bakhtin argues that Dostoevsky rejects the objectifying authorial viewpoint and replaces it with interactions between the different identities of the characters, thereby creating 'a great dialogue of interacting voices, a polyphony' (Morris, 2003, p. 89). Whereas the term heteroglossia represents stratified social languages in general, the term polyphony stands for the individual or collective voices in the novelistic genre. A character in a Dostoevsky novel is no 'mouthpiece for the author's voice' (Bakhtin, 1929/2003a, p. 89) as is the case for Tolstoy's characters. Rather, Bakhtin sees Dostoevsky's novels as platforms where a diversity of characters and themes coexist and interact. A Dostoevskian character is 'a carrier of a fully valid word and not the mute, voiceless object of the author's words' (p. 93).

Moreover, the 'voices' orchestrated in such polyphonic novels are not necessarily represented by single, individual characters. Commonly, these characters are to a greater or lesser extent defined by the community to which they belong. Consequently, the dialogue between all these different voices can be seen as an interaction between character communities. Importantly, the polyphony orchestrated by Dostoevsky's dialogic novels contains no inherent hierarchy between represented identities according to Bakhtin. The consciousness of the hero of a story exists next to 'other consciousnesses with rights equal to those of the hero' (ibid). In monologic novels such as those of Tolstoy, there is no 'connection between consciousnesses' as all characters are subordinated to the objectifying authorial consciousness (ibid., p. 95). Conversely, dialogic novels feature 'great dialogue, but one where the author acts as organizer and participant in the dialogue without retaining for himself the final word' (p. 96).[9]

Such statements invoke an image of the polyphonic novel as a radically democratic genre in which a variety of different communities are harmoniously integrated with one another. In Bakhtin's essay 'Discourse in the Novel' (1935/2003b), mentioned earlier, the novel is defined as 'a diversity of social speech types (sometimes even diversity of languages) and a diversity of individual voices, artistically organized' (Bakhtin, 1935/2003b, p. 114).[10] It is, however, rather unclear how the extent of diversity of such 'social speech types' can be assessed in a novel. As Bakhtin only provides a general framework in which novels have the potential to create a multi-voicedness, it is up to present-day scholars to find suitable methods to test this in principle alluring idea. Building on this classic literary theory, the following sections operationalize two models through which the extent of polyphony can be determined. How polyphonic are present-day Dutch novels, and by which specific criteria? As the previous two paragraphs have shown, network theory and narratology offer different criteria by which to assess the structure, function, and meaning of communities. Conjoining the empirical approach of network theory with the theoretical perspectives of Greimas and Courtés, and the Bakhtin circle, the subsequent two analyses aim to provide an integrative account of communities in literary texts with quantitative findings entering into a dialogue with qualitative readings of two individual texts.

4.4 MODEL I: COMMUNITY DETECTION

This section presents a quantitative model to statistically assess the degree of polyphony in literary texts by means of the automatic detection of communities. Community detection algorithms can be used to break down a character network into separate clusters based on statistically significant cut-off points (see section 4.2.1 of this chapter). These clusters, then, represent communities of characters who are more strongly connected to one another than they are to characters from other communities. In light of Bakhtin's concept of polyphony, such communities can be regarded as representing a specific social speech type or voice. In this view, a larger number of communities in a novel might indicate a higher degree of polyphony because there are simply more social speech types or voices present. Within a single community, however, multiple voices can also coexist, as a community can consist of characters from different social, cultural, or economic backgrounds. Both lower and higher educated, migrant and nonmigrant, older and younger, male and female characters can be part of the same community. Therefore, a great variety of voices *within* a community can also be seen as an expression of polyphony.

In other words, there is a tension between computationally detected communities and the demographic backgrounds of the characters within those communities (i.e., the social group to which they belong – men versus women, migrants versus nonmigrants, the old versus the young, the higher versus the lower educated). Communities can be seen as distinct entities representing a collective voice, but single characters also represent distinct individual voices within communities. There are ways imaginable in which the individual voices of characters cause friction with the collective voice of the character community of which they are part of. Is it possible, for instance, to speak of polyphony when a community is extremely unbalanced in terms of gender, descent, education, or age distribution? If we define the social speech types Bakhtin refers to in terms of the social, cultural, and economic backgrounds of characters, then it is hardly possible to speak of polyphony when there are, for instance, predominantly higher educated, older, Dutch, male characters in a community. In other words: the demographic composition of a community will affect its degree of polyphony. In the following two subsections a method will be presented for clustering the character networks into separate communities. The demography of these communities will then be scrutinized further in order to get a sense of how polyphonic, or dialogic, the corpus is. Building on Bakhtin, polyphonic communities are defined as having a greater social, cultural, and economic diversity of characters, whereas nonpolyphonic communities are defined as being more homogeneous in terms of their demographic composition. After the gender, descent, education, and age distributions of the detected communities are discussed, a close reading of Philip Huff's *Niemand in de stad* (2012) follows to see how a particular novel can be read in light of the observed pattern.

4.4.1 Clauset-Newman-Moore and Girvan-Newman Algorithms

None of the generic algorithms for community detection in networks, described broadly in section 4.2.1, are built specifically for analyzing character networks. It is thus a challenge to find the most suitable algorithm for detecting communities in literary texts. As there is no existing research tradition of community detection in novels, it is also not possible to fall back on best practices reported in other work.

Experiments were conducted with a variety of state-of-the-art community detection algorithms. Unexpectedly, the first experiments yielded negative results. The Clauset-Newman-Moore greedy modularity maximization algorithm (Clauset, Newman, & Moore, 2004) is based on optimizing the modularity of separate clusters of nodes (see section 4.2.1 for an explanation of modularity algorithms), and within the dataset invariably yields a number of communities equal to the size of the network. A novel with 20 characters, for instance, is broken down by this algorithm into 20 separate communities, each of which contains only one character. It is obviously not meaningful to analyze such small-size communities. The Girvan-Newman algorithm (Girvan & Newman, 2002), another state-of-the-art algorithm, aims to remove edges with high betweenness centrality to find a cut-off point between clusters (see chapter 3 'Centrality', section 2, for an explanation of different centrality metrics). Applying this algorithm to the corpus results in similar problems. This algorithm yields only two communities for every book, one of which contains one single character, the other containing all other characters – such clusters cannot meaningfully be used in the subsequent analyses. Other state-of-the-art algorithms produce similarly useless clusters.

Why do state-of-the-art algorithms fail to detect meaningful clusters of characters? Some descriptive statistics on the network structures of the novels shed light on this. Table 1 shows the means for a range of basic network features, such as the number of nodes and edges, density, clustering coefficient, and triadic closure.

Model	N	Minimum	Maximum	Mean	Std. deviation
Number of nodes	170	3	29	12.57	5.146
Number of edges	170	1	212	35.67	29.84
Density	170	0.06	1.00	0.46	0.19
Clustering coefficient	170	0.00	0.87	0.23	0.13
Triadic closure	170	0.00	1.00	0.64	0.19
Valid N (listwise)	170				

Table 1. Descriptive statistics of number of nodes, number of edges, density, clustering coefficient, and triadic closure in the corpus (N=170).

The number of nodes (i.e., characters) in novels in the corpus ranges from a minimum of 3 to a maximum of 29, with a mean of 12.57. Compared to networks used in other strands of network analysis (e.g., biological or real-world social networks), these are extremely small network sizes. One explanation of the inapplicability of, for example, the Clauset-Newman-Moore greedy modularity maximization algorithm and the Girvan-Newman algorithm is that those algorithms are designed for analyzing larger network structures. Character networks are simply too small to detect a fair number of communities with these algorithms.

Another explanation for the poor performance of these community detection algorithms is the relatively high density of the networks. Density indicates the completeness of the network; it is a measure of 'the extent to which all possible relations are actually present' (Scott, 2000, p. 32). A seminal study on real-world social networks reported that most personal networks have a low density, only one-fifth of the studied networks having a density higher than 0.50 (Wellman, 1978, p. 1215 as cited in Scott, 2000, p. 78). The character networks in the Libris corpus have a mean density of 0.46, meaning that they are relatively tightly knit. Probably, the high density of these networks makes it more difficult to separate the network into distinct, dense clusters. When everyone is connected to everyone, there is simply nothing but one tight community.

The low mean clustering coefficient (scale 0–1) of 0.23 strengthens this interpretation. This measure indicates the extent to which nodes in a network cluster together. A low clustering coefficient value 'can indicate a network with relatively small clusters compared to the overall size of the network' (Bucur, 2019). Overall, novels in the Libris corpus contain dense character networks, but they are not easily separable into dense subnetworks. Furthermore, this is supported by the scores on triadic closure, or transitivity, which measures how interconnected a graph is in terms of the ratio of actual over possible connections. The mean triadic closure of 0.64 (scale 0–1) is considerably high, and again, just as the high density, shows how tightly knit the networks are – and thus probably hard to group into distinct communities.

4.4.2 Kernighan-Lin Bisection Algorithm

Because of the low number of characters, high density and triadic closure, and low clustering coefficient, it is not meaningful to break down the character networks into a fair number of separate communities. However, it is possible to enforce a segmentation of a novel's social network into two clusters, for instance of equal size, by optimizing a separation criterion. The Kernighan-Lin algorithm (Kernighan & Lin, 1970) bisects a network into two clusters by 'iteratively swapping pairs of nodes to reduce the edge cut between the two sets'.[11] Although this results in only two communities for each novel, it seems to be the only feasible way to group the character networks into separate clusters. This is a fairly rough clustering technique, but it relies on a statistically significant cut-off point as is the case with the Clauset-Newman-Moore and Girvan-Newman algorithms.

The Kernighan-Lin algorithm thus detects two communities of equal size for every novel. Philip Huff's *Niemand in de stad*, for instance, contains 22 identified characters, and the algorithm separates these 22 characters in a community A and a community B, each containing 11 characters. Following Bakhtin, each of these communities can subsequently be regarded as a collective voice. In order to assess the diversity of individual voices – the extent of polyphony – within these communities, the gender, descent, age, and education distribution for community A and community B is computed for every novel in the corpus.[12]

Solely at the level of the individual text, this bisection allows me to qualitatively determine whether or not community A and community B are segregated in terms of gender, descent, age, and education, which will be done for Huff's novel in the close reading carried out in section 4.4.3. A hypothetical example: 20 characters were identified for novel X, of which 10 are male and 10 are female. If community A of this novel features 9 male characters and 1 female character, whereas community B consists of 9 female characters and 1 male character, then it is likely that novel X is segregated by gender: almost all male characters are grouped together in community A, and almost all female characters are grouped together in community B.

Another hypothetical example: novel Y has 10 identified characters – 1 female character and 9 male characters. Community A of this novel contains this single female character and 4 male characters, whereas community B contains all the other remaining 5 male characters. Is novel Y segregated by gender? Contrary to the hypothetical example of novel X, the character population of novel Y is already extremely unbalanced in terms of gender (90% male, 10% female); clustering these characters into distinct communities A and B will only reflect this general unbalance. Both hypothetical examples of novels X and Y illustrate that an assessment of the multivoicedness, the polyphony, cannot rely on a comparison of community A and B mutually, as it is of paramount importance to compare the gender, descent, education, and age distributions in A and B against the general distributions in the novel as a whole.

To cater to such a comparison between communities at the corpus level, so-called 'difference scores' were computed for each individual novel by subtracting the number of characters of a specific type in a community from the number of this type in the character population of the novel as a whole. For gender, for example, the following six difference scores were computed based on absolute numbers:

— the difference between the number of male characters in community A and the novel as a whole
— the difference between the number of male characters in community B and the novel as a whole
— the difference between the number of female characters in community A and the novel as a whole
— the difference between the number of female characters in community B and the novel as a whole
— the difference between the number of characters with gender unknown in community A and the novel as a whole
— the difference between the number of characters with gender unknown in community B and the novel as a whole.

Similar difference scores were computed for descent, education, and age. These scores indicate the extent to which both community A and community B reflect the overall gender, descent, education, and age distributions in the novels as a whole and more generally points at the extent to which the communities are segregated in terms of these demographic categories. If the difference between, for instance, male characters in community A and male characters in the novel as a whole is higher than the difference of male characters in community B and male characters in the novel as a whole, this may indicate that community A is more dominated by the male social speech type or voice than community B. Note that these difference scores are solely based on the bisection of communities within each of the 170 novels individually and have nothing to do with the composition of communities in other novels in the corpus.

Of course, this approach requires a move from the differences scores in communities of particular novels to generalizable statements about community formation and segregation at the corpus level. In order to assess the extent of multivoicedness or polyphony in the corpus as a whole, it was tested whether there is a significant difference between the difference scores of each of the 170 individual novels. In the case of gender, for instance, a test was conducted to see whether there is a statistically significant difference between the difference scores for male characters in community A and male in characters in community B, as well as between female characters in community A and community B, and between characters with gender unknown in community A and community B. If there indeed are significant differences between these scores, then this shows that the gender of characters is dependent on the type of community (A or B) which they are a part of – that the novels in the corpus, in other words, are segregated by gender.

The appropriate statistical test to conduct for these purposes is a repeated measures ANOVA[13], which can be used to detect overall differences between the mean difference scores of all the novels in the corpus for gender, descent, education, and age. Four repeated measures ANOVAs were conducted on the dependent variable community, one for each of the variables gender, descent, education, and age (see Appendix C for all the main and interaction effects). No statistically significant interaction between gender and community was found, $F(1, 169) = 1.002$, $p = 0.318$.[14] There was also no statistically significant interaction between education and community, $F(1.776, 300.196) = 2.036$, $p = 0.138$, $\varepsilon = 0.897$, partial $\eta 2 = 0.012$.[15] The absence of statistically significant interactions between gender and community and between education and community suggests that the novels in the corpus are not segregated by gender and education.

Significant interactions were found, however, between descent and community, and between age and community. The interaction between descent and community reached significance, $F(1.595, 269.625) = 3.521, p = 0.041$, $\varepsilon = 0.798$, but with a very small effect size (partial $\eta 2 = 0.020$), meaning that the size of the difference is relatively small.[16] Breaking down these effects by the different levels of nonmigrants, migrants, and unknown descent, Figure 3 demonstrates that the mean difference for nonmigrant characters between the communities A and B in the corpus is bigger than it is for migrant characters and for characters with descent unknown (i.e., the distance between the dark purple line [community A] and the lilac line [community B] is smaller for those categories).

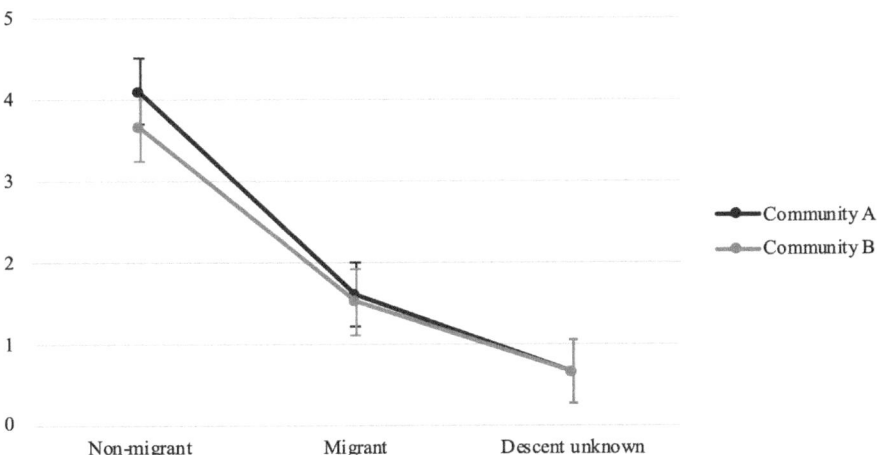

Figure 3. Interaction between descent and community of all characters (N=2,137) in the corpus (N=170). Error bars: 95% CI.

Something similar holds for age. A significant interaction effect between age and community was found $F(1.905, 321.989) = 4.156, p = 0.018, \varepsilon = 0.953$, but again with a small effect size (partial $\eta 2 = 0.024$).[17] Figure 4 shows that the mean difference for younger characters between the communities A and B and the mean difference for older characters between the communities A and B is bigger than it is for characters with age unknown.

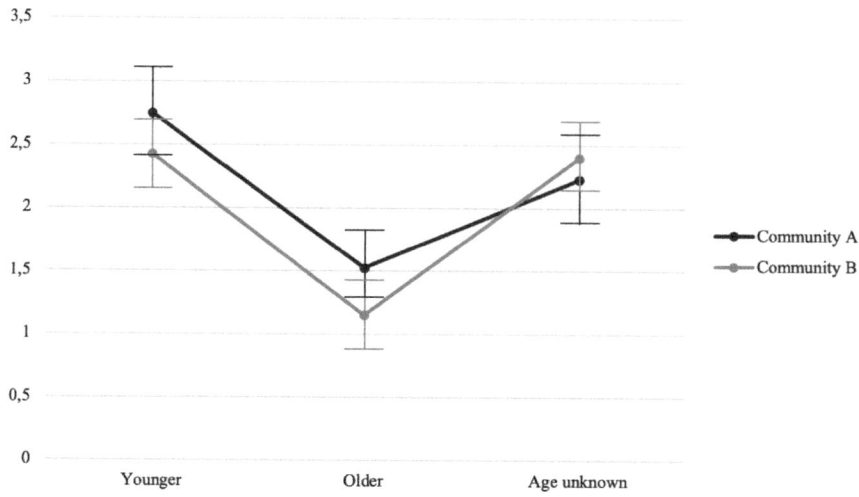

Figure 4. Interaction between age and community of all characters (N=2,137) in the corpus (N=170). Error bars: 95% CI.

In sum: although significant interactions effects have been found for both descent and age with community, the size of this effect is limited. Both descent and age are causes of segregation in the fictional characters' populations, but the extent of this segregation is low.

What does this mean with regard to the degree of polyphony in the novels? As there are no remarkable differences between the gender and education distributions within the communities compared to the books as a whole, it is tempting to conclude that the majority of the novels in the Libris corpus are polyphonic or dialogic in terms of these categories. After all, the detected communities are not significantly segregated into either male and female communities or higher and lower educated communities. Overall, both male and female voices thus tend to be simultaneously orchestrated in the same communities, as do the narrative voices of the higher and the lower educated. For descent and age, however, the tests suggest otherwise: there are significant differences between the descent and age distributions within communities A and B compared to the novels as a whole. As these results indicate that the detected communities are segregated into migrant and nonmigrant characters, and into younger and older characters, it seems legitimate to state that the corpus is *not* polyphonic or dialogic in terms of descent and age. Characters with and without a migration background tend to function within communities of their own, as do younger and older characters – connections between these social speech types are weaker than between men and women and people with different levels of education.

The results of the repeated measures ANOVA tests should be seen in relation to the negative outcomes of the tests with the Clauset-Newman-Moore and Girvan-Newman algorithms. As pointed out in paragraph 4.4.1, the inapplicability of these algorithms can be explained by basic network features of the novels, such as the low number of characters, their high density, and low clustering coefficient. But possibly, the ineffective outputs of these algorithms (e.g., a large number of extremely small size communities) are a symptom of a more fundamental problem studies on character communities face. If it is so hard to group the social networks of characters into a fair number of distinct clusters, is it even meaningful to call the bisections into two groups of characters of equal size – by the Kernighan-Lin algorithm – communities?

Perhaps not. One argument is that the small fictional worlds of present-day Dutch novels are simply communities in themselves. As the chances are relatively high that two random characters in a novel engage in some kind of a relationship, the chance that a novel can be broken down into distinct groups of characters decreases. This is exactly what is suggested by the high density of the novels: the characters are too interconnected to be meaningfully segmented into communities. Given these observations, this argument makes the case that there is just one community for every novel. From a Bakhtinian perspective, in which communities are defined as collective voices, the absence of a multitude of communities can be regarded as nonpolyphonic. Although novels with only one community might still contain a variety of narrative perspectives or social speech types, these novels are self-contained social systems in the sense that they lack a variety of collective voices. Obviously, within each single community there are interconnections between individual voices, with characters interacting on the plot level and co-occurring on the sentence level. But is this equal to a 'connection between consciousnesses' (Bakhtin, 1929/2003a, p. 95)? The existence of and interaction between multiple communities, each representing a collective voice, might be a necessary prerequisite for a novel to be genuinely polyphonic. Compared to novels such as those of Dostoevsky, containing a fairly large number of characters and perhaps a lower density, present-day Dutch novels are possibly of a radically different nature.

A second argument reverses the above line of reasoning. Instead of interpreting the high density of the networks as a negation of polyphony (because it hampers the clustering of characters into communities), it can conversely be seen as an argument *for* polyphony. Arguably, dense networks are the perfect breeding ground for a 'connection between consciousnesses' (ibid). In the tightly knit character networks in the Libris corpus, there is ample opportunity for characters with different social, economic, and cultural backgrounds to engage in contact. Although it is hard to group the characters into communities representing a collective voice, the interplay between their individual voices fosters a dialogic environment. In this second argument, polyphony, or dialogism, is a function of the demographic composition of the novels as a whole and not of the collective voices represented by distinct communities. The repeated measures ANOVA tests, furthermore, have shown that the corpus is not segregated into communities of male and female and into lower and higher educated characters, which suggests that there are sufficiently many moments of contact between characters from different genders and educational levels or social classes. However, the repeated measures ANOVA tests have also shown that the Libris corpus is segregated into migrant and nonmigrant communities and into younger and older characters, which suggests non-polyphony in terms of descent and age.

In order to assess the value of these statistics-based interpretations, a close reading of Philip Huff's *Niemand in de stad* (2012) will follow evaluating the degree of polyphony in narratological terms. This novel is selected because it explicitly thematizes community life of student fraternity members; it will be read against the background of the reported quantitative observations. Do the detected communities in this novel make sense from a qualitative perspective, and how polyphonic are they in both statistical and narratological terms?

4.4.3 Close Reading: Communities in Philip Huff's *Niemand in de stad* (2012)

Niemand in de stad has an obvious intertextual relation with Nescio's short story *De uitvreter* (1911), one of the classics of twentieth-century Dutch literature. Just as Nescio's characters Japi, Bavink, and Koekebakker, the circle of friends around Philip, the protagonist of Huff's novel, is depicted in a rather strong opposition to 'society' as a whole. In *De uitvreter*, the work-shy main characters look down upon common, working-class people because they conform to society's rules and norms. In *Niemand in de stad*, student fraternity life is represented as the last free haven before having to subsist under the yoke of society.

This sentiment is most accurately described in a key scene in which first-person narrator and protagonist Philip discusses student life with his fellow fraternity members Jacob and Matt. Idealizing his student years, Jacob characterizes the present moment as 'the autumn of [their] youth' and '[their] time in the Garden of Eden' (Huff, 2012, p. 104). Furthermore, he postulates a strict opposition between fraternity and the rest of society:

> People assume that there are no windows [in the fraternity clubhouse] so that they cannot look inside. But that is not the reason why. At least: it is only partly true. It is also about how visible the outside is seen from the inside. The club does not have any windows so that *we* do not have to look outside. We are hiding from the world, from the sheep shearers with their knives and the hunters with their guns, from our fathers and their expectations, and from our mothers and their safety-net. For just a little while. In this small, artificial, and unimportant society of ours. (p. 105)

Metaphorizing the absent windows in the fraternity's clubhouse, Jacob highlights the antagonistic relation between the insiders (the fraternity members) and the outsiders ('the world'). Remarkably, the last sentence in this quote is ambiguous: does 'this small, artificial, and unimportant society of ours' refer to society as a whole ('the world') or to fraternity life specifically? The impossibility of disambiguating between the first and the second option obstructs an analysis in terms of Greimas and Courtés's distinction between paradigmatic and syntagmatic collectives (see section 4.3.1 of this chapter). If fraternity life is the object of reference in this sentence, then the narrative world of *Niemand in de stad* can be framed as a paradigmatic collective in which society as a whole is placed higher in the hierarchical order than the community of fraternity members, the latter being merely a 'small, artificial, and unimportant' suborder of that society. When the sentence is interpreted as referring to society in general, then the fraternity is simply part of 'this small, artificial, and unimportant society of ours'. In this interpretation, the novel conversely depicts a syntagmatic narrative world in which there is no explicit hierarchy between the fraternity and 'the world' as such. Because of the sentence's ambiguity, both options are left open.

There are, however, less ambiguous text fragments that reinforce a strong, hierarchical opposition between fraternity and society. Most obviously, this is illustrated by the fraternity's strong emphasis on the importance of being part of a group, a collective, a community. As the most eloquent member of the group, Jacob points out that Philip and his friends should use '[Their] right to surrender to the group' (p. 27). Authenticity and individual identity, in other words, have to be sacrificed for the sake of the collective. In fraternity, Jacob contends, people are 'the role [they] play'. 'Yes, of course', Philip passively complies (ibid.). One of the main goals of this collective is to remain intact. This is exemplified by Matt's dissatisfaction with the quality of the beer in the clubhouse, about which he jokingly fears that 'in this way, we will not be able to drink enough to feel connected' (p. 19).

The importance of the social cohesion within the fraternity collective conflicts with the social ties Philip has with people outside of it, most importantly with his high-school girlfriend Elisabeth. When Elisabeth visits the 'Weeshuis', the residency of Philip and his fellow fraternity members, the clash between inside fraternity and outside is foregrounded. Hannes, Jacob, and Bart encounter Elisabeth and Philip having sex when they enter his room unannounced, after which they make ironic jokes about Elisabeth's pubic hair. Elisabeth is, quite expectedly, not amused. But more strikingly, she seems to hold Philip responsible for her confrontation with the rudeness of his friends: 'Elisabeth turned her face to the wall. [...] When I touched her shoulder, she pushed away my hand' (p. 33). Being part of this community, Philip indeed is in a sense responsible for the norms and values he implicitly upholds by being a member of it. One of these implicit norms is to have a variety of sexual contacts. Because he has a girlfriend, Philip has a hard time conforming to this expectation. Again, this highlights the hierarchical opposition between fraternity life and the outer world, here represented by Elisabeth, who is described by Philip as '[his] home' (p. 36). In the course of the novel, the fraternity gradually replaces Elisabeth as Philip's 'home'.

Network visualizations of the two communities as detected by the Kernighan-Lin algorithm (see section 4.4.2) help to gain a more general insight into the novel's segmentation into distinct groups. Figures 5 and 6 show the networks of the two detected communities.

With some exceptions, the bisection of the novel's character network into these two communities by the algorithm is understandable from a close reading perspective. Community A (Figure 5) contains most of the fraternity insiders. Philip, Jacob, Matt, Paulus, Bart, Hannes, and Tom are all residents of the 'Weeshuis'. Karen is also part of the student organization and has an affair with Philip. Simon is the organization's praeses. Only Elisabeth, Philip's girlfriend, and Tessa, Matt's girlfriend, are not part of the same organization. However, as Elisabeth and Tessa interact frequently with both Philip and Matt, it seems logical that they are grouped into the same cluster by the algorithm.

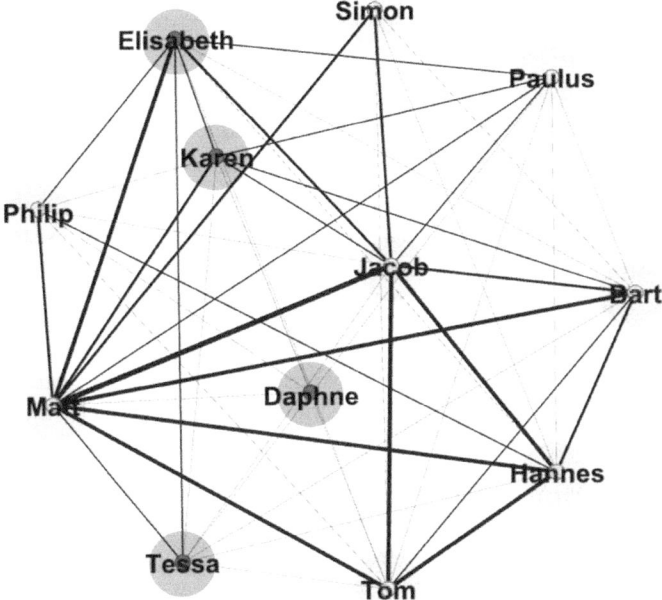

Figure 5. Network visualization of community A as detected by the Kernighan-Lin bisection algorithm. Node size is equal for all nodes, node color indicates gender (light color = male, dark color = female). Edge size indicates weight.

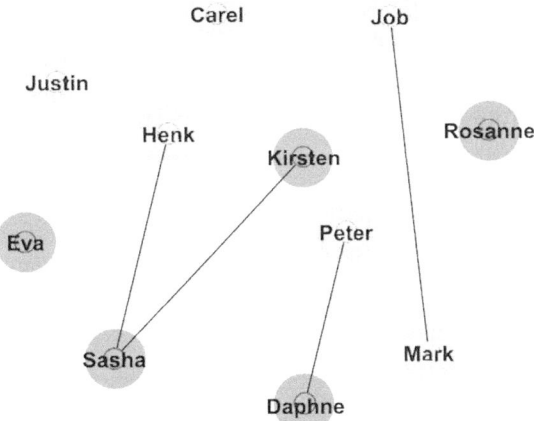

Figure 6. Network visualization of community B as detected by the Kernighan-Lin bisection algorithm. Node size is equal for all nodes, node color indicates gender (light color = male, dark color = female). Edge size indicates weight.

Most of the outsiders are part of community B (Figure 6). Sasha and Henk are coworkers of Philip and Matt at their part time job at the casino. Mark and Job are both older ex-fraternity members. Peter is Matt's older brother, and Daphne is his stepmother. Carel is Jacob's father, and Justin is Jacob's nonfraternity friend with whom he supposedly has a romantic relation. Eva is a stripper whom Philip encounters in Prague. Less logical from a thematic point of view is that Rosanne and Kirsten are grouped in this community as they are part of the same students' organization. But as they have only a minor role in the novel and thus do not interact frequently with the main characters, there are probably no statistical reasons for the algorithm to group them in the other community.

Looking at these network visualizations, it is immediately clear that there is a strong difference in the extent of interconnectedness between community A and B. This is supported by the density of both networks: the insiders' community has a density of 0.70, whereas the 'outsiders'-community has a density of only 0.07. In other words, people belonging to the circle around Philip and his fellow fraternity members are drastically more interconnected than people less close to this circle. Narratologically, this can be explained by the simple observation that the outsiders are relatively minor characters compared to the insiders: they are not as fully characterized as the insiders and are less visibly dispersed in the narrative. As a key descriptive statistic related to the network structure, the density of the communities thus reflects the importance of social cohesion and collective spirit thematized by the fraternity members in the novel.

Is the thematic opposition between fraternity and society reflected in the gender, descent, education, and age distributions of the two communities? An opposition in terms of education or descent is not apparent. Tables 2 and 3 show that the descent and education distributions in both the insiders' community (A) and the outsiders community (B) are close to the overall distributions in the book as a whole. This is a result of the fact that migrant and lower educated characters are fully absent in the novel. The only differences in descent and education distribution in the communities is due to the degree of descent and education that is unknown for certain characters.

	Descent	*Relative distribution*
Book	Nonmigrant	0.92
	Migrant	0.00
	Unknown	0.09
Community A	Nonmigrant	1.00
	Migrant	0.00
	Unknown	0.00
Community B	Nonmigrant	0.82
	Migrant	0.00
	Unknown	0.18

Table 2. Relative descent distributions for Niemand in de stad as a whole compared to the two detected communities (A and B).

	Education	*Relative distribution*
Book	High	0.82
	Low	0.00
	Unknown	0.18
Community A	High	0.91
	Low	0.00
	Unknown	0.09
Community B	High	0.73
	Low	0.00
	Unknown	0.27

Table 3. Relative education distributions for Niemand in de stad as a whole compared to the two detected communities (A and B).

It is tempting to regard this as an indication of the absence of polyphony, or dialogism, in terms of descent and education. After all, the novel only includes higher educated and Dutch characters, which can be interpreted as an obstruction of the diversity of social speech types with regard to these demographics. An important side note, however, is that the homogeneity in terms of descent and education in both communities is a direct result of the homogeneity of the book as a whole. Subsequently, this overall homogeneity results in a narrative world in which there is no possibility for a segregation into communities of higher and lower educated, and migrant and nonmigrant, characters. When all characters in a novel are higher educated and of the same descent, no (hierarchical) opposition between groups of characters can arise. However, this is only true in the most direct, literal sense and does not account for the full complexity of the represented identities in the novel. Philip and Jacob, for instance, are both annotated in the database as higher educated, but there is an obvious class difference between the two: Philip comes from a broken family and receives little financial support, whereas Jacob has a wealthy family with its own seal ring. Reducing them both to higher educated characters does not do justice to such differences. Statistically, there is no opposition in terms of descent and education in the detected communities, but it would be reductionistic to conclude that these identity categories play no part at all in the thematic opposition between fraternity and society as presented in *Niemand in de stad*.

A slightly different image emerges for age and gender. Tables 4 and 5 show that the relative age and gender distributions in the insiders' community (A) and the outsiders' community (B) deviate more strongly from their overall distributions in the novel as a whole than is the case with descent and education. The insiders' community is relatively young and male in light of the age and gender distribution in the novel's narrative world as a whole. Whereas almost all characters in this community are below the age of 25, the outsiders community has more variance in age categories. The novel's overall male-female ratio is 0.64–0.36, whereas 73% of the characters in the insiders' community are male as opposed to only 55% of the characters in the outsiders' community.

	Age	Relative distribution
Book	<25	0.64
	26–35	0.00
	36–45	0.14
	46–55	0.00
	56–64	0.05
	65+	0.05
	Unknown	0.14
Community A	<25	0.91
	26–35	0.00
	36–45	0.00
	46–55	0.00
	56–64	0.00
	65+	0.00
	Unknown	0.09
Community B	<25	0.36
	26-35	0.00
	36–45	0.27
	46–55	0.00
	56–64	0.09
	65+	0.09
	Unknown	0.18

Table 4. Relative age distributions for Niemand in de stad as a whole compared to the two detected communities (A and B).

	Gender	Relative distribution
Book	Male	0.64
	Female	0.36
	Unknown	0.00
Community A	Male	0.73
	Female	0.27
	Unknown	0.00
Community B	Male	0.55
	Female	0.45
	Unknown	0.00

Table 5. Relative gender distributions for Niemand in de stad as a whole compared to the two detected communities (A and B).

Although being young seems to be a crucial part of student culture, it is not specifically thematized in the novel other than through an idealization of youthful fraternity life in general such as exemplified by Jacob in the quote above. Being male does not seem to be a necessary prerequisite for entering this supposedly last free haven of fraternity life. However, *Niemand in de stad* is a story about boys rather than about girls. 'Boys we were, but nice boys,'[18] the opening line from Nescio's short story *De Titaantjes* (1911/2018), and one of the most famous lines from twentieth-century Dutch literature, constantly looms in the background. The comings and goings of Philip, Jacob, Matt, and other fraternity members should first and foremost be read in light of the book's nostalgic yearning for a time when boys could just be boys without having to bother about careers, marriages, parenting, and mortgages.

This image of naive boyhood trickles down to the way in which the female characters are depicted. Most women in the novel function as catalysts for the burgeoning sexual desires of Philip and his friends. This is first of all apparent in the characterization of the female characters. Although physical descriptions are often a key element of characterization, the bodily features of the women in the novel are remarkably more foregrounded than those of the men. For instance, Philip introduces Elisabeth to the reader by emphasizing her appealing looks rather than her fine character traits: 'She was small, blonde, large breasts, and wore black glasses. Especially those glasses excited me.' (p. 29). Furthermore, the first scene she features in is the above-described uncomfortable sex scene, highlighting her physicality rather than her psychology. Philip's fascination with Karen is also primarily a fascination with her body, which is exemplified by his description of her looks (e.g., 'She has full, striking lips that highlight her sensuality' [p. 71]), as well as by Matt's reaction on Philip talking with such a 'hot chick' (p. 75): 'Last night, you were having extremely lengthy conversations with those tits of Karen Ricks' (p. 74). When Philip is worried about Elisabeth finding out about his affair with Karen, he subtly makes clear that he has an affair with her body rather than with her mind: 'And Karen's body was not here to calm me down' (p. 263).

The foregrounding of the bodily features of Elisabeth and Karen does not stand on its own; it is exemplary of a pattern. Philip and his friends conform to the fraternity stereotype of striving for as much sex as possible. Although Philip is rather troubled about having an affair, the dominant morale of fraternity is accurately described by Matt stating that 'you have to fuck those chicks out of your system. Satisfying the need' (p. 184). When Philip and Matt visit Matt's stepdad, this again becomes clear through Philip's sexualization of Daphne, Matt's stepmom: 'She wears a short, purple dress without a bra. Her large, heavy breasts are firm and look good in the fabric' (p. 175). In line with the present analysis, Philip is aware that this desire is part of a pattern: 'It seems as if Karen opened up a door of desire to strange, unreachable women' (p. 178).

Whereas descent and education are not particularly highlighted, and age only partly, as a component of the thematic opposition between fraternity life and society, gender definitely creates a distance between the insiders' community and the outsiders' community. Not only does the insiders' community feature more men than the outsiders' community, female characters also have a different status in the novel than male characters. The idealization of the free-haven of fraternity goes hand in hand with an objectification and (hetero)sexualization of female bodies. 'Boys should be boys' here also denotes a permission to surrender to raw, hormonal desires for sexual fulfilment. Furthermore, the frustration of this desire has the potential to result in covert aggression toward female characters. Most strikingly, this is illustrated in a scene where Philip is robbed by stripper Eva in a private session. Being frustrated in his sexual desire and upset about the robbery, Philip aggressively masturbates while thinking about Eva in terms of a 'Bitch' (p. 66), a 'Goddamn whore' (p. 66), and a 'Stealing whore' (p. 67). In a similar vein, Philip is hostile toward Elisabeth when she criticizes his friend Matt for having such loose sexual morals ('That boy is a Neanderthal' [p. 118]). As a result of his girlfriend's criticism of the fraternity's implicit norm of sexuality, a quasi-ironic desire to kill her emerges in his mind: 'I feel like pushing Elisabeth. *Boy kills girlfriend in hotel room*' (ibid., emphasis in original quote). As if criticism against the collective he belongs to desexualizes, Philip then promptly loses his sexual interest in Elisabeth (p. 119).

The male voice or social speech type is arguably more dominant in *Niemand in de stad* than the female. It is narrated from the perspective of a young man who finds himself in the middle of a male-centered, masculine community in which women are primarily regarded in terms of their sexuality. Prioritizing the male perspective, the novel can be taken as being quite non-polyphonic, or non-dialogic, in terms of gender: a genuine 'connection between consciousnesses' (Bakhtin, 1929, p. 95) does not seem to take place between the male and the female social speech types. These qualitative observations are backed up by the novel's algorithmic bisection into an insiders' community and an outsiders' community, of which the first features more male than female characters. That Elisabeth and Karen are grouped into this insiders' community does, however, not conform smoothly with the present qualitative analysis, as these characters are not genuinely part of the community of (male) friends around Philip, and they have a rather instrumental function in the narrative.

A closer look shows that the novel deliberately seems to create this schematic opposition between groups such as fraternity and society, and men and women. This is subtly expressed through the metaphor of the casino where Philip and Matt work as a croupier, which is ironically called 'the firm Sly & Fraud' (p. 120). In a briefing before their work shift, their boss motivates the croupiers by saying that '[they] are going to unite people and bring them fun. Decorate lives' (p. 54). This euphemism can be read as a critical reference to fraternity: claiming to unite and decorate the lives of their members, the fraternity collective possibly tricks people into avoidance behavior in the same way gambling does. Whereas Philip seems to have little problem with fraternity as such, he dabbles with the ethics of being an employee of the casino:

> We do not work here to deceive people, I say to myself in the stairway.
> We are here to facilitate. It is their choice to be here. (p. 111)

Repeating the logic he learned at the casino, Philip deceives himself. In truth, he knows very well that the casino fosters an environment of abuse, addiction, and avoidance. His attitude toward the casino can be interpreted as symbolizing his latent attitude toward the fraternity. Deep down, it is suggested, Philip knows that the strong opposition between fraternity life and society leads to self-deceit as well, which becomes painfully clear when his friend Jacob appears to have lived a life of deceit for years and finally commits suicide. The casino claims to help those at the margins of society ('There is nobody in town who cares more about those people than we do' [p. 226]). Similarly, the fraternity community also claims to cater to young people who do not have to be part of society yet. Both the casino and the fraternity are deceitful in postulating a divide between them and society in the first place. Although it is not stated explicitly in the novel, reading between the lines shows that the narrative self-consciously plays with this schematic opposition between groups.

'Exclusively thinking in oppositions is an indication of intellectual laziness' (p. 134), Jacob states in one of his conversations with Philip. This can be read as hidden meta-commentary on the narrative as a whole. Statistically and narratologically, the bisection into an insiders' community and an outsiders' community creates a framework for analyzing the novel in oppositional terms. Such an oppositional, schematic analysis indeed shows a hierarchy in the novel's representation of certain social groups, between fraternity and society, as well as between men and women. This very opposition, however, is also thematized in the novel through, for instance, the metaphor of the casino. As such, the narrative seems to play with these observed statistical and narratological patterns. This is not to say that these patterns are meaningless: the novel still contains an obvious opposition between fraternity and society, as well as an absence of gender polyphony. But although the novel does conform to these statistical and narratological patterns, the literary stylistic mechanisms of metaphors, symbols, and subtle metacommentary open up possibilities for deconstructing those same patterns. In this sense, the oppositions can be interpreted as a form of critical mimesis[19]: although the opposition between fraternity and society is represented as highly schematic, such literary stylistic mechanisms call into question the moral scheme associated with it.

4.5 MODEL II: HOMOPHILY

Whereas the former section studied polyphony in character communities by detecting subgroups of characters in all of the 170 networks, the present section focuses on the similarities between individual characters. The current analysis thus reverses the order of the analysis carried out in the former section. Instead of breaking down the networks into smaller portions and then computing frequency distributions of gender, descent, education, and age of those portions, the point of focus now lies on the similarity of these demographic categories between any two characters sharing edges. As such, this section presents an alternative model for analyzing polyphony in narrative communities to the model proposed in the previous section. Whereas the former analysis approached polyphony in terms of top-down detected communities, the present analysis studies polyphony through the concept of homophily (see section 4.2.2). A high degree of homophily on gender, descent, education, or age indicates that a novel is segregated with regard to these demographic categories. In a novel where, for instance, older characters are mostly connected to other older characters, there is no dialogic interaction between characters from different age groups. High homophily thus suggests a low degree of polyphony: there is not so much a 'connection between consciousnesses' (Bakhtin, 1929/2003a, p. 95) in terms of, for instance, older and younger characters. Conversely, low homophily can be framed as indicating a high degree of polyphony. When connections between older and younger characters occur relatively often, there is arguably a greater dialogic interaction between characters with different ages, and thus a higher degree of polyphony with regards to age.

An important side note is that this operationalization of polyphony via the statistical metric of homophily is obviously based on a pragmatic, but reductionist, take on the voices or social speech types present in a novel. A character may inhabit many voices that are not necessarily reducible to their demographic features: youthful characters, for instance, can speak with an older voice inherited from their ancestors. In order to gain a fuller account of the multivoicedness in a novel, the narratological evaluation of the statistical results devotes attention to such voices falling outside the model's scope. In the following, the methodological design of the analysis is first described, after which its results are reported. In order to assess the relevance of these results, a novel from the corpus is read through the lens of homophily related to age. *Liefde heeft geen hersens* (2012) by Mensje van Keulen is selected as a case study because of its thematization of youth, old age, and death, as well as for its problematization of fixed age categories.

4.5.1 Dyad Assortativity

Homophily in networks can be studied by computing the assortativity for specific node attributes such as gender, descent, education, and age (see section 4.2.2). For each of the 170 character networks, the Python software package Networkx was used to compute four so-called assortativity coefficients related to gender, descent, education, and age of the characters.[20] These assortativity coefficients are the Pearson correlation coefficients for each dyad of characters sharing edges. The result is a number between -1 and 1, with positive values indicating a correlation between characters with similar gender, descent, education, or age, and negative values indicating a correlation between characters with different gender, descent, education, or age. For instance, the assortativity coefficient related to gender for *De lichtekooi van Loven* by Ineke van der Aa is -0.05. If the gender assortativity coefficient were 1, then this novel would feature exclusively same-sex relations (male-male and female-female). Conversely, if the gender assortativity coefficient was -1, then the novel would only feature opposite-sex relations (male-female, female-male). In reality, *De lichtekooi van Loven* has a gender assortativity coefficient close to 0, indicating that both same-sex and opposite-sex relations occur relatively equally.[21] Table 6 shows the means for each of the four computed assortativity coefficients in the corpus. On average, the assortativity coefficients for gender (-0.11), age (-0.07), and education (-0.06) show negative values, indicating that the corpus contains more character pairs differing in gender, age, and education. For descent, this is the other way around: the positive mean of the assortativity coefficients (0.18) indicates that there are more pairs of characters with the same region of descent.[22]

	N	Minimum	Maximum	Mean	Std. Deviation
Gender assortativity	170	-1.00	1.00	-0.11	0.21
Age assortativity	170	-0.60	1.00	-0.07	0.26
Education assortativity	170	-0.50	1.00	-0.06	0.27
Descent assortativity	170	-0.61	1.00	0.18	0.48
Valid N (listwise)	170				

Table 6. Descriptive statistics of the assortativity coefficients of gender, age, education, and descent in the corpus (N=170).

How to evaluate the meaning of these numbers? Section 4.2.2 of this chapter described general findings of research on homophily. Homophilous associations with regard to race and ethnicity have demonstrated to be most prominent in contemporary societies (Marsden, 1987, 1988). The positive mean assortativity coefficient for descent suggests that segregation on this demographic factor is also apparent in present-day Dutch literary fiction. However, this segregation pattern is probably less dominant than it is in present-day Dutch society, which is demonstrated by a previous comparison of a part of the present dataset with a dataset on real-world networks of Dutch people showing that the fictional networks are significantly less segregated by means of descent than real ones (Volker & Smeets, 2019).

Divides in society are also caused by homophilous associations with regards to education (Marsden, 1987; Verbrugge, 1977). The negative mean of the assortativity coefficient for education suggests that this is less so in the fictional worlds of Dutch characters. Age homophily in society is rather high in specific networks such as marriages, but differs depending on setting (McPherson et al., 2001, pp. 424–425). In Dutch literary fiction, age homophily is more on the lower than on the higher end of the spectrum. Segregation in society is the least fueled by gender, part of this is due to opposite-sex marriages (Marsden, 1988). On average, opposite-sex relations are more present in the corpus than same-sex relations.

Still, it is up for debate how the findings on gender, descent, education, and age homophily in the corpus should be assessed. Which scores on these assortativity coefficients are reasonable to expect? Research on homophily in real-world networks is one of the possible baselines. Given such real-world findings, how extraordinary are the homophily patterns in Dutch literary fiction? This baseline is used in the comparison above and is operationalized and analyzed – for a portion of only 65.4% of the present dataset – in Volker and Smeets (2019). Testing the present results against results for social networks of actual people presupposes a particular idea about the extent to which the societies portrayed in literary fiction resemble real social structures. How reasonable is it to expect literary fiction to mirror segregation patterns in societies? Leaving this question aside for now, a more neutral and formal baseline is to conduct a so-called permutation test, or randomization test,[23] to estimate the chance that the observed mean positive degree of descent assortativity (0.18) and the observed mean negative degrees of gender (-0.11), age (-0.07), and education (-0.06) assortativity are found given the same descent, gender, age, and education ratios of the nodes and the same number of edges. The goal of this permutation test is to single out the possibility that the found assortativity values are just a random effect of the distributions of these classes. The fact, for instance, that there are more men than women in the corpus (a 60:40 ratio), increases the chance of finding more male-female pairs than female-female pairs. The permutation test is conducted by randomly reassigning the descent, gender, education, and age labels of the characters in the corpus 1,000 times, while keeping the ratios the same. The male-female ratio, for instance, remains 60:40, but the specific characters who are male or female change with every random permutation. Then, for every of the 1,000 random permutations, the assortativity coefficients are recalculated. Finally, the assortativity values as observed in the actual dataset are compared to the values resulting from these random permutations. The question, then, is whether or not the actual assortativity values differ significantly from these random assortativity values. If it does, then this is an indication that the actual assortativity values are not just a random effect of the gender, descent, education, and age ratios.

Following the approach by Kraicer and Piper (2019), 1,000 permutation tests were conducted, and the assortativity coefficients for each of these permutations were calculated.[24] Then, the means of the 1,000 permuted assortativity coefficients for gender, descent, education, and age were computed. In four one sample t-tests[25], the actual means – the gender, descent, education, and age assortativity coefficients for the actual dataset – were compared with these four permutation means as a baseline to determine whether the actual means are significantly different from these permutation means. The mean gender assortativity of the novels in the corpus ($M = -0.11$, $SD = 0.21$) is slightly higher than the permutations' mean gender assortativity of -0.12 ($SD = 0.02$). There is, however, no statistically significant difference between the actual observed mean gender assortativity in the corpus and the permutations' mean gender assortativity, $t(169) = 0.55$, $p = 0.586$, 95% BCa CI [-0.23 to 0.04]. This suggest that the extent of gender homophily in the corpus is likely to be just a random effect of the 60:40 male-female ratio of characters. In other words: the found negative gender homophily seems to be from the result of the relative amount of male and female characters rather than signaling hetero- or homonormative gender interaction patterns.

This is different for descent, education, and age. For descent, there is a strong difference between the actual mean assortativity and the assortativity of the 1,000 permutations. Whereas the actual descent assortativity in the corpus is a positive value of 0.18 ($SD = 0.48$), indicating more interactions between characters with the same descent, the mean descent assortativity of the 1,000 permutations shows a negative value of -0.11 ($SD = 0.018$), which is a statistically significant difference ($t(169) = 8.010, p < 0.0001$, 95% BCa CI [0.23 to 0.37]). As descent homophily does not appear to be a random effect of the ratio of non-migrants and migrant characters in the corpus (± 90:10, excluding the portion of characters with descent unknown), the interactions between characters with the same descent thus seems to be a signal of segregation by descent. Characters with the same descent, in other words, tend to flock together.

The mean education assortativity ($M = -0.06$, $SD = 0.27$) is higher than the mean education assortativity of the 1000 permutations of -0,13 ($SD = 0.012$), which appears to be significantly higher ($t(169) = 3.734$, $p < 0.0001$, 95% BCa CI [0.04 to 0.12]). Something similar holds for age: the mean age assortativity ($M = -0.07$, $SD = 0.26$) is significantly higher than the mean age assortativity of the 1000 permutations ($M = 0.15$, $SD = 0.009$), $t(169) = 3.647$, $p < 0.0001$, 95% BCa CI [0.04 to 0.10]. In the narrative worlds of the 170 novels, the interactions between characters from both different age groups and different educational levels are thus not a random effect of the age and education distributions. On average, there is significantly more integration and less segregation between ages and classes in the corpus.

Another way to evaluate the extent of homophily is by looking at features related to the network structure. To what extent do network structure features such as network size (i.e., the number of characters in a novel) and density predict the extent of gender, descent, education, and age assortativity? Before this question can be answered, the Pearson correlations between all the variables related to the network structure of the novels were computed in order to see how they are interrelated (see Appendix D). Figure 7 shows a scatterplot matrix representing the correlations between the number of words of the novel ('tokencount'), number of characters ('nrnodes'), number of edges between these characters ('nredges'), the density, the triadic closure, and the clustering coefficient. A more diagonal fit line between a variable on the X axis and a variable on the Y axis represents a stronger correlation – a positive correlation when the line goes upward, a negative correlation when the line goes downward.

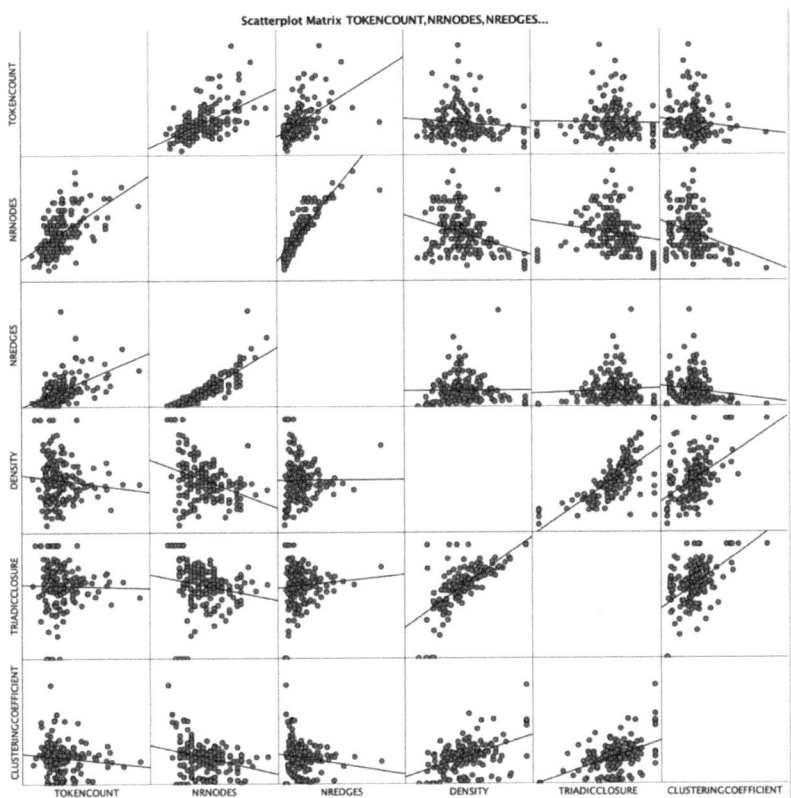

Figure 7. Scatterplot matrix showing the correlations between the following variables relating to network structure: tokencount, number of nodes, number of edges, density, triadic closure, and clustering coefficient.

Unsurprisingly, the variables that were used to explain the problem of detecting communities in section 4.4.1 show a significant correlation. There is a negative correlation between density and number of characters ($r = -0.352$, $N = 170$, $p < 0.01$), meaning that the density of the character networks decrease when there are more characters present. This is understandable: for example, a Dostoevsky novel with a great number of characters might be less fully interconnected than a novel with just a few characters. There are positive correlations between density and triadic closure ($r = 0.713$, $N = 170$, $p < 0.01$), as well as between density and clustering coefficient ($r = 0.713$, $N = 170$, $p < 0.01$). More dense networks are thus more fully interconnected in terms of triadic relations, and show more clustering. Whereas the positive correlation between density and triadic closure is imaginable, it would have been more logical if density and clustering coefficient would have correlated negatively instead of positively, as a combination of high density and low clustering was given as an explanation for the problem of community detection in section 4.4.1. The variables number of nodes and number of edges show multicollinearity ($r = 0.862$, $N = 170$, $p < 0.01$), meaning that they are so strongly correlated that it does not make a difference whether one or the other is used as a predictor in a multiple regression analysis. Therefore, only the number of nodes is used in the subsequent analysis.

Does the likelihood of gender, descent, education, and age homophily increase when there are more characters in a novel, when a novel has more words, or when a novel has a higher density, clustering coefficient, or triadic closure? Hypothesizing that this is the case, four multiple linear regressions were conducted to predict 1) gender assortativity, 2) descent assortativity, 3) education assortativity, and 4) age assortativity based on the tokencount, number of nodes, density, triadic closure, and clustering coefficient. No significant results were found for descent assortativity, education assortativity, and age assortativity. As features related to the network structure, tokencount, density, triadic closure, and clustering coefficient are thus no predictors for the extent of descent, education, and age homophily. It is not the case that, for instance, a denser character network leads to, for instance, more same-age character pairs.

A significant regression equation was only found for gender assortativity ($F(5, 7135) = 2.361$, $p = 0.040$), with an R^2 of 0.067 and number of nodes as the only significant predictor. The predicted gender assortativity is equal to a B value of -0.107 + 0.008 (number of nodes) (see Table 7), indicating that gender homophily increases for each additional character in a novel. The number of characters in a novel is thus a predictor of the degree of gender homophily. More characters result in more same-sex pairs. The chance of gender segregation, in other words, increases when the fictional population of a novel is larger. This pattern is not easily interpretable. In nonfictional, real-world social networks, gender homophily – or gender segregation – is relatively low, mostly because of the dominance of heterosexual romantic relations (Marsden, 1988). Compared to the descent, education, and age homophily, the extent of gender homophily is also relatively low in the fictional networks in the corpus. Why does it increase when more characters are staged?

	Unstandardized B	Coefficients std. error	Standardized coefficients Beta	t	Sig.
(Constant)	-0.107	0.016		-6.673	0.00
C Token Count	4.803E-8	0.000	0.039	0.427	0.670
C Number of nodes	0.008	0.004	0.205	2.067	0.040
C Density	-0.145	0.129	-0.129	-1.124	0.263
C Triadic closure	0.068	0.126	0.061	0.541	0.589
C Clustering coefficient	0.140	0.146	0.087	0.958	0.340

Table 7. Linear model of predictors for gender assortivity. Only number of nodes produces a statistically significant effect.

For example, *Kunstroof* (2012) by Raymond Rombout has 29 identified characters, which is the highest number of characters in any of the novels in the corpus. Its gender assortativity coefficient is 0.007, which is relatively high in light of the mean gender assortativity coefficient of -0.11. In this novel, conforming to the general pattern, a larger population of characters goes hand in hand with more gender segregation. Why? Any theoretical explanation of this pattern seems bound to speculation as it does not relate to intuition or any literary, cultural, sociological, or other kind of theory. It seems that only a qualitative reading of this particular novel could inform the observed gender homophily. Possibly, certain thematic or stylistic dimensions of this novel might clarify why it is likely that more same-sex interactions emerge when more characters are staged.

More generally, the regression analyses carried out in this section invoke the image that it is challenging to find a sound, data-driven explanation for the degree of gender, descent, education, and age homophily in literary fiction. This is best exemplified by the lack of significant results for the regression analyses in which it was tested whether or not tokencount, density, triadic closure, and clustering coefficient are predictors of descent, education, and age homophily.

Furthermore, the observed effect of the number of characters on the extent of gender homophily is statistically significant, but is hard to explain from a literary-theoretical point of view. This suggests that features related to the structure of the character networks do not seem to offer sound explanations for the extent of homophily in the corpus.

In order to evaluate the statistical patterns narratologically, the close reading below offers a qualitative assessment of homophily, and subsequently of polyphony, in terms of form and content. In the following section, the extent of age homophily in Mensje van Keulen's *Liefde heeft geen hersens* (2012) is assessed in light of the observed mean age homophily in the corpus as a whole.

4.5.2 Close Reading: Homophily in Mensje van Keulen's *Liefde heeft geen hersens* (2012)

In which ways can love bridge the gap between the young, the old, and the deceased? This question is raised by Van Keulen in *Liefde heeft geen hersens* without giving a final answer. The question can be reframed in Bakhtinian terms as: how can love create a dialogic interaction between, or a polyphony of, characters from different age groups? As it is a central demographic category in the narrative world portrayed by Van Keulen, the primary focus of the current close reading is on age. How does the detected age homophily in the novel relate to its thematization of youth, old age, and death? Are there thematic or stylistic dimension that might explain or inform the extent to which the characters in the novel are segregated, or integrated, by means of their age?

The novel alternates between the first-person narrations of Romy, a (probably) middle-aged employee at a funeral home, and Harro, the forty-three year-old concierge of Romy's apartment block who is secretly obsessed with her. A simple detective-like plot kick-starts the narrative when Romy finds her eighty-year-old neighbor Irma dead at her home. Romy suspects her son Christian, Harro suspects Romy. At the end of the novel, it is still unclear whether Irma was a murder victim or died a natural death. It does not really matter who did it, as the plot line primarily serves to illustrate the interrelations between a variety of characters. Irma's death invokes in Romy a reflection on her problematic relation with her grown-up son Christian and daughter Blanca, as well as on her relationship with her deceased abusive husband, Louis. For Harro, Irma's death fuels his obsession with Romy and makes him reflect on his cohabitation with his old-aged mother.

What does it mean to be either young or old in this narrative world? At first sight, the novel foregrounds stereotypes related to people of a certain age. Neighbor Irma is focalized by Romy as a stereotypical old lady who is physically impaired ('Her eyes and ears, her memory, it seems as if she succumbed to old age' [p. 7]), querulous ('She complains and growls' [ibid.]), and suspicious ('It is annoying that she became suspicious, she already accuses me of theft' [ibid.]). Something similar holds for Harro's mother, who is described in Harro's chapters as a stereotypical old lady who is xenophobic ('They invade our country, they are impolite, they are mostly analphabetic, but they feel superior because of their joyless religion that brainwashes them, because of that they disregard the original inhabitants and harass them' [p. 67]) and longs for death ('She says she is currently always cold, that this is a precursor of death, which she says to welcome' [p. 128]). Conversely, the young Christian and Blanca are portrayed by Romy as immature and in need of parental protection. Romy feels that she must talk her daughter Blanca out of her romantic relation with a man who is twenty years older than she is. Given her son Christian's robbery of Irma when he was young – 'a youthful indiscretion' (p. 8), according to her – she fears that her son Christian is the one who robbed and murdered Irma.

A closer look at the age representation in both Romy's and Harro's first-person narrations shows that such stereotypes do not cover the full extent of what it means to be either young or old in this novel. In light of Greimas and Courtés's concept of the hierarchically ordered, paradigmatic collective (see section 4.3.1), the position of the characters in the age hierarchy keep shifting depending on the perspective taken. On a scale from birth to death, Romy and Harro are probably positioned somewhere in the middle. But Romy is old in the eyes of her son ('This not appropriate for older people' [p. 51]), whereas she sees him as young ('For young people such lines are both an opinion and an invocation' [p. 48]). However, she still views herself as a 'young widow' (p. 71) as she lost her husband at a relatively young age. Conversely, she characterizes herself as old when she utters the wish to go to 'a grand cafe where not only young people come' (p. 8). Furthermore, she is still among the living and is thus further to the left on the birth-death spectrum than the deceased Irma and Louis. Harro is young seen from the perspective of his elder mother but is then relatively old to still live in the same house with her. Being young or old is not a fixed label but a matter of perspective in this narrative world. Subsequently, the position of the characters in the narrative's paradigmatic collective in terms of age is not set in stone but is fluid. In order to understand the ways in which characters from different age groups connect with one another, the statistically detected age homophily of this novel, i.e. the assortativity coefficient for age, can be compared with the mean age assortativity coefficient of the corpus (see Figure 11 in section 4.5.1). Interpreting the novel's age assortativity coefficient with the mean age assortativity coefficient for the corpus as a baseline, it is possible to describe the extent to which this particular case deviates from or conforms to the overall pattern; to determine, in other words, how unique or peculiar the narrative is in this respect. The mean age assortativity coefficient is -0.07, indicating a weak negative age homophily for the corpus as a whole (with 1 indicating same age group relations only, and -1 different age group relations only). On average, relations between characters from same age groups and different age groups occur relatively equally in the corpus, as the mean age assortativity coefficient is close to 0[26]. The age assortativity coefficient for *Liefde heeft geen hersens* is -0.23, indicating that there are more connections between characters with different ages than is the case in the corpus as a whole. Numerically, there is thus more integration and more dialogic interaction between younger and older characters than the overall trend indicates, suggesting that there is a relatively strong polyphony of different age groups.

These statistical findings are compatible with the novel's thematization of bridging the divides between the young, the old, and the deceased. 'Love has no brains': the repeatedly mentioned key sentence, and the title of the novel, illustrates this perfectly. Although quarrels, dissatisfactions, and traumas have resulted in divides between certain characters, the story demonstrates how love has the potential to create a genuine 'connection between consciousnesses' (Bakhtin, 1929/2003a, p. 95). The middle-aged Romy has a hard time reaching out to both younger, older, and deceased characters. Her daughter Blanca left the house to live with an older man in the same apartment block, who Romy despises because of his tattoos and his unhealthy lifestyle, focalized by her as a 'giant of meat and fat, who lets her [Blanca] take care of him, and commands her' (p. 88). Romy cannot seem to get in contact either with Blanca or with her son, Christian, who does not want to talk with her about the deceased Louis, her abusive husband and his abusive father. In response to one of Christian's rants about his father, Romy suggests that his fierce attitude is due to his age: 'If I am I right, you are out of puberty now' (p. 60). 'Age has nothing to do with this', Christian answers, 'there are plenty of old men who still get crazy when they think about their father' (p. 60). But although Romy is not able to connect with her children through her words and actions, a strong, biological urge ties her to them: 'Awful, most awful, is that I cannot see my children anymore when I die' (p. 74).

In a similar vein, Romy's relation with both the older (and then deceased) Irma and the deceased Louis is problematic. As described above, Romy focalizes Irma as querulous and suspicious and tries to cover up her death, which she thinks was caused by Christian. But in covering up her death, she is respectful and loving to Irma's dead body, promising her to take care of her cat (p. 76). The relation between Romy and her deceased husband Louis is even more problematic, as he physically and psychologically abused her for years. Despite this, however, love keeps connecting her with him: 'I did love him' (p. 60).

Harro primarily interacts with his old, aged mother and Romy. Living together with his mother gets on his nerves to such an extent that he fantasizes about killing her: 'The thought gives me visions. Whistling painters in the house, the smell of paint, a terrace in the garden, a benevolent silence, but also music, a smile' (p. 118). The fantasy almost becomes reality at the end of the novel when he pulls her out of her chair and hits her in response to her asking him about his whereabouts. But when he sees her lying on the ground, a feeling of affection washes over him: 'Mother…" I caress her cheek. "Oh, what a soft skin you have' (p. 189).

Love thus indeed bridges divides between characters from different age groups. It bridges the divide between Romy and the younger Christian and Blanca, and between Romy and the older, or deceased, Irma and Louis. It also bridges the divide between Harro and his older mother. However, it does not bridge every divide in the novel. In light of the relatively negative detected age homophily of -0.23, it is remarkable that the only unbridged divide is between Harro and Romy, who are close in age (Harro is forty-three, Romy's age is not made explicit but is probably somewhere between 45–55). As the tie between Romy and Harro is quite homophilous in terms of age, their separation conveniently supports the argument that the novel primarily integrates people with different ages and not people who are of a relatively equal age. The narrative structure with the alternating perspective of Romy and Harro caters to the separation between these two characters. It becomes gradually apparent through Harro's focalization that he is obsessed with Romy. In trying to get close to her, he steals objects belonging to her, such as her glove and a drinking glass she used (p. 111). Conversely, Romy's perspective shows that she does notice Harro positively ('Harro takes off his jacket, it strikes me how muscled he is' [p. 107]), but she does not notice or answer his love interest in her at all. The novel climaxes when Harro secretly observes Romy through a security camera in the elevator and catches her making out with a strange man (p. 179). In his despair, his obsession transforms into a revengeful attitude when he thinks about turning her in for covering up Irma's death: 'An autopsy. If there is nothing to prove, then seeds of doubt at least have been sown' (p. 185).

This qualitative assessment of the divides between characters in Van Keulen's novel can explain this extent of segregation better than the multiple linear regressions conducted on the whole corpus (see section 4.5.1). Statistically, the non-homophilous ties between the younger and older characters result more in an integration than a segregation of different age groups. The middle-aged Romy differs in age from her children, as well as from the older and deceased Irma and Louis. The same holds for the forty-three-year-old Harro, who is differentiated from his mother by means of his age. However, the novel's negative homophily of -0.23 suggests that there are more relations between older and younger characters than the overall trend in the corpus indicates. Thematically, one of the driving forces of this integration is the love motif through which the non-homophilous associations between the above-mentioned characters are bridged. In light of real-world studies arguing that homophily tends to lead to integration rather than segregation, the relation between Romy and Harro serves as a counterexample. As Romy and Harro are close in age, their interaction in the novel's character network subsequently leads to a rather homophilous relation. However, there is a strong thematic divide between them, as Romy does not answer Harro's love interest. The extent to which love plays a role in either the segregation or integration of people with different demographic profiles can hardly be taken into account in real-world studies on homophily. In the narrative world of *Liefde heeft geen hersens*, however, love appears to connect characters who are non-homophilous in terms of their age, while the absence of love poses a divide between characters who are demographically similar.

Parallel to this love motif, a death motif furthers the divide between Romy and Harro. Both Romy and Harro are confronted with death, in the first place through Irma's passing away, but they have a diametrically opposed stance toward it. Romy is confronted daily with death at her work at the graveyard but is extremely avoidant and fearful of it ever since she was little:

> As a child I had to bite in my blanket in order to not scream because of my death agony. I could not endure words such as death, dying, end, and when I read those words today, something in my eyes pushes them away. I turned away from funeral cars, let alone that I dared to look at it. (p. 16)

Her work at the graveyard does not normalize her feelings toward death at all. Quite the contrary: 'I don't know if I can keep working here, I don't want to be smothered by death' (p. 42). Conversely, Harro's ultimate fantasy is to be joined in death with Romy: 'To be lying with her, finally, on that graveyard, not far from that arcade and the luminous grass ...'(p. 188). Furthermore, he more than once fantasizes about killing his mother (p. 118). Death, in other words, has a totally different connotation for Harro than for Romy. Whereas Romy cannot bear or accept the idea of dying, Harro would be glad to die alongside Romy and to send his mother to the afterworld.

How do these thematic cues relate to the observed causes of homophily in the real-world? Geographic space and family structure are two important causes of real-world homophilous associations (see section 4.2.2). For age, the spatial environment of the classroom most obviously fosters homophily, but families are usually non-homophilous in terms of age as both children and parents live together. In *Liefde heeft geen hersens*, geographic space seems to foster the non-homophilous age relation between neighbors Romy and Irma. Quite obviously, living in the same neighborhood is not a guarantee of having contacts with people from the same age, as both older and younger people can live in an apartment block. Family structure is a cause of the non-homophilous age relation between Romy and her children, as well as between Harro and his mother: families usually consist of both older and younger people. The love motif ties in nicely with this: it can be argued that geographic space and family structure are a perfect breeding ground for the love that bridges the initial divides between Romy and her children, Romy and Irma, as well as between Harro and his mother.

Whereas geographic space seems to fuel the non-homophilous age associations between Romy and her children, and between Romy and Irma, it simultaneously creates a fertile environment for the homophilous age relation between Harro and Romy. As Harro is the concierge of Romy's apartment block, they meet frequently. But geographic space falls short of explaining the thematic divide between Romy and Harro. Their narrative perspectives do not converge smoothly just because they see each other on a regular basis in the apartment block. This divergence can very clearly be traced back to the absence of mutual love. More subtly, their conflicting stances toward death – Romy avoids its, Harro is open to it – reinforces their divergence of souls. Putting this love motif and death motif in dialogue with the found statistical pattern of age homophily shows that the thematic dimension of the novel is an important force behind the extent of segregation or integration. Statistically, the age assortativity coefficient of -0.23 suggest a relatively high polyphony of characters from different age groups in this novel. But this is only partly backed up by the present narratological analysis of the novel. The thematic structure is obviously not taken into account in the data-driven, statistical analysis of age homophily in the novel, but it does provide a sound explanation of why certain characters are segregated or integrated by means of their age. The love motif fuels a dialogic interaction between Romy and her children, Romy and Irma, as well as between Harro and his mother. However, the same love motif, in parallel with the death motif, sets the divergence between Romy and Harro in motion.

4.6 CONCLUSION TO THIS CHAPTER

In this chapter, an attempt was made to gain a closer insight into the ways in which community co-shapes the representation of social groups in present-day Dutch literary fiction. Building on classical social theory by Tönnies, Durkheim, and Simmel on what it means for people to be united in a community, it explored both network theoretical and narratological concepts and techniques to study community in narrative fiction. For the analysis of the literary representation of social groups, community proved to be particularly useful for assessing how integrated or segregated these groups are. Building on Bakhtin's concept of polyphony, two models were presented through which the extent of integration or segregation in the corpus could be analyzed statistically, and close readings of two novels followed to evaluate the meaning of the statistical patterns. Based on the output of these models and their narratological evaluations, at least two conclusions can be drawn as to how community co-shapes the literary representation of social groups in contemporary Dutch literature.

First, segregation by descent and age was found through use of the first model. Based on a community detection algorithm, the model divided each of the 170 novels in the corpus in two distinct groups and computed the gender, descent, education, and age distribution for each of these groups. Running a range of statistical tests revealed that these communities are not segregated by gender or education, but rather by descent and age: characters with the same descent (either migrant or nonmigrant) and from the same age group (either between age 0–45 or from age 46 and upward) tend to flock together. These patterns of segregation suggest that characters from different descent and age groups tend to be represented in oppositional terms. Statistically speaking, a line can be drawn between migrant and nonmigrant characters and between older and younger characters. Based on these results, it can be argued that these groups of characters are depicted as distinct, separate entities in present-day Dutch literary fiction.

A close reading of communities in Philip Huff's *Niemand in de stad* was conducted to assess the meaning of these results at the level of the individual text. As this novel presents a strong opposition between an insiders' community of fraternity members and an outsiders' community, this case study was selected to assess which patterns of segregation the model detected in a novel thematizing divides between groups. Because of its absence of lower educated and migrant characters, no segregation by education or descent takes place between the characters populating the novel. Conforming to the overall pattern for the entire corpus, the novel's communities are segregated by age, but contrary to this overall pattern, these communities are most notably segregated by gender. Although an opposition between male and female characters is highlighted by the thematic structure, the novel seems to self-consciously reflect on its staged oppositions through literary stylistic mechanisms such as metaphors, symbols, and metacommentary.

Secondly, an alternative take on community was presented in the second model, which computed for every two characters how similar they are in terms of gender, descent, age, and education. This so-called homophily, or assortativity, score can be seen as an indication of segregation on the level of any two individual characters. Based on a range of statistical tests, it was argued that segregation by descent, education, and age is apparent in the (non-)homophilous associations between characters. These segregation patterns are partly in line with the first model's finding that descent and age cause divides between characters, but this second model suggests that divides are also caused by education. Gender is in neither of the two models put forward as cause for divides. According to the second model, characters with different educational levels are also represented as distinct, separate entities, just as characters from different descent and age groups (as the first model also suggested). This finding, indeed, only holds true in a statistical sense, and it remains open as to what the meaning of this overall trend is in the context of an individual novel. A qualitative, narratological assessment of segregation by age in Mensje van Keulen's *Liefde heeft geen hersens* demonstrated how a particular narrative relates to such a statistical pattern. As one of the novel's main themes is age and everything associated with it, it proved to be a useful case study to analyze against the general backdrop of the statistical trends in the corpus as a whole. In general, Van Keulen's novel is an outlier: while on average segregation by age in the corpus is high, it is relatively low in this novel. At first glance, the novel indeed thematizes integration between people from different age groups. A closer look at the love motif in the novel shows that while divides between the young and the old are bridged for specific characters, a divide is installed between two characters from the same age group. This close reading highlights the importance of love in bridging or posing divides between characters from different social groups.

Emphasizing the interrelations between the macro and the micro levels of literary representation, this chapter has shown how the notion of community plays a part in the depiction of social groups in present-day Dutch literary fiction. Confronting statistical trends for the corpus as a whole with close readings of individual novels, it demonstrated how segregation of communities affects the representation of social groups. Most notably, the extent to which groups are segregated by a certain demographic category reflects the extent to which such groups are presented as either distinct or connected.

CHAPTER 5

CONFLICT

5.1 INTRODUCTION: NARRATIVE CLASHES

How do conflicts between characters co-shape the representation of the social group(s) in which they function? In this chapter, the representation of social groups will be studied through the concept of conflict. Just as with the concepts of centrality and community in the previous chapters, conflict is used as an umbrella term. Here, it denotes a variety of negatively loaded relational notions such as 'dislike', 'disrespect', 'avoidance', 'hate', 'hostility', 'confrontation', 'violence', and 'strife'.

Conflict as a narrative mechanism has been studied by formalists such as Vladimir Propp in the 1920s and Algirdas Julien Greimas in the 1960s, both of whom devised models of narrative action in which conflict has a vital function (Propp, *Morphology of the Folktale*, and Greimas, *Sémantique structurale*). Although these classic narratological models have made the idea that conflict is a driving force behind narrative action common knowledge, a specific in-depth conceptualization and a practical, replicable operationalization of conflict in narrative fiction has not been on the forefront of contemporary literary scholarship. The two models of conflict proposed in this chapter fill this gap while building on Propp and Greimas. In order to do so, a range of typologies, concepts, terms, and tools are conjoined from a variety of research traditions such as narratology, network theory, conflict studies, social psychology, and theater studies. By close reading three novels from the corpus in light of the output of these models, this chapter aims to gain insight into how conflict situations co-shape the representation of characters belonging to a certain social group.

What is conflict? This chapter turns to the field of peace and conflict studies to pinpoint some central assets of the concept. For a first working definition, it draws upon the work by Johan Galtung, founding father of the field, who defines conflict in strong association with violence:

> Whenever there is violence there is an unresolved conflict. Unresolved conflict means that there is an incompatibility of goals, including means, that has not been resolved, superseded, transformed, or transcended. That conflict can be direct, between actors who have conscious goals, or structural, between parties that have their interests. In other words, if you don't like violence solve the conflict. (Galtung, 2010)

According to this definition, violence is a meaningful marker of conflict. Conflict is not a sufficient but a necessary condition for violent practices: there can be conflict without violence, but there cannot be violence without conflict. It makes sense, therefore, to integrate the notion of violence into this chapter's conceptualization of narrative conflict. Furthermore, this association with violence highlights the hierarchical nature of conflict. From an ideological point of view, conflicts between characters generally indicate representational hierarchies through which a form of physical, verbal, or ideological violence is expressed. Such hierarchies between (groups of) characters, then, determine the dynamics and outcome of conflicts: arguably, there is a tendency for more powerful actors or parties to be the dominant party in the conflicts. Often, this is exemplified by a dominance of one representational category over another – e.g., male over female, Western over 'exotic', higher over lower class. Following Galtung's definition, narrative conflict will be used in this chapter in both a direct sense and a structural sense. In the direct sense, it refers to explicit, conscious conflicts between (groups of) characters. In the structural sense, it refers to implicit, sub- or unconscious conflicts between interests, principles, ideologies incorporated or expressed by (groups of) characters, via inner conflicts, or through artistic literary devices such as metaphors and symbolism.

A second characteristic of conflict is its fundamental relational mechanism, as it is always manifested between an X and a Y – it takes (at least) two to conflict. In the field of social psychology, a distinction is made between interpersonal and intergroup conflict (Tajfel & Turner, 1979, p. 33).[1] For *interpersonal* conflicts, theories have primarily focused on the nature of e.g. frustration or aggression (ibid.). The realistic group conflict theory (R.C.T.) is a seminal theory of *intergroup* conflict (originally formulated in Campbell, 1965). The theory puts forward the idea that

> opposed group interests in obtaining scarce resources promote competition, and positively interdependent (superordinate) goals facilitate cooperation. Conflicting interests develop through competition into overt social conflict. It appears, too, that intergroup competition enhances intragroup morale, cohesiveness, and cooperation [...] Thus, the real conflict of group interests not only create antagonistic intergroup relations but also heightens identification with, and positive attachment to, the in-group. (Tajfel & Turner, 1979, p. 33)

The 'scarce resources' can be anything from material sources such as food and money, to immaterial sources such as prestige and respectability. In works of narrative fiction, a competition for scarce resources can be represented explicitly through, for example, the opposing armies in *Game of Thrones* trying to reign over a geographical area, or implicitly through, for example, the different ethnic groups in Özcan Akyol's *Eus* (2012) struggling for respect in their social environment.

A remarkable feature of this theory is that people in intergroup conflict will behave as a function of their group as it 'heightens identification with, and positive attachment to, the in-group'. A sense of *intra*group cohesion can arise when social groups are in conflict with each other. The protagonist in Philip Huff's *Niemand in de stad* (2012), for instance, belongs to a group of student fraternity members that are clearly in opposition to members of society outside of their fraternity, which results in a positive attachment and identification with the student in-group. If this holds true for narrative fiction, then characters can be expected to act according to their social identity as they 'will not interact as individuals, on the basis of their individual characteristics or interpersonal relationships, but as members of their groups standing in certain defined relationships to members of other groups' (Tajfel & Turner, 1979, p. 35, italics in original quote).

Conflict thus has the potential to co-shape social identity. If we accept the premise that fictional worlds are modeled after real-world social and psychological patterns, it is reasonable to expect that narrative conflict also functions as a way to shape the identity of characters and the groups they function in. Hypothesizing that conflict has a similar function in narrative fiction, this chapter examines the ways in which conflicts are co-constitutive of the literary representation of social groups. To ensure that the models presented here are applicable (and generalizable) to a broad range of narrative fiction, basic narratological insights are integrated with the formal tools of social network theory. Whereas narratology offers a conceptual framework, social network analysis provides some practical instruments to formalize and analyze conflicts between characters on a larger scale. Before presenting the models, then, this chapter describes how conflict has been studied in both the fields of narratology and network theory. Insights from both of these fields are used in the construction of the models. The first model focuses on conflict between two characters, the second model on conflict between three characters. Each of these models is subsequently described in detail and applied to the corpus of 170 novels as a whole. For both these models, close readings from individual novels from the corpus are used to exemplify their relevance.

5.2 CONFLICT IN NETWORK THEORY

In network theory, conflicts in networks are studied from a variety of different angles. Most obviously, conflicts are expressed through negative edges between nodes in a network. As in every network, relations between characters in a novel can have either positive or negative implications. Positively connotated edges are represented by, for instance, friendship relations, whereas negatively connotated edges are represented by (for example) enemy relations. In general, each edge exists on a negative-positive spectrum; the positivity/negativity of the edge is always relative to the overall social dynamics in the network. Furthermore, it should be noted that the nature of relations can change over time, as friends can become enemies and vice versa.

Although negative ties are not taken into account in most network analyses, some studies address the issue (e.g., Bohn, Buchta, Hornik, & Mair, 2014; Box-Steffensmeier & Christenson, 2014; de Jong, Curşeu, & Leenders, 2014; Smith, McPherson, & Lovin, 2014; van de Camp & van den Bosch, 2012). Researchers have recently proposed ways to reframe network analytic techniques and concepts for the analysis of negative ties as a response to the fact that positive and negative ties are usually treated in the same way by researchers in the field (Everett & Borgatti, 2014; Kaur & Singh, 2015). Networks consisting of negative relations are typically sparse, highly disconnected, and have no clustering, all of which tends to make the analysis of centrality harder if not impossible. For some centrality measures, negative ties pose no problems. The application of degree centrality to negative ties, for instance, 'require[s] few alterations in interpretation but [is] applicable in both ties' (Kaur & Singh, 2015, p. 41). But basing the computation of betweenness and closeness centrality on negative ties is problematic as these measures 'rely on network flows and thus cannot be applied on negative ties where flow among nodes of a network is minimum' (ibid.). The analysis of negative bonds in a network thus requires some customization of existing techniques. Everett and Borgatti (2014) provide such a customization. They formulate h^*, a negative centrality measure 'in which a node gets a high centrality score if they have few negative ties to central others' (Everett & Borgatt, 2014, p. 119). In this conception, characters who have fewer enemies would be considered more central, whereas characters with more enemies would have lower centrality values.

A network in which both positive and negative edges are ascribed to social relations is called a signed network (Doreian, 2011). Unsigned networks pay no attention to features of signed relations such as like/dislike, respect/disrespect, and love/hate. Signed networks are often associated with (structural or social) balance theory, of which social psychologist Fritz Heider laid the foundation in the 1940s. In a seminal essay he sets out the basis of the theory:

> Attitudes towards persons and causal unit formations influence each other. An attitude towards an event can alter the attitude towards the person who caused the event, and, if the attitudes towards a person and an event are similar, the event is easily ascribed to the person. A balanced configuration exists if the attitudes towards the parts of a causal unit are similar. (Heider, 1946, p. 107)

This densely formulated theory is best explained by the common expression 'The enemy of my enemy is my friend'. In Figure 1, the rationale behind this maxim is visualized in what became known as Heider's model of social balance. Imagine that a person P is in a hostile relation with a person O. There is a state of social balance, as both have the same negative attitude toward each other. Then, a third person X enters the scene, who also happens to dislike O. In order to maintain social balance, P and X should become friends, based on the fact that they share a negative attitude toward O. Heider's theory asserts that there is social *balance* whenever a triadic relationship consists of either two negative relationships and one positive relationship as in this case, or when all relations between P, O, and X are positive.

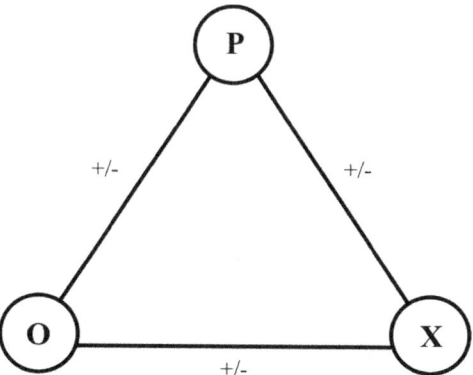

Figure 1. Heider's model of social balance. Adopted from Khanafiah and Situngkir (2004, p. 2).

Conversely, a state of social *imbalance* arises when P likes O and X but finds out that O and X dislike each other. There is social imbalance as there are now two positive relations and one negative relation in this triad. This imbalance is resolved if P either starts to dislike X just as O does, or when X and O become friends. Social imbalance occurs when there are two positive relations and one negative relation in a triad, or when all relations are negative.

Following Heider, balance theory has served as an inspiration for research on signed networks. It has been formalized and further refined in the 1950s and 1960s (Cartwright & Harary, 1956; Davis, 1967). However, although balance theory sparks one's imagination and has proved to be a fruitful point of departure for formal network methodologies, it does not necessarily hold empirically. The simple premise that signed networks strive toward balanced structures is simply not always true, as there are numerous signed networks containing imbalanced triads in the real world (Doreian, 2011). For the present study, it remains to be seen to what extent the balance theory applies to the fictional worlds of characters in novels, which are studied in section 5.5 of this chapter. To consider narrative conflict in terms of social balance enables this study to go beyond the classic protagonist-antagonist or hero-villain duality. While the first model presented in this chapter works with this duality (see section 5.4), the second model transitions to a triadic conception of narrative conflict by testing Heider's balance theory (see section 5.5).

5.3 CONFLICT IN NARRATOLOGY

For a theoretical understanding of conflict in narrative texts, a starting point is provided by a variety of interrelated lemmas in the seminal analytic dictionary of semiotics by Greimas and Courtés. As in most handbooks and encyclopedias of literary analysis, the lemma 'Conflict' is nonexistent, but the lemmas 'Confrontation', 'Polemical', and 'Constraint' cover elements that are directly related to it.

What stands out in the description of these lemmata are multiple references to the 'subject' and its relation to the 'anti-subject'. Confrontation is said to occur 'when the goal of the narrative program [of the subject] is contrary to the goal of the narrative program of the anti-subject' (Greimas & Courtés, 1979, p. 70). This clash of two narrative programs can result in three situations: 1) a domination of the subject or anti-subject over the other, 2) an exchange between the subject and the anti-subject, or 3) a (mutual) contract between the subject and the anti-subject. In case the clash is of a polemical nature, the narrative typically contains 'the figure of the [...] opponent as a metonymic manifestation of the anti-subject' (p. 324). Characters who oppose one another can be a manifestation of subject and anti-subject in a direct sense, but the subject/anti-subject opposition is broader as two clashing narrative programs in a novel might also take shape in the form of two opposing political ideologies, e.g., the confrontation in Orwell's *1984* between the ruling totalitarian regime and the more liberal conviction of its protagonist. Furthermore, clashing narrative programs can also occur within a single character. In the slipstream of experiments by modernist writers, inner conflicts have arguably become one of the characteristic features of modern literature (Katz, 1995).

But most obviously, the subject and the anti-subject are performed by two or more characters who are engaged in a hostile relation. It is important to stress that such a relation is hierarchical in case the conflict is resolved by a domination of the subject over the anti-subject, as the anti-subject is then subjugated to the narrative program of the subject. This can be characterized as a situation of semiotic constraint, which is defined as 'a range of voluntary or involuntary, conscious or unconscious, obligations which the individual takes up through its involvement in a semiotic practice' (Greimas & Courtés, 1979, p. 200). It is comparable to the subject or the anti-subject accepting certain 'rules of play' (ibid.). In a concrete sense, this can be thought of as a character – either willingly or unwillingly – accepting the norms and values of another character.

In Orwell's *1984*, this is illustrated by Winston Smith's inescapable submission to Big Brother's totalitarian ideology: the protagonist has no choice but accepting his rules of play. Constraint, in all its manifestations, indicates a hierarchical opposition expressed through conflict.

For more practical applications of the concept of conflict, theater studies offer some points of departure. In his *Dictionnaire du théâtre* (2004), leading theater scholar Patrice Pavis stresses that conflicts between characters expressed on stage have often social, political, or philosophical causes:

> Tout conflit dramatique repose, selon une théorie marxiste ou même simplement sociologique, sur une contradiction entre deux groupes, deux classes ou deux idéologies qui se trouvent être, à un moment historique donné, en conflit. En dernière analyse, le conflit ne dépend pas de la seule volonté du dramaturge, mais de conditions objectives de la réalité sociale dépeinte. (Pavis, 2004, p. 66)

Conflicts are not exclusively motivated by personal issues between characters but can often be traced back to the 'conditions objectives de la réalité sociale dépeinte'. The depicted social reality has certain possibilities and constraints that the character on stage must obey. For instance, a female character in a play that is set in an era where women's rights were marginal has a priori more disadvantages than male characters. As such, the nature of a possible confrontation between her and patriarchy is already predefined by the 'conditions objectives' of that particular sociohistorical reality. Pavis provides a typology of five different forms of conflict (2004, p. 66):

1. Rivalry between two characters because of money, love, morality, politics, etc.
2. Two conflicting worldviews or irreconcilable moral conceptions.
3. (Inner) conflict between e.g. passion and reason.
4. Conflict between the particular and the general, e.g., between the individual and society.
5. A moral or metaphysical conflict between a character and a principle such as God or an ideal.

This typology ranges from the most concrete, direct type of conflict (type 1) to the most abstract type (type 5). Each type defines two elements that are in conflict: two characters (type 1), two world-views (type 2), two conflicting feelings of thoughts (type 3), the particular and the general (type 4), and a character and a principle (type 5). In the statistical analyses and close readings of the novels that will follow, this typology will be used to specify the type of conflict at stake. As there is a wide variety of different types of conflict, it will prove useful in the analyses to make explicit what type of conflict we are talking about. This is not only relevant for clarification but also helps keep track of the shifts between types of conflict that can take place within a narrative, such as an inner conflict of a single character leading to a rivalry between two characters.

As mentioned in the introduction to this chapter, conflict has an important function in two closely related classic narratological models, first described in the 1920s by Vladimir Propp in *Morphology of the Folktale* (1928/1968) and further developed in the 1960s by A. J. Greimas in *Sémantique structurale* (1966). Propp was the first to analyze narrative structures using a 'morphological' method referring to the analysis of all constituent elements that comprise a narrative. His method is based on the assumption that 'it is possible to make an examination of the forms of the tale which will be as exact as the morphology of organic formations' (Propp, 1928/1968, Foreword). Although his model is based on a distinct collection of 100 Russian fairytales and therefore is not necessarily generalizable to fictional narratives in general, Propp's conviction that 'the labyrinth of the tale's multiformity' can be reduced to 'an amazing uniformity' (ibid.) still seems rather universalistic.

On the basis of four axioms, he defines 31 narrative units he calls 'Functions' that range from 'Absentation' (the hero is introduced as he leaves the safe environment of his community) to 'Wedding' (the hero is rewarded for his conquest and marries the princess). According to Propp, the number of these functions are limited to 31, they follow an identical sequence, and all fairy tales conform to the proposed structure. This model is remarkably similar to a narrative template used in comparative mythology: that of the Hero's journey, also known as the Monomyth (Campbell, 1949). Furthermore, these functions are believed to revolve around seven general character types, which he calls 'dramatis personae': the villain, the donor/provider, the helper, the princess (and her father), the dispatcher, the hero, and the false hero (pp. 79–80). Although Propp contends that the distribution of these character types can shift between characters, he has a structuralist conviction that all characters must fall in one of these seven categories.

From a contemporary point of view, such a formalistic, universalistic approach seems outdated and of little use for analyzing the diversity and complexity of present-day (Dutch) novels. Propp's model is clearly modeled after the action that takes place on the level of plot. This works probably better for fairy tales than for novels, as the first are generally more plot-oriented, whereas style is typically a more central asset of the latter. However, Propp's first axiom – 'Functions of characters serve as stable, constant elements in a tale, independent of how and by whom they are fulfilled' (pp. 21–23) – is relevant for the conceptualization of conflict in novels. The building blocks of novels are typically characters who perform certain functions, although these characters are obviously not always 'stable, constant elements'. More precisely, conflict situations often take the form of a function in which the villain and the hero are confronted with one another.

Propp's concept of the seven dramatis personae served as an inspiration for Greimas, who turned it into a more general abstraction commonly known as the actantial model (Greimas, 1966; see Figure 2). Just as in Propp's morphology, this model focuses primarily on action taking place at the level of plot. It can be used to reduce every narrative action to a set of six components: the subject, the object, the helper, the opponent, the sender, and the receiver. Each of these actants revolve around three axes. The subject and object are located at the axis of desire; e.g., in Goethe's *Die Leiden des jungen Werthers* (1774), Werther (subject) wants Lotte (object). This relationship between subject and object is called a junction and can take the form of a conjunction when the subject and object are brought together, and the form of a disjunction when the subject is being freed of the object. The axis of power is where the helper and the opponent are centered; e.g., Lotte's sisters (helpers) help Werther (subject) come closer to Lotte (object), but Lotte's fiancé Albert (opponent) obstructs Werther (subject) in his wish to possess Lotte (object). At the axis of knowledge, also known as the axis of transmission, resides the sender who asks for the junction between subject and object, and the receiver who profits from this junction. E.g., Werther (subject/sender/receiver) requests that he might one day marry Lotte (object), in which case he would be the one benefiting (receiver) from this request (sender).

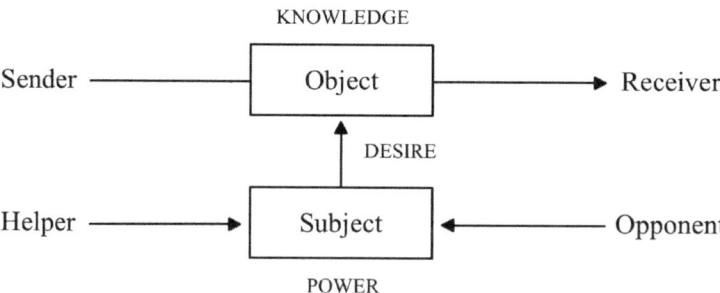

Figure 2. Greimas's actantial model. Adapted from Greimas (1966).

Point of view is a crucial aspect in establishing an actantial model for narrative actions. Greimas underscores that there is no final, definite model, but that a range of different models can be devised for the same sequence of actions as different points of view are taken into account (Greimas, 1966, pp. 172–191). The above-used example from *Die Leiden des jungen Werthers* is modeled on the perspective of protagonist Werther, whose subject-role predetermines the establishment of all other roles in the model. From the perspective of Lotte, the model looks completely different, as she has other desires than Werther and other characters contributing to and obstructing the fulfilment of those desires. Besides, multiple roles can be played by the same character, as Werther can be simultaneously subject, sender, and receiver.

The axis of power is of particular relevance for this chapter, as conflicts center around this axis. For that reason, it will be reframed here as the axis of conflict, although the original name also makes sense as conflicts typically denote hierarchical power relations in which a form of semiotic constraint is present. The roles of helper and opponent roles are reframed here as friends and enemies of the subject. More generally, the helpers and opponents might be conceived as being each other's enemies, as they have conflicting goals, i.e., either helping or opposing the subject. An inner conflict can arise when a character is either subject and opponent at the same time (e.g., a drug addict (subject/opponent) wishing to be clean (object) but who keeps taking drugs), or helper and opponent at the same time (e.g., the character who is a sobriety coach and a drug dealer at the same time). Finally, it is noteworthy that actants do not necessarily have to be characters, as values, principles, belief systems, and ideologies can also take up the role of an actant. As a general scheme, the actantial model will serve in the close readings as a structural point of departure in framing the type and mode of conflict relations at stake.

5.4 MODEL I: HIERARCHIES IN ONE-ON-ONE CONFLICTS

On the axis of conflict, hierarchies between characters take shape. According to Galtung's thesis, violence is the result of unresolved conflict (see the first section of this chapter), and violent practices commonly lead to a domination of one of the involved parties over the other. The model presented in this section operationalizes hierarchies between characters by establishing for every pair of conflicting characters who the more powerful party in the conflict is. Then, it will be tested whether one of three identity categories – gender, descent, level of education – is a predictor of a character's dominance or subordination in the conflict. Are, for instance, Dutch or male characters more dominant in conflict situations than non-Dutch or female characters? In order to make sense of the resulting statistical pattern, the numbers will be confronted with a close reading of a case that is selected for the reason that it simultaneously conforms to and deviates from that pattern. The type of conflict under consideration in this section is exclusively focused on two characters and thus relates to the first type offered by Pavis's typology (see section 5.3): rivalry between two characters because of money, love, morality, politics, etc.

5.4.1 Conflict Scores

A first challenge is to define under which specific conditions characters are in conflict. As these conditions may vary endlessly in nature and intensity, it was decided to not settle this in a data-driven way, but rather to use the top-down relational labels assigned to characters by annotators, which are stored in database EDGES.[2] From the five relational labels – friend, enemy, lover, family, colleague – enemy is the only label that explicitly points at a hostile relation between characters. Sometimes friends, lovers, family, and colleagues are in conflict with one another; in those cases, double labels were assigned, such as colleague_enemy. Double labels were also assigned when the nature of the relation changed over time, such as friends becoming enemies. The labels friend and enemy are the only mutually exclusive labels. Two characters can be enemies and colleague, lovers, or family, but they cannot be enemies and friends at the same time. In case a double label friend_enemy or enemy_friend was assigned, the order of the labels reflects the change in those relations, e.g., the relational label 'friend_enemy' denotes that the relation was initially friendly but later became hostile.

How to establish which party is the most powerful one in the conflict? In order to tackle this problem, the results of the character rankings model presented in the third chapter are taken into consideration. In that chapter, all 2,137 characters in the corpus were ranked on the basis of five centrality metrics, each of them indicating a specific form of centrality. As explained in detail in that chapter, a character's position in the rankings is a sign of its importance in the narrative and possibly of the power it exerts over other characters. In this line of thinking, the higher-ranked character in a conflict can be perceived as the dominant party in that conflict. Framed in terms of the actantial model, characters with higher centrality scores than their enemies arguably have better chances of fulfilling their goals than their enemies.

In order to gain insight into the social dynamics between characters who are in conflict, this section introduces the 'conflict score'. This score is based on the idea that, in situations where characters show hostility or antagonism toward one another, their respective network centralities is a proxy of their dominance in the conflict. While simply counting the number of enemies of a character indicates the extent to which a character is involved in antagonistic relations, the conflict score of a character is an indication of the power a character exerts over their enemies.

Thus, for every two characters annotated as enemies, it was automatically established who of them has a higher degree, betweenness, closeness, eigen vector, and Katz centrality.[3] The resulting 'conflict score' of a character is increased by one in case that character has a higher score on one of these centrality measures. Some characters have more conflicts than others (i.e., have more enemies), and the likelihood of a higher conflict score therefore potentially increases for characters with multiple enemies. An example: in the novel *Heldhaftig* by Britta Bolt, there are nine characters who show enmity to other characters, but not every character has the same number of enemies. The character named Najib has six enemies, whereas the character named Posthumus has only two enemies. This means that Najib's conflict score for each of the centrality measures can be 6 at a maximum, as there are potentially 6 points which he can 'earn'. Conversely, Posthumus's maximum conflict score for each centrality measure is only 2. Table 1 shows the computed conflict scores for both Najib and Posthumus.[4]

	Conflict score degree	Conflict score betweenness	Conflict score closeness	Conflict score eigenvector	Conflict score katz	Composite conflict score (mean)
Najib	5	6	4	5	5	5.0
Posthumus	2	1	1	2	2	1.6

Table 1. Example of computation of conflict scores for characters Najib and Posthumus from the novel Heldhaftig *by Britta Bolt.*

Najib's conflict score for betweenness centrality is 6, which means that he was ranked higher than all his six enemies for this particular centrality measure. For closeness centrality, Najib's conflict score is 4, which means that two of his enemies were higher ranked than him for this measure. Finally, the means of all five conflict scores are brought together in a composite conflict score, which is an average indication of the power characters exert over other characters in conflict situations. Based on this composite score, Najib (score: 5.0) is more central than Posthumus (score: 1.6) in terms of conflict.

5.4.2 Results of Multiple Linear Regression

Are gender, descent, and/or education predictors of characters' conflict scores? It would be interesting to see if characters with a certain demographic profile have higher conflict scores than other types of characters, as that would indicate a dominance of, e.g., the male over the female, the Dutch over the non-Dutch, or the higher educated over the lower educated in conflict situations. As there is no previous research on this topic, there are no strong reasons to formulate hypotheses about which identity categories will likely have an effect on a character's position in conflict situations. Nevertheless, cultural theory provides a vantage point for an informal hypothesis.

Similar to the hypothesis tested in chapter 3, it is hypothesized that male, Dutch, and higher educated characters have better chances to end up high in the scores, as ideological approaches to (Dutch) literature have repeatedly suggested that these have favorable positions in representational hierarchies (e.g., Meijer, 1996a, 1996b, 2011; Meijer & van Alphen, 1991; Minnaard, 2010; Pattynama, 1994, 1998). This informal, cultural-critical hypothesis fits in a general scheme of binary oppositions of which the first known example in Western culture is the Pythagorean Table of Opposites referenced in Aristotle's *Metaphysics* A. The table contains ten opposites, among which male-female, of which Aristotle morally prefers the left part over the right, such as male over female. The current hypothesis builds on the common knowledge that Western culture implicitly prioritizes one side of those binary oppositions (Kristeva, 1969, pp. 65, 183; Cassin, 1994, pp. 151–276).

A multiple linear regression was conducted to predict characters' composite conflict scores based on their gender, descent, and education. Gender is coded as 0 for male and 1 for female. Descent is coded as 0 for nonmigrant and 1 for migrant. Education is coded as 0 for higher educated and 1 for lower educated. With the composite conflict score as a dependent variable, this resulted in a regression model in which only education featured as an effective independent variable. Gender and descent were excluded as independent variables by the model as they do not produce significant effects. A significant regression equation was found ($F(1, 363) = 7.362, p < 0.01$), with an R^2 of 0.020. Characters' predicted conflict score is equal to a B value of 0.933 + 0.405 (Education) (see Table 2). This means that lower educated characters scored 0.405 higher than higher educated characters on their composite conflict scores. Education is thus a predictor of characters' conflict scores. Characters who are lower educated have significantly higher conflict scores than characters who are higher educated.

Model		Unstandardized coefficient		Standardised coefficient		
		B	Std. Error	Beta	t	Sig.
1	(Constant)	0.933	0.083		11.246	0.000
	Education	0.405	0.149	0.141	2.713	0.007

Table 2. Linear model with the composite conflict score as dependent variable. Gender, descent, and education were entered as independent variables. Only education generated statistically significant effects.

What is the relevance of this observed pattern in terms of the representation of social groups? If education is considered as a proxy for socioeconomic class (without suggesting that education and class always coincide), then a possible, Marxist-oriented interpretation is that conflict situations are a place where characters from lower classes effectively rebel against their fixed socioeconomic position. In the fictional worlds in which they are depicted, lower class characters have less socioeconomic status, but more central roles are ascribed to them in situations where they are in conflict with characters who are higher up the socioeconomic ladder. In this line of thinking, the dominance of the lower classes over the higher classes can be framed as a protest of the underdog.

An alternative interpretation of the statistical pattern, and one that is diametrically opposed to the former, is that lower educated characters have limited social and intellectual skills, increasing the likelihood of them using violence quicker than higher educated characters. This is line with research suggesting that people who are more educated tend to be less involved in violent and/or criminal activities (Lochner & Moretti, 2004; Barrera & Ibánez, 2004). The inclination of lower educated characters toward violence could subsequently lead to a more dominant, and thus central, position in the network. In this interpretation, the lower educated characters conform to a rather stereotypical image of the lower social classes. As opposed to the former interpretation, these characters do not resist their fixed socioeconomic position but rather reinforce the rigidity of that position.

It is particularly at the level of the individual text that one of these interpretations might demonstrate their relevance. In order to illustrate the narratological value of these statistical results and their interpretations, I briefly demonstrate below how dyadic conflict between characters from different social classes in one novel from the corpus can be read in light of this section's findings.

5.4.3 Close Reading: Class Conflicts between Two Characters in Bart Koubaa's *De Brooklynclub* (2012)

The cult novel *Fight Club* (1996) by American author Chuck Palahniuk clearly served as an inspiration for Bart Koubaa's *De Brooklynclub* (2012). Similar to Palahniuk's novel, Koubaa's story centers around a secret club where people from all layers of society get together to fight. Co-founder of this so called Brooklynclub is the novel's nameless first-person narrator (hereafter: the protagonist), who is locked up in prison and unfolds the story of the events that led to his imprisonment. Next to the protagonist, the most prominent characters are his (former) girlfriend Lauretta and real-estate giant Mayer. A central event in the story is when Mayer rapes Lauretta in front of all the people present at the Brooklynclub at that moment, after which Lauretta then paradoxically leaves the protagonist to marry Mayer.

Violent conflict is the central tenet of the novel and is symbolized through the metaphor of the fight club. More specifically, the novel centers around a conflict between the protagonist and Mayer, which can be seen as a metonymic expression of a clash between the higher and lower socioeconomic classes. Being employed in environments such as an abattoir, a restaurant, a bar, and as an elevator operator, respectively, the protagonist is undoubtedly part of the lower socioeconomic classes of society. As a successful businessman who is one of the most powerful persons in the world of real estate (the young Donald Trump comes to mind), Mayer is undoubtedly upper class. Furthermore, 'Mayer' is a speaking name: alluding to the word 'mayor', it emphasizes his influential societal status.

How does social class tie in to the (violent and hostile) relation between the protagonist, Mayer, and Lauretta? This is most clearly understood by singling out the axes of conflict of three different actantial models, each of which has one of these three characters as a subject.

— Axis of conflict 1: The protagonist (*subject*) wants to build Lauretta's dream house (*object*), but first has to destroy Mayer (*opponent*). He receives help from his friend Paaluk (*helper*). The plot of the novel build toward the kidnapping of Mayer by Paaluk, a friend of the protagonist. The protagonist prepares for what he calls his 'masterpiece: destroying Mayer *and* taking the ransom, with which [he] will build a West coast house for Lauretta' (Koubaa, 2012, p. 57).[5] By striving for that goal, the protagonist hopes to achieve 'rehabilitation' (p. 64) for the moral degradation that he suffered because of Mayer's raping of his girlfriend. He wants to 'purify Lauretta's name' by not 'only humiliating Mayer, but to affect him deeply in his soul' (ibid.).

— Axis of conflict 2: Mayer (*subject*) wants total financial and societal power (*object*). It is not made explicit who his helpers and opponents are, but it is clear that the protagonist (*opponent*) forms an obstacle to this goal as Mayer is murdered by him. The monofocal perspective of the novel does not allow for a genuine counterperspective from Mayer's side of the story. Based on the information that the protagonist provides us, Mayer comes across as a power-hungry, immoral animal, which makes his character rather flat.

— Axis of conflict 3: Lauretta (*subject*) wants to have her dream house on the American West coast (*object*). Again, it is not made explicit by whom she is helped or opposed, but it is clear that the protagonist (*helper*) helps her to realize her wish. Because of his raping her, Mayer (*opponent*) can be conceived as someone who counteracts her.

Throughout the novel the protagonist repeatedly talks about Lauretta's wish for her dream house:

> Lauretta had a dream: she wanted a house at the West coast. She closed her eyes when she described it while she laid down her head on my lap: a white villa like the deck of a steamship on top of a hill with a seaside view, large windows, blowing curtains, and a shell shaped pool everything surrounded by palm trees. (p. 61)

Most of these descriptions are focalized by the protagonist, so it is unclear if this genuinely is Lauretta's big wish. As is the case with Mayer, the absence of a counterperspective from Lauretta's side results in her being depicted as a rather flat character.

The protagonist explicitly states that his goal coincides with Lauretta's goal: 'Lauretta's dream was also my dream' (p. 63). At first glance, this seems to have nothing to do with his social position. But at a specific moment in the story, it is suggested that his social status is the driving force behind his actions:

> After having taken advantage of others for more than sixty years, I felt that it was time to do something back, something that I was good at and what, as opposed to my work as elevator operator, served a higher goal. (p. 64)

What this 'higher goal' exactly is, remains ambiguous. But what the protagonist does make explicit is that he has a 'social debt' (p. 65) to pay off.

This social debt can best be interpreted in the historical economic context that is foregrounded in the narrative. The Brooklynclub was founded in the aftermath of the Vietnam War and the American economic recession of the early 1980s that followed. Mayer symbolizes the prototype of the evil capitalist for whom economic gain is a primary goal. As if that is not enough, the protagonist states that Mayer contributed to the fall of the American economy: 'He [Mayer] helped bring America down the tube through his lobbying, and the real estate bubble is largely a result of his work' (p. 41).

In light of this historical economic context, the conflict between the protagonist and Mayer can be perceived as a metaphor for class hierarchies in capitalist, neoliberal societies. The slogan of the Brooklynclub is 'Union is strength', which is subverted by Mayer when he joins the club:

> I longed for shivers. Mayer had transformed those shivers into blind violence by considering the fights as games while, except for a few people, no member of the club wanted to prove their superiority. We didn't care about losing or winning a fight, but Mayer was so vain that he assumed that he was under attack in the ring. He regarded it as criticism when someone hit him. By betting with extremely high amounts of money and by exploiting Cass and Gordon, he created confusion and strife. (pp. 85–86)

Before Mayer entered the scene, the Brooklynclub was a place of social anarchy where people would fight each other noncompetitively – hence the slogan 'Union is strength'. With the arrival of Mayer, the Brooklynclub transforms into the opposite: a place of competition and strife.

In the resulting competitive situation, the conflict between the protagonist and Mayer symbolizes the class struggle of those people who occupy a lower place on the social ladder. The protagonist represents the underdog who is dominated by his societal superior Mayer. The raping of Lauretta by Mayer serves as an illustration of that fact: Mayer is so powerful that he can take away the most precious 'possession' of the protagonist. By murdering Mayer, the protagonist not only takes revenge on his enemy but also breaks open the power hierarchies that are a result of his and Mayer's socioeconomic positions.

This reading of the novel fits in the overall statistical pattern in which lower-class characters are more central in conflict situations than higher-class characters. In this particular novel, the conflict between the lower-class protagonist and the higher-class Mayer is indeed reflected by their conflict scores: the protagonist has a composite conflict score of 2.75, Mayer has a composite conflict score of 1.5. On the level of plot, the discrepancy in these scores is exemplified by the protagonist's murdering of Mayer, which is the ultimate victory over one's enemy.

However, this conformation of the novel to the statistical pattern only holds in this schematic, plot-based reading. An alternative reading of the novel sheds a different light on the nature of the conflict between the protagonist and Mayer. There are instances in the novel where it is subtly suggested that the protagonist and Mayer are actually very much alike, despite their different socioeconomic positions. First, there is the seemingly strange coincidence that the two characters are lookalikes on a physical level. The protagonist takes advantage of this coincidence in his 'masterpiece' of letting the kidnappers think that it is Mayer who they kidnap, although in reality it is the protagonist who earlier killed Mayer in his apartment.

Furthermore, the protagonist is fairly startled by the deep spiritual connection he has with Mayer:

> I waited sixty years to pay off my social debt, and forty-two years to avenge Lauretta. Initially, Mayer appeared in my thoughts a few times every day. Every morning I had to fight against the daunting image of his drool dripping on Lauretta's back while he clenched his rough hands around her waist in the Buick Riviera; an image that filled me with horror at the moments when I recognized myself in it, I used to cool down my self-hatred and shame by spitting on the mirror after I washed my face and brushed my teeth. (p. 65; emphasis added)

The classic metaphor of the mirror serves to underline the protagonist's resistance toward introspection that is sparked by his recognition of the similarities between him and his enemy. A few pages later, this metaphoric logic is repeated:

> I had no single mirror in my house in Queqertarsuup Tunua, and when I coincidentally saw my reflection in a window or a piece of ice, I turned away from myself as a dog from his own shit. The last time I felt disgusted by my own appearance was when they showed a picture of Mayer on television. (p. 67)

The foregrounding of the physical similarities between the protagonist and Mayer creates a tension in the plot. It is not only that the protagonist has similar looks as Mayer, but he is also able to picture himself vividly as the rapist of his own beloved, which fills him with genuine disgust. As such, the question arises as to whether or not the protagonist and Mayer actually are two different characters. The coincidence of their physical similarities and the plot twist of Lauretta marrying her rapist are so odd that the protagonist's reliability as a narrator is called into question. Does Mayer exist at all or is he a product of the protagonist's imagination?

This 'Doppelgänger' motif opens up an alternative reading to the one presented above. The initial reading considered the conflict between the protagonist as belonging to the second type of Pavis's typology: rivalry between two characters because of money, love, morality, politics, etc. Taking the Doppelgänger motif as a point of departure, however, this conflict can be reframed as conforming to the third type of the typology: (inner) conflict between, e.g., passion and reason. A possible interpretation is that the protagonist's real enemy is his own Self. Externalizing this inner conflict, the protagonist has created Mayer in his imagination as the ultimate Other. The class hierarchy between the protagonist and this imagined character of Mayer is a politicization of his personal problems. By viewing the conflict he has with his own Self in terms of a class conflict, the protagonist is able to make sense of his personal misery and blame it on his position on the social ladder. Eventually, he realizes that his defeat over Mayer is in reality a personal defeat: 'It occurred to me that by destroying my doppelganger I emasculated myself permanently' (p. 149).

In this more resistant reading of the narrative conflict, *De Brooklynclub* escapes the observed statistical pattern subtly. By looking at what happens between the lines as opposed to what happens at the surface of the text, indeterminacies are found that undermine a schematic reading of the text. Statistically, it is true for the corpus of 170 novels in general that characters with a low education are more central in conflicts than characters with a high education. From a Marxist point of view, this statistical pattern can be interpreted as a rebellion of the lower class to their fixed socioeconomic position. In a surface-like analysis that stays close to how the narrative is presented in terms of plot, Koubaa's novel is a perfect illustration of that statistical pattern. By murdering his higher-class enemy Mayer, the lower-class protagonist becomes the central party in their mutual clash.

However, a reading that is resistant to the state of affairs as presented by the first-person narrator reveals that the nature of the conflict is more complex. Possibly, Mayer is a product of the protagonist's imagination. Read from this point of view, the conflict at stake is not a socioeconomic clash between the high and the low class, but rather an inner conflict taking place within the boundaries of the protagonist's own psyche. In this second reading, *De Brooklynclub* is not primarily a story about a lower-class character taking revenge on a higher-class character, but rather a novel about a confused underdog fighting against the person in the mirror. While conflict between the higher and the lower classes is still prevalent in this reading of the novel (although only in the protagonist's imagination), it shows how literary mechanisms such as the Doppelgänger motif enable a subtle deconstruction of observed statistical patterns.

5.5 MODEL II: SOCIAL BALANCE IN TRIANGULAR CONFLICTS

Now that there is a clearer image of the nature of hierarchies exposed through conflicts between two single characters, a closer look at broader network structures in conflict situations is warranted. In the statistical analyses carried out in the former section, the conflicts at stake encompass only the first type offered by Pavis's typology (see section 5.3): rivalry between two characters because of money, love, morality, politics, etc. This is a logical consequence of a focus on enemy pairs consisting of only two characters. In theory, the second type of conflict from Pavis's typology – two conflicting worldviews or irreconcilable moral conceptions – can also be expressed through dyadic relations, as two characters could have conflicting worldviews resulting in them becoming enemies. But this more abstract type form of conflict generally involves more than two characters, as worldviews and moral conceptions can be expressed metonymically by multiple characters belonging to a group with shared values.

A focus on more than two characters potentially lays bare broader network dynamics that are at play in narrative conflict. Such dynamics are also relatable to the fourth type of Pavis's typology: conflict between the particular and the general, e.g., between the individual and society. It is imaginable that the intragroup morale leads to a clash with an individual belonging to that group. Furthermore, it might also relate to the fifth type: a moral or metaphysical conflict between a character and a principle such as God or an ideal. A group can, for example, have ideals that an individual has trouble accepting or refuses to adopt.

In order to limit this potentially large and heterogeneous subject of conflict in which more than two characters are involved, this section only considers subnetworks of three characters, also called triads. Triads are the second smallest network structure after dyads (two nodes linked by one edge). According to sociologist Georg Simmel, the transformation from a dyadic to a triadic network is the most radical, phase-shifting relational change.[6] Following Simmel, the shift of focus from dyads to triads makes it possible to research character conflicts in two fundamentally different – dyadic and triadic – contexts.

An empirical testing of Heider's social balance theory (see section 5.2 of this chapter) can lead to insight into the effect that conflicts have on relationships between more than two characters. As explained above, the social balance theory poses that triadic signed networks are either balanced or unbalanced depending on the composition of the nodes' positive and negative attitudes toward the other nodes. Kraicer and Piper (2019) offer a clear visualization of the theory (Figure 3). In the analysis below, positive relations are represented by friendship relations, negative relations by enemy relations.

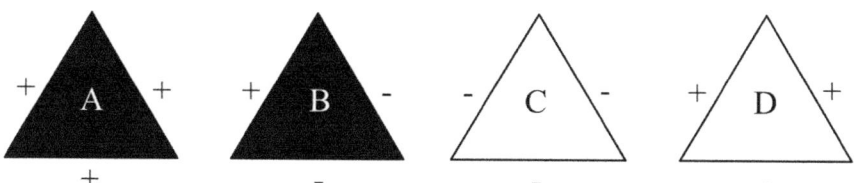

Figure 3. Visualization of Heider's social balance theory, adapted from Kraicer & Piper (2019). Triangles A and B are balanced, triangles C and D are imbalanced.

To what extent are triadic relationships in the corpus balanced (triangle A or B in Figure 3) or imbalanced (triangle C or D in Figure 3), and what are the consequences of social (im)balance for the representation of social groups?

According to Heider, imbalanced structures strive to balanced states. If the theory applies to character networks as well, then the corpus should contain few imbalanced triads. In the following, social balance theory will serve as the framework for the analysis of character triads. As such, a general pattern will be presented, which will be subsequently explored in depth through a close reading of a novel that has both balanced and imbalanced triadic subnetworks.

5.5.1 Automatic Modeling of Social Balance in Enemy/Friend triads

For every triad consisting of either friends and/or enemies, it was automatically established whether or not it is balanced or unbalanced.[7] First, from database EDGES only those characters that have either an enemy or a friend relation were selected.[8] Then, it was automatically determined whether or not the observed triads fall into the balanced or the unbalanced category. The relative distribution of social (im)balanced states show that the majority of these triads is balanced: 65% of the observed triads is balanced, as opposed to only 35% of imbalanced (N = 560). The absolute distributions of the (im)balanced categories friend-friend-friend (balance), friend-enemy-enemy (balance), enemy-enemy-enemy (imbalance), and enemy-friend-friend (imbalance) are shown in Figure 4.

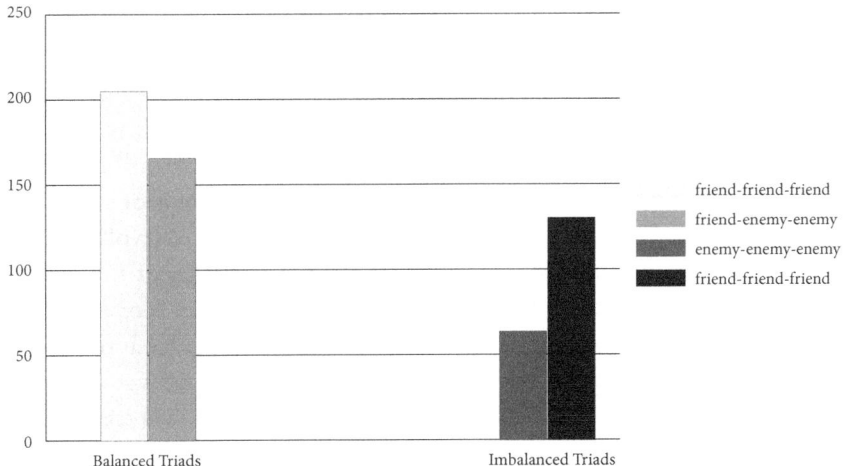

Figure 4. Absolute distribution of social (im)balance for all enemy/friend-triads in the corpus divided by type (N =560).

These results broadly confirm Heider's theory, but with some counterexamples. It remains a question how generalizable these results are beyond the 170 novels in the present research corpus. Up to the present, as far as I am aware, there is only one other study that uses social balance theory for framing interactions between characters in literary texts (Kraicer & Piper, 2019). This study focuses on a corpus of 1,333 contemporary English novels and reports a distribution of 53% balance as opposed to 47% imbalance. However, their method for detecting negative and positive relations deviates from the method used here. The authors of this study automatically detect negativity/positivity of character relations bottom-up by using sentiment analysis, which results in a fairly rough and partly inaccurate estimate of the nature of those relations. The present research uses top-down expert annotations of negative and positive relations between characters and comes arguably closer to how readers would frame those relations. In order to make generalizable statements on social balance in literature, comparative research has to be conducted on several corpora, preferably from other language fields and other time periods, using the same method.

Although there has been some critique on the generalizability of the theory, as imbalanced triadic structures have been reported in social networks (Doreian, 2011), this is not the place to make assertions on the general tenability of the social balance theory. Presuming that Heider's theory has some truth in it, it is remarkable that 65% of the character triads in the corpus conform to it. In the context of Greimas's actantial model, it would be more likely that fictional networks do not strive to social balance in the same way as real-world networks do. In fictional social networks, an alternative organizing principle might be in place that does not prefer social balance over social imbalance. This intuition appeals to the idea that disparity and divergence are driving factors behind the fictional worlds of novels, which can be associated with the axis of conflict in Greimas's actantial model. Action in fictional narratives is said to revolve around three axes (knowledge, desire, power/conflict), but the roles of the helpers and opponents, or friends and enemies, at the axis of conflict is of particular importance in terms of keeping the story interesting for the reader. If the desires of the subject are not frustrated by any opponents at all, a tedious story would be the result. More generally, an overrepresentation of imbalanced triads in the corpus might be an indication that stories tend not to evolve smoothly but rather evolve with a necessary amount of squirming and irritation.

However, this appears not to be the case for the present data, as there is an overrepresentation of balanced triads as opposed to imbalanced triads. One interpretation of this unexpected outcome is that social structures in fictional worlds tend to resemble real-world structures. If one follows Heider's theory that in actual societies social balance is more present than social imbalance, these results can be used as an argument for the mimetic powers of literary worlds, which can be traced back all the way to Aristotle's account of literature being a reflection of the world in which it is produced (Aristotle, 335 BC/2013). Also in modern times, the idea that literature is a medium in which societal tendencies are reflected continues to be popular (Anjana & Bhambhra, 2016; Auerbach, 1946/2003; Hoggart, 1966), In order to make a solid case for this interpretation, social (im)balance would have to be measured in contemporary Dutch society and compared with the present results.[9]

An alternative interpretation of the overrepresentation of social balance is that only a minimum of action can take place at the axis of conflict. One could argue that, in order for the story to evolve at all, the subject should have ample opportunities for reaching his goal. If there is too much social imbalance, too much activity at the axis of conflict, the story could not gain any momentum. Referring back to Propp's example of fairy tales: too much social imbalance would possibly result in the hero not even leaving his castle to save the princess, as he would be stuck in socially imbalanced structures at home.

The possible explanations of this pattern will be left aside for now, and its value will be evaluated through a case study. The observed general pattern of social (im)balance will be confronted with close readings of two novels from the corpus for which balanced triads have been reported. In the following subsection the effect of these balanced triads on the representation of social groups in the novels will be assessed. This qualitative reading will then be contextualized through the quantitative results in order to put the social (im)balance in the novel in a broader perspective.

As case studies, two novels from the corpus are used in which there is a clear conflict between ideologies. The state of social balance in the first case study, Leon de Winter's *VSV of daden van onbaatzuchtigheid* (2012), creates a rather schematic opposition between a group of Dutch characters and a group of characters with a Moroccan and Muslim background. Such a schematic opposition also seems to be present in the second case study, Tommy Wieringa's *Dit zijn de namen* (2012), but the social imbalance in certain specific character triads complicates that view. In both qualitative readings, Greimas's actantial model will be used to (de)construct the specific conflicts at stake in the novels.

5.5.2 Social Balance in Leon de Winter's *VSV, of daden van onbaatzuchtigheid*

Conflict is definitely a driving force behind Leon de Winter's *VSV of daden van onbaatzuchtigheid*. The novel's general setting is the polarized Dutch political climate that came into being after the murders on politician Pim Fortuyn (2002) and film director Theo van Gogh (2004). Both of them were outspoken critics of Islamic fundamentalism and were assassinated by people who were offended by their criticism. *VSV* is set in a country still recovering from the aftermath of these tragic events. Through the narrative perspectives of eleven different characters, a plot is set in motion that recalls the ideological conflict between religious fundamentalism and freedom of speech that lay at the heart of the Dutch public debate in the early 2000s. This is done specifically through the staging of actual people who played a role in sparking those debates, such as Theo van Gogh and his assassinator Mohammed Boujeri. By staging himself as a character, author Leon de Winter brings back to memory the personal quarrel he had with Theo van Gogh, which revolved around De Winter's accusation that Van Gogh harbored anti-Semitic ideas.

The story commences with the perspective of Theo van Gogh, who got stuck in what he calls a 'barrack building'[10] (De Winter, p. 14) after his death, and which is strongly reminiscent of the purgatory. The military metaphor of the barrack building can be associated with the unfinished strife that Theo has to settle before entering into heavenly spheres. This strife is a political one: Theo has 'to finish a movie about a hero, Pim Fortuyn' (p. 10). As was the case in reality, Theo supported Pim Fortuyn's campaign for freedom of speech and his criticism on the Islam. In the novel, Theo repeatedly refers to Moroccan people with the term 'kutmarokkanen' ('damn Moroccans'), as well as with terms as 'goat fucker' (p. 9) and 'religious fool' (p. 17). He calls his assassinator Mohammed Boujeri 'a bearded monkey in a sack-like dress' (p. 8). On a general level, character Theo seems to incorporate the beliefs of the historic person Theo van Gogh:

> Nowadays there were too many of them [bearded monkeys] in the city. Lunatics who were only able to endure the trip from the desert to the filthy city through abiding by the norms and values of nomads from the seventh century. Everyone has his madness. But these fools did not tolerate other people's madness. (ibid.)

From the first chapter onward, an opposition between the ideology of Islamic fundamentalism and Dutch liberalism is thus postulated. This activates a conflict in the structural sense that falls into the second category of Pavis's typology: two conflicting worldviews or irreconcilable moral conceptions.

The liberal ideology is expressed most explicitly by the character of Theo van Gogh, the Islamic extremist ideology most explicitly by the character of Mohammed Boujeri. More generally, this structural conflict divides the novels into two groups of characters who (implicitly or indirectly) side with one of the ideologies. This division between characters is based on their ethnic background and is represented by Moroccan characters on the one hand and non-Moroccan characters on the other.

Leon de Winter, among others, belongs to the group of non-Moroccans. Compared to the real-world quarrel between the actual Leon de Winter and the actual Theo van Gogh, it might seem odd that both are placed in the same camp. However, Van Gogh and De Winter shared similar ideas regarding the dangers of the Islam, and so do the characters modeled after them. Furthermore, the character of gangster Max Kohn, to whose narrative perspective most chapters are dedicated, can also be associated with this group. Although he says that he is not interested in 'the whole phenomenon of Muslims who feel wronged' (p. 216), he exemplifies the typical prejudices against Muslims. When he hears an explosion the 'prejudices were immediately invoked: this was a deliberately caused explosion, and therefore caused by terrorists, and therefore caused by Muslims' (ibid.). Besides Van Gogh, De Winter, and Kohn, the notorious ideas of politician Geert Wilders make the character through which Wilders is represented also part of this group. The characters of former Dutch politicians Piet Hein Donner and Job Cohen represent the Dutch political status quo in the novel and are as such also part of this group.

The five characters with a Moroccan background – Mohammed Boujeri, Sallie, Frits (Firas), Karel (Kareef), and Kichie – are to a greater or lesser extent associated with the ideology of Islamic extremism. Mohammed killed Theo van Gogh and is represented as the stereotypical Muslim extremist. He repeatedly quotes from the Quran, defies non-Muslims, and is proud of the killing of Theo van Gogh:

> It is thus completely acceptable to silence unreformable slanderers. Warnings should be made, but one day the sword of the true believer will cut the throat of the slanderer, and repentance is no reason to stop the vengeance. Our devotion to the Prophet (Sallallahu alaihie wa Sallam) is so strong, that we cannot ever let him be insulted with impunity. (p. 77)

Similarly, Sallie, Frits, and Karel are portrayed as typical Muslim extremists, committing three terrorist assaults in Amsterdam driven by religious motives. Kichie (Kicham Ouaziz) is Sallie's father and is characterized as a 'Berber in search of the rituals of his people before it was wiped out by the Arabs and their Islam' (p. 248). Although he is not represented as a Muslim extremist – he is focalized by Mohammed Boujeri as an 'apostate dog' (p. 253) and claims repeatedly that he is 'no religious extremist' (p. 263) – among his most defining features is his Moroccan ethnic background. Another of his defining features is his criminal background. It is noteworthy that each of these characters is a terrorist or a criminal. Numerically, of all identified Moroccan characters in this novel, 100% are involved in criminal activities. This fact only already creates an a priori moral scheme in which non-Moroccan characters such as Theo van Gogh and Leon de Winter are on the moral, and the Moroccan characters on the immoral, side of the spectrum.[11]

The clash between these two groups of characters can be formalized through two different actantial models, of which these are the axes of conflict:

— Axis of conflict 1: The non-Moroccans (*subject*) want a free and peaceful country (*object*) but are frustrated in reaching that goal by the Moroccans (*opponent*).
— Axis of conflict 2: The Moroccans (*subject*) aim to satisfy the commandments of the Islamic faith (*object*) but are hampered by the non-Moroccans (*opponent*).[12]

Below, a closer inspection of one particular character triad in the novel will demonstrate how this general clash between two conflicting sociocultural belief systems is embodied through a direct, face-to-face conflict between three characters.

5.5.1.1 Balanced Triad Sallie-Karel-Kohn

On a micro level, the balanced triad shown in Figure 5 exemplifies the intergroup conflict between Moroccans and non-Moroccans. Max Kohn has a hostile relation with both Sallie and Karel, whereas Sallie and Karel are close friends and fellow terrorists. The triad is balanced because the enemy of Sallie's/Karel's enemy, i.e., Kohn, is Sallie's/Karel's friend, i.e., Karel/Sallie.

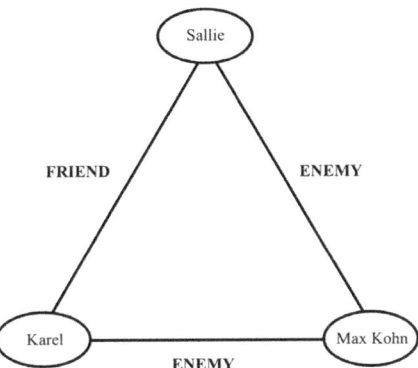

Figure 5. Imbalanced triad in Leon de Winter's VSV, with characters Sallie (a.k.a. Salheddine Ouaziz), Karel (a.k.a. Kareef) and Max Kohn.

The hostility between Sallie and Max Kohn has old roots. Sallie's father, Kichie, used to work as a hitman for Max Kohn. Early in the novel, Sallie focalizes Kohn as 'a tough guy, who fled the country unharmed' and repeats the fact that his father 'took all the punches for the gangster' (p. 145). Although this is not the reason why Sallie and Kohn become enemies, their personal history is brought back into memory when a direct, physical conflict between Sallie and Kohn takes place.

The setting for this conflict coincides with a scene in which the action climaxes. Sallie, Karel, Frits, and others have occupied a school and held a group of children hostage, among which is Kohn's son. Politicians Piet Hein Donner and Job Cohen have asked Kohn and Kichie to take back control over the situation. When Sallie sees Kohn, he says: 'Hey, you are that Jew from the underworld, right? The boss of my pa-pa' (p. 398). This recognition sparks an anger in Sallie that kick-starts the hostile events that follow, and in which Kohn eventually holds Sallie at gunpoint (p. 402).

A similar direct, physical conflict is at work between Kohn and Karel, who is also one of the hostage takers. Kohn physically assaults Karel and takes his gun (p. 401). Their mutual conflict climaxes when Kohn shoots Karel in the shoulder:

> Kohn pulled the trigger and the shot sounded dry. The boy briefly shocked and then remained silent. Blood was dripping from his arm. (p. 405)

The social balance in this Sallie-Karel-Kohn triad serves as a strengthening of the general intergroup conflict between the Moroccans and the non-Moroccans.

The scene described above fits perfectly in the central tenet of the novel: acts of altruism lead to the good, whereas acts of egoism result in the bad (hence the novel's subtitle *Acts of Altruism*). As a guardian angel, the character of Theo van Gogh has been commissioned to have the previously immoral Max Kohn do something morally good, in which Kohn succeeds by stopping the terrorist attack carried out by Sallie and his friends. As such, the enemy/friend relations in this particular triad are exemplary of a moral scheme in which the Moroccans are morally perverted and the non-Moroccans (become) morally enlightened.

Furthermore, the Sallie-Karel-Kohn triad does not stand on its own; it is representative of a pattern. There is a range of other balanced triads in the novel for which the same argument can be made. Sallie and Karel not only feature in a balanced triad with Kohn, they also feature in similar balanced triads with the following non-Moroccan characters: Nathan Verstraete (Kohn's son), Sonja Verstraete (Kohn's ex-lover), Job Cohen, Marijke Hogeveld (Cohen's lover), and Geert Wilders. On top of that, Sallie and Frits – another member of Sallie's group of terrorist friends – feature in the exact same balanced triads as Sallie and Karel. In total, twelve balanced triads occur that are all indicative of the same two conflicting worldviews.

These twelve observed balanced triads fit perfectly in two different actantial models in which the Moroccans and non-Moroccans function as each other's opponents on the two axes of conflict (see section 5.5.2). In other words, each of these balanced triads stands in a metonymic relation to a general actantial model with either the Moroccans or the non-Moroccans as a subject. No imbalanced triads are observed that potentially complicate these highly schematic moral oppositions between both groups. Instead, the intragroup morale in these twelve balanced triadic subnetworks confirm an overall moral scheme in which the Moroccans are good and the non-Moroccans are bad. Subsequently, this is not only an opposition in terms of descent, it is also an opposition in terms of belief systems. The fact that these balanced triads strongly conform to such broadly defined actantial models makes *VSV* ideologically biased toward the cultural values of Dutch liberalism rather than those of Islamic fundamentalism.

5.5.3 Social Imbalance in Tommy Wieringa's *Dit zijn de namen*

Just as in his most recent book *De heilige Rita* (2017), the notions of East and West and their borderland play a pivotal role in Tommy Wieringa's Libris prize–winning *Dit zijn de namen* (2012). The setting of the novel is Michailopol, a fictional frontier town that symbolizes the gateway from East to West, although it remains unclear where the town is exactly located. There are two main perspectives in the novel that alternate per third-person narrated chapter. The novel commences with the perspective of Pontus Beg, a middle-aged police officer who works in Michailopol. The other perspective lies with a group of initially nameless refugees with varying backgrounds who are on their way to the West, and eventually end up at Michailopol where they are caught and interrogated by Pontus Beg. In the chapters in which the refugee perspective is adopted, the focalization lies with one of the individuals from the refugee group consisting of five men, one woman, and one boy. At various instances in the novel, the idea is foregrounded that prosperity can be found in the West. This may occur very explicitly: 'They had to keep on going to the West, the man said' (Wieringa, 2012, p. 14). Or it might do so more implicitly, through e.g., the metaphor of a pack of cigarettes from the brand 'Western' that the little refugee boy finds and which gives him false hope of quickly arriving at the promised Western land.

Ironically, Pontus Beg, who tries to prevent the refugees from the East entering the West, is highly obsessed with Eastern philosophy, such as the teachings of Confucius and Zhuang Zi. As someone living on the border between East and West, he appears to be more strongly attracted to the East, as is illustrated through quotes such as 'Confucius was a man of order, someone who provides guidance. Honoring the elderly, the rituals and the Road, his love for the true word; Beg sometimes regretted that he did not live in the China of the Master' (p. 50). Furthermore, throughout the novel Pontus Beg has numerous conversations with rabbis as he is interested in gaining more knowledge on his Jewish roots ('He intended to read everything that he needed to know, and then to decide if he would become a religious Jew or only a Jew from birth' [p. 206]). As Judaism originated in the Middle East, this motif strengthens Pontus Beg's obsession with spiritual teachings from the East.

This general framework serves as the core of the conflict between Pontus Beg (and the town of Michailopol which he represents) on the one hand, and the group of refugees on the other. It is a conflict in the structural sense which can be associated with the second type of Pavis's typology: Two conflicting worldviews or irreconcilable moral conceptions. The general worldview incorporated by the refugees is that the West is the desired place to be, whereas Beg incorporates the worldview that spiritual wisdom lies in the East. Although these two worldviews do not necessarily have to be conflicting, they form the axis of conflict in two different actantial models of the novel, of which the subjects, objects and opponents can be represented in the following way:

— Axis of conflict 1: Refugees (*subject*) want happiness in the West (*object*) but are hindered to fulfill that goal by Pontus Beg (*opponent*)
— Axis of conflict 2: Pontus Beg (*subject*) is in search of spiritual salvation (*object*) but his search is obstructed by refugees entering his hometown (*opponents*)

The role of helper has been left out of these two representations of the axis of conflict because it is rather ambiguous who helps who. A closer inspection on two imbalanced triadic relationships in the novel helps to pinpoint how conflict co-shapes its representation of different social groups.

5.5.1.1 Imbalanced Triad Samira-Ethiopian-Akmuhammet

In Figure 6, the imbalanced triad of three of the refugee characters is shown. Two of them are named at the end of the novel: Samira Uygun (who was earlier referred to as 'the woman') and Akmuhammet Kurbankiliev (who was referred to as 'the man from Asjchabad'). 'The Ethiopian' remains nameless, being only referred to with downgrading terms such as 'Africa', 'the black man', 'the negro', and 'dog'.

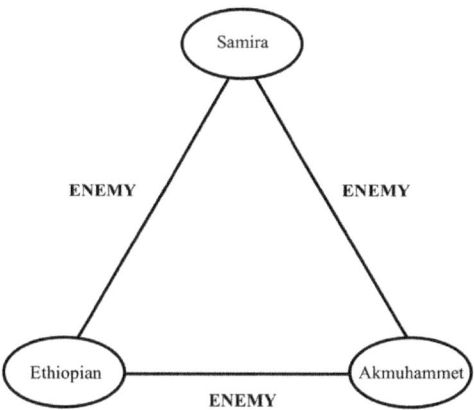

Figure 6. Imbalanced triad in Tommy Wieringa's Dit zijn de namen, with characters Samira Uygun (a.k.a. 'the woman'), 'the Ethiopian' (a.k.a. 'Africa', 'the black man', 'the negro', 'dog'), and Akmuhammet Kurbankiliev (a.k.a. 'the man from Asjchabad').

All relations in this signed triadic network are hostile, and therefore imbalanced according to Heider's theory. 'The enemy of my enemy is my friend' is not applicable in this triad, as the enemy of a character's enemy is its enemy and not its friend. This example poses a problem for the assignment of the roles of helper and opponents in an actantial model of the novel. In a general sense, all individuals in the group of refugees are each other's helpers, as they are in the same situation and would benefit from a joint effort to reach their shared goal. However, the social imbalance of some triads within the general network of refugees potentially obstructs the fulfillment of this common goal. This is illustrated by the triadic relationship between Samira, Akmuhammet, and the Ethiopian, which forms a separate network with an intragroup morale that deviates from the general interests of the group of refugees. As such, some of the refugees are both opponents to the group as well as opponents to the goals of the individuals within that group. On a micro-textual level, the clash between this particular triad and the overall refugee network is expressed through Wieringa's highlighting of both the shared goal of the refugees and the hostility between some particular individuals in that group. The shared interest is expressed by the anonymous narrator through descriptions such as the following:

> Despite the bitter disappointment, the village gave them new courage; it seems as if they walk faster than before. It can't possibly be the only settlement in the area. Communities are never that isolated. *The village ahead* becomes their chief point of focus. They see tractors on the fields, smoking chimneys, the cattle. The friendly beehives at the edge of the village... They only have to walk toward it ... (p. 30)

The narrator frames the situation in such a way that it seems as if everyone in the group is on the same page and has the same object of focus (i.e., '*The village ahead*'). The phrase 'communities are never that isolated' can be read as the shared hope that their finding of the earlier village might be a sign that another village will be near. However, the phrase can also be interpreted as an ironic comment on the situation in their group: as refugees they are isolated, forming a distinct group that will likely be closed off from any new society they might encounter. Furthermore, within the group of refugees there are multiple isolated subgroups that are in conflict with the collective ideals of the group as a whole.

One of those isolated subgroups is the imbalanced triadic relationship between Samira, Akmuhammet, and the Ethiopian. Throughout the novel, intragroup hostility between certain members come to the fore. This is made clear through comments by the narrator such as:

> The woman, the boy, and the negro occupy a different role. Prey. Victim. Spectator. It is best if they make themselves invisible. (p. 31)

As a 'Prey', Samira (or 'the woman') has a special status in the group: she is repeatedly raped by Akmuhammet, also known as 'the man from Asjchabad whose prey she was at night' (p. 132). Furthermore, the 'negro', or 'the Ethiopian', is allocated the role of 'Spectator' as he is more generally excluded by different members of the group. Time and again, he is downgraded and physically assaulted by Akmuhammet in particular (p. 148). A scene in which the little boy is the focalizing subject illustrates the Ethiopian's position in the group:

> The dog in the tail of the caravan. A dog – although they keep beating him, he keeps coming back, begging for attention and mercy. They will beat him even harder, just as long as he finally understands that he does not fit in. That he is a stranger, a bearer of mystery. There is no place for him in the group, he will need to make the trip alone. [...] He must understand that the group now poses a bigger threat to him than lonely wandering the plains. (p. 150)

Although the Ethiopian is part of the same endeavor to find a better life in the West, he becomes more and more isolated from the group, to such an extent that the group turns on him and 'poses a bigger threat to him than lonely wandering the plains'. He has been excluded from the group of which he initially was a part: 'The distance between them became unbridgeable in a short while. Not long ago, he had warmed his hands at the same fire' (p. 176).

The imbalanced triadic relationship between Samira, Akmuhammet, and the Ethiopian demonstrates a key element in the intragroup hierarchies of the refugees. In a very broadly defined actantial model, the five men, the woman, and the boy represent a common subject striving for the shared goal of finding a new life in the West. In that model, all refugees are each other's helpers. However, from the narrower perspective of single character triads, an alternative actantial model can be outlined. The imbalance in this particular triad indicates the dominance of Akmuhammet over both Samira and the Ethiopian. In terms of gender and race, this hierarchy is represented as a dominance of the male (Akmuhammet) over the female (Samira) and the non-black (Akmuhammet) over the black (the Ethiopian).

5.5.3.2 Imbalanced Triad Pontus-Samira-Akmuhammet

The overall clash between Pontus Beg and the refugees takes place in the part called 'Winter'. At this point in the narrative the surviving refugees reach Michailopol. As the officer in chief, Pontus Beg is a general representative of the town. When the arrival of the refugees creates disquiet in the town, it is Beg's responsibility to reestablish the peace. In a chapter where the focalization lies with the people of Michailopol, the refugees are framed as 'tramps' (p. 183), 'the dead' (ibid.), 'fucking tramps' (ibid.), 'shadows' (ibid.)', 'the untouchables' (p. 185), 'lepers' (ibid.), 'starvelings' (p. 186), and 'Jews from the camps' (p. 189). These descriptions create a first hierarchical opposition between the people of Michailopol and the refugees: the negatively connoted terms serve to subjugate the refugees to a hostile and downgrading vocabulary.

Although the refugees did not do any particular harm, they are arrested and imprisoned at the police station where Pontus Beg works. Here, a power mechanism is at play that can be observed in actual frontier towns such as Lampedusa: refugees are subjected to the law system and bureaucracy of the country where they arrive. Beg takes their freedom away and makes them potential suspects to a crime of which they were not previously aware. Their criminalization is amplified when the head of the Ethiopian character is found in their luggage and each of the refugees is subjected to an official interrogation.

This situation of criminalization gives rise to the imbalanced triad between Pontus, Samira Uygun, and Akmuhammet Kurbankiliev (see Figure 7). As was already discussed in the previous subsection (5.5.3.1), Samira and Akmuhammet are in a hostile relation with one another. When their relation is triangulated with Pontus as a third member, a situation arises that is unlikely to occur according to the social balance theory. It would be in line with the theory, had Pontus been a friend to either Samira or Akmuhammet. This is, however, not the case, as Pontus Beg becomes their enemy by imprisoning them and suspecting them of a crime.

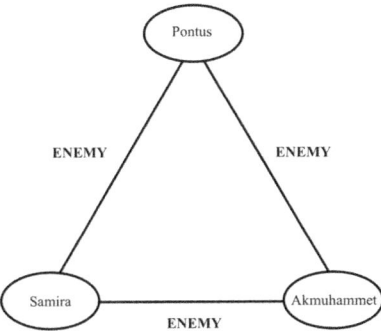

Figure 7. Imbalanced triad in Tommy Wieringa's Dit zijn de namen, with characters Pontus Beg, Samira Uygun (a.k.a. 'the woman'), and Akmuhammet Kurbankiliev (a.k.a. 'the man from Asjchabad').

In the context of an actantial model that has Pontus as a subject, this triad can raise two conflicting conceptions of who are the opponents and the helpers. Pontus's goal in the novel can be framed as a search for spiritual salvation. On the one hand, his hostile relation with both Samira and Akmuhammet distracts him from reaching this goal. In this conception, the imbalanced triad serves as a strengthening of the statement that these two refugees are his opponents. On the other hand, the hostile environment in which Pontus, Samira, and Akmuhammet are engrained is a breeding ground for Pontus gaining spiritual insight:

> Isn't it ironic, he said, that this happened to him precisely at the moment that he set his first steps toward the Eternal: a group of people who, in a sense, had been reliving the journey of the desert generation with nothing above their heads than the empty sky. They fled poverty and oppression, the desert generation escaped from the Egyptian slavery. Different, incomparable, and yet the same. Mankind, lost in the wild, looking up at the sky in despair: Lord, help us, protect us. (p. 276)

The refugees coming into his life are thought of by Pontus as an allegory to his own spiritual journey. Just as Pontus is in search of a deity's protection, the refugees are in need of salvation. Pontus's realization of the similarities between him and the refugees deconstructs an actantial model in which Samira and Akmuhammet are his opponents. In this alternative interpretation of the novel they are rather his helpers. This would mean that they no longer are his enemies and that they become his friends. Interestingly, and perhaps coincidentally, the shifting of these relational roles would still result in an imbalanced triad, as the triad would then be friend-friend-enemy.

In all cases, the imbalanced triadic relation between Pontus, Samira, and Akmuhammet is a clear example of a power mechanism in which hierarchies between characters belonging to groups of different descents and classes are at play. Obviously, the hierarchy between Pontus on the one hand, and Samira and Akmuhammet on the other is in greater part the result of the fact that Samira and Akmuhammet have different origins and subsequently other rights than Pontus has. Furthermore, the hierarchy is amplified by Pontus having a prestigious job, whereas Samira and Akmuhammet are not ascribed a professional identity other than 'refugee'. In general, such oppositions between descents and professions (as indicative of classes) fuel the antagonism in this particular imbalanced triad.

5.6 CONCLUSION TO THIS CHAPTER

This chapter examined how the conflicts of characters co-shape the representation of their social groups. Propp published *Morphology of the Folktale* in the 1920s; almost 40 years later Greimas published *Sémantique structurale*. More than fifty years later, their classic models still serve as an inspiration for any structural analysis of narrative action. Recent developments within cultural analytics have opened up possibilities to take the ideas of Propp and Greimas to the next level. Computational and statistical analysis have the potential to fill the gap since Propp and Greimas, and enables a conceptualization and an operationalization of (the analysis) of conflict both at the level of the corpus and at the level of the individual text. Synthesizing typologies, concepts, terms, and tools from a variety of research domains, this chapter thus presented a method to study conflict in literary texts. This method was used to analyze the extent to which narrative conflict shapes the representation of social groups in present-day Dutch literary fiction. Two models of conflict were presented testing two hypotheses related to the literary representation of genders, descents, and classes. Analyzing the research corpus with these models, two general conclusions can be drawn as to the role of conflict in the representation of social groups in today's products of Dutch literary fiction.

First, dyadic conflict was modeled by computing a conflict score for every pair of hostile characters in the corpus, which is an indication of the dominance of characters in such two-way conflicts. It was hypothesized that male, Dutch, and higher educated characters would have higher conflict scores. Surprisingly, gender and descent turned out to have no effect on a character's importance in a conflict. Education is the only statistically significant predictor of the height of these scores; lower educated characters scored significantly higher than higher educated characters. In order to assess the relevance of this macro pattern, it was contextualized through a close reading of a novel from the corpus. The violent clash between the protagonist and antagonist in Bart Koubaa's *De Brooklynclub* seems to reflect the dominance of the lower over the higher classes. However, a less schematic, more resistant reading of the novel shows that the conflict between the lower-class protagonist and the higher-class antagonist can also be read as an externalization of the protagonist's inner conflict. Whereas at the level of the whole corpus, education seems to install class hierarchies in conflicts between two characters, at the level of the individual text these class hierarchies are either reflected or subtly nuanced through various stylistic mechanisms, as is shown by the reading of Koubaa's novel.

Second, going beyond this classic protagonist-antagonist conflict, this chapter examined triadic conflict by modeling the extent of social balance between all possible triangular configurations between enemies and friends in the corpus. Contrary to what one might expect on the basis of Greimas's actantial model, the majority of these triads turned out to be socially balanced. Two possible interpretations were given for this pattern. Based on the assumption that the balance theory generally holds true and that most real-world triangular relations are thus balanced, the dominance of social balance in present-day Dutch literary fiction provides an argument for a mimetic understanding of Dutch literature. In this interpretation, social balance in a particular society seeps through in its products of narrative fiction.

An alternative interpretation is that too much antagonism – defined as social imbalance – holds back narrative progression at the level of plot: a fair amount of social balance is perhaps needed to keep the story going. The relevance of this pattern for the representation of social groups was assessed through a close reading of social balance in both Leon de Winter's *VSV of daden van onbaatzuchtigheid* and Tommy Wieringa's *Dit zijn de namen*. For case study *VSV*, reading triads of enemies in light of Greimas's actantial model revealed a highly schematic opposition between two groups of characters of different descents. In this particular narrative, social balance in a range of triangular character relations functions as an amplification of the more general intragroup conflict between a group of Moroccan and a group of non-Moroccan characters. Whereas social balance in *VSV* leads to schematic (moral) opposition between social groups, this at first also seems to be the case in *Dit zijn de namen*, in which social balance between particular characters fuels antagonism between descents and genders. However, the presence of social imbalance between three other characters complicates such a schematic reading of the novel. While this particular example of social imbalance can be interpreted as fueling hierarchies between characters of a certain descents and class, two alternatively defined actantial models for these three characters suggest that these seemingly opposed groups are perhaps closer to one another than is presented at first. The readings of these two novels thus demonstrate how the extent of social (im)balance in the narrative affects how hierarchies between different social groups take shape.

Both the dyadic and the triadic model of conflict provide data-driven insights into the mechanism of narrative conflict. For the representation of social groups, the models have proven to be useful in exploring and mapping out hierarchies between characters with different demographic profiles. As was already stressed in the previous chapters, the full potential of such models lies in the integration of their statistical results with a contextualization and assessment of the results through close readings of individual works. As was shown in the close readings in this chapter, such qualitative assessments can either conform to or deviate from the observed statistical patterns. By emphasizing the interrelations between the micro and macro levels of representation, a broader insight was thus gained into how conflict co-shapes the representation of social groups in present-day Dutch literary fiction.

CHAPTER 6

CONCLUSION

6.1 FINDINGS OF THE BOOK

Character Constellations examined how the representation of social groups in present-day Dutch literary fiction is shaped by the centrality, communities, and conflicts of 2,137 characters populating the 170 novels in the research corpus. In doing so, it has contributed to a closer understanding of literary representations of men, women, migrants, nonmigrants, the lower educated, the higher educated, the young, and the old. The book's main argument is that hierarchies in the representation of these social groups are reflected in the relational dynamics between characters. While readers tend to see a variety of different, often conflicting images in the patterns between characters, each of these images is based on what I have called 'character constellations': the positions characters occupy in the narrative's linguistic structure relative to the position of other characters. By generating data-driven blueprints of the character constellations in a large, representative sample of today's Dutch literary fiction, this book has led to a range of insights into the dynamics between characters representative of a particular group of people. Highlighting a different aspect of these dynamics in each individual chapter (centrality, community, conflict), I have argued that the literary representation of social groups is structured by means of the more or less central position characters occupy in their networks, the integration or segregation of characters into distinct groups, and the clashes between characters.

While contributing to an academic tradition of critiques of literary representation,[1] *Character Constellations* responds to a threefold methodological problem within this field of inquiry. Character-based critiques of literary representation often start from the assumption that hierarchies, biases, asymmetries, or inequalities can be found in the ways in which certain groups of people are depicted as opposed to others. Although this is a reasonable assumption in light of Marxist, feminist, postcolonial, and other ideological strands of theory, its operationalization is limited in the following three ways. 1) Most of these studies rely on in-depth qualitative close readings of one or a few individual texts. While such small-scale approaches can do justice to the multilayered complexity of individual texts at the local level, their findings are not representative of developments or trends at the overall level of literary output (e.g., based on a sample corpus of texts published in one year). 2) Critiques of representation based on close reading lack a general norm to compare their findings against. Without such a baseline, there is no way to assess how 'normal' or 'peculiar' a qualitatively observed pattern of representation is. What, in other words, do we expect to find in terms of literary representation? 3) Methodological choices often remain implicit. Just as literary representations are always mediated in the sense that someone has shaped it in a particular way,[2] the *study* of literary representation is also mediated, as the scholar shapes his or her reading of the original text in a particular way to arrive at concluding statements. Explication of such mediating steps tends to be lacking in qualitative character-based critiques.

In order to overcome these methodological issues, this book has developed a methodology for a *data-driven* critique of literary representation.[3] Inspired by recent developments within the field of cultural analytics, it has incorporated the notion of modeling into the study of the representation of social groups. As an attempt to move beyond narrowly defined, schematic oppositions between close and distant reading, recent scholarship within cultural analytics has proposed a shift from measuring to modeling (e.g., Piper, 2018; Underwood, 2019).[4] By presenting, applying, and qualitatively evaluating data-driven models of literary representation, *Character Constellations* has attempted to find a solution for the threefold methodological problem described above. It has done so in three ways. 1) Upscaling the research object from one or a few texts to a corpus of 170 novels enabled a more representative view on how social groups are represented in present-day Dutch literary fiction. As the corpus consists of almost 40% of Dutch literary fiction published in one sample year,[5] it was possible to more convincingly generalize about patterns and trends of literary representation. 2) Statistical patterns generated for the corpus as a whole have provided a baseline against which individual works could be read. While determining the extent to which single novels either conform to or deviate from these patterns, the close readings assessed the peculiarity of the case studies in light of these statistical norms. 3) This study has attempted to do justice to the fundamentally mediated nature of the study of literary representation by making explicit how each model was constructed. Emphasizing the mediatedness of the presented insights resulted in more methodological transparency.

Each of the chapters assessed one aspect of the representation of social groups in present-day Dutch literary fiction. Based on qualitative character-based critiques of literary representation, hypotheses were formulated and then tested through the models. While these models generated statistical insights into the dynamics of the representation for the level of the corpus, qualitative close readings were conducted to assess the meaning of these patterns at the level of the individual text. With this methodological framework, the book draws on Susan Suleiman's distinction between poetics and criticism. In her view, poetics is about finding 'the resemblances between works and [seeking] to disengage their common traits' (1983, p. 15), whereas criticism determines 'what is specific or unique about each work' (ibid.). *Character Constellations* used poetics to come up with models at the level of the corpus and used criticism to see how specific works confirm, contradict, or criticize those models at the level of the individual text.

Below, the answers to each of the sub-questions are summarized.

1. How does the centrality of characters co-shape the representation of the social group(s) which they function?

While qualitative studies on literary representation have viewed centrality, importance, or dominance of characters in narratological terms (e.g., Minnaard, 2010), quantitative studies have considered it in terms of their frequency of occurrence (e.g., van der Deijl, Pieterse, Prinse, & Smeets, 2016). In the third chapter, a third approach to the centrality of characters was introduced. Defining centrality in terms of the positions of characters in their social networks, the chapter presented a fundamentally relational take on the question of what makes a character central in a narrative. Each individual character was ranked according to a range of centrality metrics from network theory, after which statistical tests were conducted to determine which types of characters end up high in these rankings. Based on descriptive statistics presented in chapter 2, it was hypothesized that male characters and characters with a Dutch or Belgian descent would end up as more central in these rankings, as these types of characters have a relatively high frequency of occurrence. Contrary to what was hypothesized, female characters and characters with a migration background in fact take up more central positions. This finding invoked a clash between different definitions of centrality: while the frequency with which characters are presented in literature affects the visibility of the groups they represent, these groups are not necessarily more central in terms of their social networks. Although they occur less often in the corpus than male and nonmigrant characters, female and migrant characters have both more relations in general and *more* relations with *important* characters.[6] The close reading of gender and descent in Özcan Akyol's *Eus* has, moreover, shown that centrality in narratological terms might also clash with centrality in terms of either frequency of occurrence or network position. In line with the general pattern for the corpus as a whole, characters with a migration background are statistically more central in this novel than characters without a migration background, and they are also more central in terms of narration and focalization. However, as the narrator is resistant toward any fixed sociocultural identity, the narrative seems to subtly disrupt or escape the statistical baseline that migrant characters are more central than other types of characters. Contrary to the general pattern, furthermore, female characters are less central in this individual narrative than male characters in both statistical terms (i.e., their position in the network) and narratological terms (i.e., narration, focalization).

2. How do the communities in which characters function co-shape the representation of the social group(s) in which characters function?

The main finding of the fourth chapter is that community formation affects how certain types of characters are either integrated into the same group or segregated into distinct groups. More specifically, two different models of community (the first based on a community detection algorithm, the second on assortativity scores) were developed to determine the extent to which the novels were segregated by gender, descent, education, or age. Neither of these models suggests that gender is a cause for segregation in the corpus. Both models do suggest that descent and age are causes for divides between characters, and the second model also adds education as having a statistically significant effect on segregation. Based on these results, it can be argued that present-day Dutch literature stages a divide between migrant and nonmigrant characters, older and younger characters, and higher and lower educated characters. In statistical terms, it is safe to say that these social groups are depicted as separate collective entities. Narratologically, however, segregation between groups is more complex than the data-driven models suggest. Case studies *Niemand in de stad* by Philip Huff and *Liefde heeft geen hersens* by Mensje van Keulen are both outliers: gender is the main cause of segregation in the first (but has no effect on segregation at the global level of the corpus), age leads to integration between groups in the latter (whereas for the corpus as a whole it is a cause for segregation). Furthermore, close reading these cases shows that although plot and themes might invoke divides between groups, other literary stylistic mechanisms potentially problematize schematic oppositions in the novels.

3. How do conflicts between characters co-shape the representation of the social group(s) characters function in?

In the fifth chapter, antagonism, friction, and clashes between characters representative of a social group were demonstrated to install representational schemes in which some are more dominant than others. Models of both dyadic conflict (one-on-one conflict between two characters) and triadic conflict (conflict between three characters) were developed to determine which demographic categories affect the position of characters in conflict situations. Hypothesizing that male, migrant, or higher educated characters are dominant parties in conflicts, the first model computed a conflict score for every pair of enemies in the corpus. Education appeared to be the only significant factor; lower educated characters demonstrated to be more dominant than higher educated characters in these one-on-one conflicts. At the local level of the individual text, this statistical pattern does, however, not necessarily hold. Close reading Bart Koubaa's *De Brooklynclub* exemplifies the various ways in which hierarchies within conflicts can be presented as well as deconstructed through literary-artistic means. Moving beyond this protagonist-antagonist, or hero-villain, conflict, the second model computed the extent of social balance between all triangular relations of either enemies or friends. While a classic narratological model such as Greimas's actantial model (1966) suggests that conflict is a driving force behind narrative action, the model on triadic conflict has demonstrated that social balance (the absence of conflict) occurs in the vast majority of triadic manifestations of conflict. In light of Greimas's narratological models, close readings of Leon de Winter's *VSV of daden van onbaatzuchtigheid* and Tommy Wieringa's *Dit zijn de namen* were conducted to determine how social (im)balance in conflicts between three characters take shape at the level of the individual text. Whereas social balance in the first novel fuels schematic oppositions between groups, social (im)balance in the second novel problematizes initially established hierarchies in the text. Both models, and their narratological contextualization, highlight the ways in which hierarchies are manifested through antagonistic relations between characters belonging to a certain group.

Conjoining the answers to each of the three sub-questions leads to the central conclusion that the representation of social groups in present-day Dutch literary fiction is hierarchically structured. Representational hierarchies are reflected in the centrality, community, and conflict of characters: some types of characters occur more often or occupy a more central position in their social network than others, some are part of a distinct group from which others are excluded, and some are more dominant in conflicts than others. While the finding of representational hierarchies is in line with the assumptions of most qualitative, close reading-based critiques, the present study came to this conclusion on the basis of a representative research corpus, statistical baselines, and methodological transparency. In whichever way one might interpret depictions of women and men, migrants and nonmigrants, the higher and the lower educated, the old and the young, such interpretations are rooted in the actual encounters between characters in the words on the pages. By providing an empirically informed overview of these concrete social dynamics, *Character Constellations* has attempted to create a data-driven basis for discussions on the representation of groups of people within today's society.

Whereas critiques of literary representation based on close reading tend to focus on individual identities within individual narratives, this study has alternatively proposed to view the representation of social groups in terms of character constellations, i.e., the relative positions characters occupy in their social networks. This approach allows for interpretations of the position and social function of the novel in society. More specifically, the above-described results from the individual chapters exemplify the ways in which major societal themes such as (in)equality and emancipation (chapter 3, Centrality), integration and segregation (chapter 4, Community), and social mobility and class struggle (chapter 5, Conflict) are reflected in the genre of the Dutch novel. Although it might seem common sense that the novel is a medium in which such societal issues resonate, systematic quantitative research as conducted in this book is required to gain genuine insights into the ways in which these issues are foregrounded, replicated, criticized, or distorted in works of art such as novels.

In light of the relation between literature and society, the findings from each of the chapters can be interpreted in the following ways. The extent to which certain types of characters are present or central in narrative fiction might be taken as an indication of the equality or emancipation of social groups in society. The descriptive statistics in chapter 2 show, among other, that female characters and characters with a migration background are less present, and thus less visible, in present-day Dutch literary fiction than male and migrant characters. If one holds the mimetic view that literature is a mirror of society, it seems to make sense that a smaller part of the characters in the corpus has a migration background, as the portion of people with a migration background in Dutch society is also relatively small. However, the imbalance between male and female characters conversely invokes the question why the gender distribution in literary fiction does not reflect the (roughly) 50–50 ratio of male and female Dutch citizens. Does the under- or overrepresentation of certain social groups in fiction imply a cultural or aesthetic bias regarding these groups? How, then, should we define under- or overrepresentation? Do we, furthermore, expect to find demographic distributions in fiction similar to those in society?

There is no simple answer to such questions. It is, however, controversial, if not unattainable, to assume that demographic distributions within fictional populations of characters mirror real-world demographics or social dynamics. Based on the descriptive statistics outlined in the second chapter, one could claim that the relative absence of female characters and characters with a migration background is a result of their unequal status in society – more emancipation of these groups would possibly lead to a stronger presence of these groups in works of fiction. In this interpretation, the novel is a rather conservative medium that only reflects the societal status quo. The findings from the third chapter on centrality, however, problematize such a straightforward, perhaps naive mimetic assumption. Despite the imbalances in the gender and descent distributions, female characters and characters with a migration background occupy a relatively central position in their fictional social networks. Contrary to a mimetic interpretation of the demographic distributions in the corpus (i.e., the relative absence of certain social groups in fiction is a result of their unequal status in society), this finding calls for an anti-mimetic interpretation. Although the emancipation of women and people with a migration background still has a long way to go,[7] Dutch literary fiction grants these social groups a relatively central position. This is not a reflection but rather a distortion, or perhaps even a criticism, of societal trends. Moreover, this finding highlights the progressive potential of the novel. Although there are indications that the genre is a conservative reflection of existing societal inequalities (based on chapter 2), the statistical patterns described in the third chapter on centrality suggests that narrative fiction can also shake up the status quo.

The results from the fourth and fifth chapters similarly allow for such a two-sided interpretation. As in real-world social networks, descent, age, and education are causes for divides in fictional social networks. The finding that segregation patterns in society seem to be mirrored in literary fiction provides an argument for the interpretation that the Dutch novel is a mimetic genre in which real-world dynamics are reflected. This interpretation, however, calls into question the notion of a baseline: against which norm should these fictional segregation patterns be compared? How reasonable is it to compare fictional social dynamics with actual social dynamics? In order to explore this question, sociologist Beate Volker and I compared a dataset of personal social networks of Dutch citizens with a part of this study's dataset of fictional social networks (Volker & Smeets, 2019).[8] The findings presented in that study invoke a more progressive, anti-mimetic image of the Dutch novel: although descent, among other factors, is a cause for segregation in both real-world and fictional social networks, the networks of fictional characters in Dutch literature are considerably less segregated than the networks of Dutch citizens. If this pattern will appear to hold true more generally, then this suggests that narrative fiction is a domain in which the integration of social groups take shapes more strongly than in society.

Finally, the results from the fifth chapter on conflict fuel interpretations with regard to (class) struggle and social mobility. This chapter has shown that education is the only statistically significant factor at play in one-on-one conflicts between characters. A Marxist, mimetic interpretation of this pattern is that the struggle between social classes (a fundamental organizing principle in capitalist societies according to Marxist theory) is mirrored in literary fiction. More specifically, the chapter has demonstrated that lower educated characters take up a more dominant position in one-on-one conflicts than higher educated characters, which might be an indication that the lower social classes in fiction are prone to climbing the social ladder. Another result from this chapter, however, allows for an alternative, anti-mimetic interpretation. The majority of the triangular conflicts (between three characters) exist in a state of social balance according to Heider's theory, which suggests that class struggle or conflict in general is a less important factor in the fictional populations of Dutch literature than it would be in Dutch society according to a Marxist line of thinking. In this view, in other words, there are fewer clashes between social groups in fiction than there are in society.

Without a systematic comparison between real-world social dynamics and fictional social dynamics, however, interpretations of the representational hierarchies as observed in this study remain up for debate. *Character Constellations* is a first step toward a more profound insight into the intricate ways in which societal issues are reflected in fiction. To that end, it has not only laid bare surprising patterns of representation in a sample corpus of present-day Dutch literary fiction that can be used to formulate hypotheses on how fiction reflects societal trends, but it has also developed a methodology that can be applied to other corpora from different time periods and different language fields. In order to gain insight into the changing dynamics between fiction and society throughout literary history and across national literatures, the next step is to work more closely with sociologists. A first attempt to align research questions and methodologies from the cultural study of narrative fiction with the sociological study of people is presented in Volker and Smeets (2019). As the findings from *Character Constellations* invoke the fundamental question of what function fiction has with regard to societal issues such as (in)equality and emancipation, integration and segregation, and class struggle and social mobility, it stresses the need for a stronger synthesis between the study of fiction and the study of society.

6.2 PUBLIC DEBATES ON LITERARY REPRESENTATION

Character Constellations intervenes in recent public debates on the representation of social groups in (Dutch) literature by contesting three firmly ingrained ideas. First, it challenges the idea that characters should not or cannot be treated as if they were real people. In a response to two previous studies by myself and others in the spirit of this book,[9] critic and writer Kees 't Hart argued that this type of character-based scholarship wrongfully confuses fictional characters with real people (2019).[10] In his view, ascribing real-world demographic labels to characters does not do justice to the fact that they are rhetoric constructs.[11] While this book does not deny the text-like qualities of characters (in fact, its analyses are text-based), it does contend that their person-like qualities are crucial for a fuller understanding of literary representation. As Toril Moi recently argued, the taboo on treating characters as if they were real people is a result of 'the modernist-formalist assumption that [character criticism] always presupposes a naive realism' and 'rests on no sound philosophical grounds' (2020, pp. 61–62). To be clear, characters are obviously not real people, but there should be no taboo on acknowledging their resemblances to creatures of flesh and blood. Moving beyond this taboo, the analyses of characters presented in the previous chapters exemplify 'that literary forms always come embedded in world-building language that conveys specific meanings, themes, and subject matter' and 'that texts are never just forms but also expressions, actions, and interventions' (p. 67). Characters, in other words, are not only words on a page but also human-like. Focusing on both their textual and person-like qualities, the present book was able to make claims on how groups of actual people are represented by means of their fictional, textual analogues.

The second idea this book contests is closely related to the first. A central argument against character-based critiques of literary representation is that literature is immune to any ideologically oriented criticism as it functions within an autonomous sphere. As was shown in the introductory chapter, this argument has been used by writers Joost Zwagerman and Robert Vuijsje to defend their depictions of black women against ideological objections.[12] In 2014 critic Carel Peeters similarly alluded to the autonomy of literature in response to an essay by literary scholar Saskia Pieterse. She observed an absence in the Dutch literary field of multidimensional, dialogic novels that move beyond stereotypical representations of particular social groups (2014). In accusing her of political correctness, Peeters suggests (and deplores) that, in her view, 'Novels cannot be anything in and of itself'.[13] The idea that literature operates in an autonomous domain separated from political and social reality has a complex history with roots in eighteenth-century Romantic aesthetic ideals (Van Rooden, 2019). While *Character Constellations* does not dispute the idea that the organization of narrative elements in a literary text constitutes a world in its own right, it does stress the interconnections between textual form and extraliterary social context. More specifically, the book explored the fictional populations of characters (form) in terms of real-world social dynamics (extraliterary context). Extracting social networks from the novels in the corpus and analyzing the centrality, community, and conflict of characters in these networks, its methodological framework bears similarities to that of sociological research on social networks of actual people. By conducting what might be called a 'sociology of literary representation,'[14] the book has demonstrated that characters can function as mediators between text and world. As fictional, text-based analogues to human beings, characters are tied to the literary form in which they are embedded, but they are simultaneously vehicles for literary reflections, criticisms, or distortions of real-world social dynamics.

The third idea this book contests is that counting characters and measuring aspects of their social dynamics is reductionist. In response to an article in Dutch newspaper *Trouw* by Sander Becker (2018) on the type of research carried out in *Character Constellations*, writer Philip Huff asserted that 'a novel becomes flat when you use it for a tally sheet' (2018).[15] As it is one of the major arguments against data-driven, computational approaches to literature, Huff's point of criticism does not stand on its own. In a notorious article in the *L.A. Review of Books* in which algorithms are compared to fascism, writer Stephen Marche stated that literature cannot meaningfully be treated as data. The problem is essential rather than superficial: literature is not data. Literature is the opposite of data. (Marche, 2012)

More recently, literary scholar Nan Z. Da sparked a vivid debate on the online platform of journal *Critical Inquiry* with a polemical article titled 'The Computational Case against Computational Literary Criticism', in which she contends that data-driven approaches to literature suffer from 'a fundamental mismatch between the statistical tools that are used and the objects to which they are applied' (2019, p. 601). In a general sense, Huff's, Marche's, and Da's argument that quantifying literature does not do justice to its intricate complexity is true. The statistical trends of literary representation presented in this book rely on formalizations of the social dynamics of characters that are inherently reductive. There is obviously more to characters than their interactions on the sentence level; their meaning and function do not coincide with how often they occur with whom. Irony, ambiguity, symbolism, and other literary stylistics strategies could not be taken into account in this book's proposed statistics-based models of literary representation as they cannot be computed automatically in a reliable way and were not annotated in the data. This is, however, no reason to abandon quantification and data analysis for literary studies altogether. As Andrew Piper noted in the opening article of *Journal of Cultural Analytics*, a distinction should be made between the local and the global level:

> There is an aspect of reductiveness to all of this that is understandably hard for many to accept. For cultural critics, things are always more complex than they seem. That may in fact be one of the most elementary definitions of "culture" – a practice or artifact that conveys more than one meaning, that has at its base a commitment to something more than self-evidence. *But such reductiveness is the cost of scale and scale is the price of generalization. We cannot know something at the general level as complexly as we can at the local level.* There is an inverse relationship between the number of things considered and the complexity of what can be known about them. (2016; emphasis added)

By combining both macro analysis at the global level (statistical analysis on the corpus as a whole) and micro analysis at the local level (close readings of individual works in the corpus), *Character Constellations* has produced (inherently reductive) generalizations on the literary representation of social groups while simultaneously acknowledging the complexity of individual novels.

6.3 FUTURE RESEARCH

While this book's research corpus represents a large share of the literary fiction written in the Dutch language in sample year 2012 (36.9%), it has two main limits.

First, the corpus of all 170 submissions to the Libris prize 2012 is confined by genre. As this prize targets literary novels for adults (NUR-code 301), the findings of *Character Constellations* are not representative of narrative fiction as such but apply only to relatively highbrow books. Applying the book's models to children's literature, thrillers, fantasy, science fiction, regional novels, or other genres might result in different insights. It might very well be the case that the social dynamics between characters in one of these other genres are fundamentally different from those observed in the books of literary fiction within the Libris corpus. Some differences in social dynamics are possibly genre specific. Children's literature, for instance, expectedly features a higher number of younger characters, which probably would result in patterns of segregation or integration between age groups other than those observed for the Libris corpus. Fantasy or science fiction, to give another example, often portrays fundamentally *other* worlds, which not only problematizes the categorization of characters in actual demographic categories (what to do with wizards, elves, orcs, or dragons?) but would possibly also conform less to real-world social dynamics than the predominantly psychological-realist books in the Libris corpus. Comparative research into different book genres can shed light on the inter-genre variability of the representation of social groups. In a similar vein, comparative research into the representation of groups of people in films, television series, comics, or video games, can reveal inter-media variability of the fictional social dynamics studied in this book.

Second, *Character Constellations* is a synchronic study of one year of literary production taken to be representative of present-day Dutch literary fiction. Just as most natural, social, or cultural phenomena, literature changes over time. Diachronic, longitudinal research is warranted to gain insight into changes within the representation of social groups in books of literary fiction over the years. Insights in shifts within literary representation is then also a convenient point of departure for a study on how these literary representations conform to or deviate from changing dynamics in the society in which these books were written. A hypothesis worth testing is that demographic changes within actual populations affect the fictional populations in products of fiction. Waves of migration of people from a particular country might, for instance, result in more depictions of people with this specific migration background in literary fiction. An increase in the number of people with higher educational levels, for example, might result in a different status of the higher or the lower educated within fictional social networks. More generally, such diachronic research enables a broader understanding of the supposedly mimetic nature of literary fiction, as it might provide an empirically informed overview of how actual social dynamics are reflected in books written in different periods. The crowdsourced database 'de Personagebank' is a first attempt to diachronically track changes within literary representation.[16]

While *Character Constellations* responds to existing methodological problems prevalent in character-based critiques of literary representation, it invokes at least three new methodological issues. First, the book relies on a very specific hermeneutical strategy: every chapter first presents a macro analysis for the corpus as a whole and then transitions to micro analysis of individual works in light of the patterns that emerged from the macro analysis. By doing so, it introduced a statistical baseline, a norm, against which the peculiarity of individual novels was assessed. The use of a statistical baseline in character-based critiques of literary representation is, however, controversial. More specifically, it is up for debate how the relation between statistics-based analyses on the corpus as a whole (macro) and qualitative readings of individual novels (micro) should be understood. Whereas the present study starts and ends at the macro level, it would be valuable to explore what would happen if these steps were to be reversed. Alternatively, future research could start with qualitatively assessing the representation of social groups in an individual novel and formulating hypotheses based on this reading (micro), then test these hypotheses through data-driven, statistical analysis on a larger corpus (macro), and finally interpret the confirmation or refutation of these hypotheses in light of a qualitative re-reading of that particular individual novel (micro). Such a hermeneutical strategy, in which the individual novel has the first and the last word, probably calls for a rethinking of the notion of 'baseline' compared to the way in which it has been used in this book

Second, the statistical baselines generated in this book more generally invoke a discussion on the very notion of a baseline within critiques of literary and cultural representation. While it seems clear that the present book's introduction of statistical baselines to the field is unprecedented, this does not mean that close reading–based critiques of representation do not work with baselines in any sense whatsoever. A baseline is used to compare findings against a general norm in order to assess the extent to which they conform to or deviate from it. Close reading–based critiques of representation also tend to focus on certain norms or build on ideological or value-laden hypotheses that are explored and questioned in the course of an analysis. Unlike the present study, these are not based on statistical analysis but often implicitly coincide with terms such as archetype, stereotype, template, or 'cultuurtekst' (Meijer, 1996b) that are used to denote how recurring cultural representations of particular groups of people jointly establish a norm to which individual representations inevitably have to relate. For instance, the recurring cultural representation of the 'femme fatale' establishes a template, a 'cultuurtekst', that comes into play with every new representation of destructive or seductive female characters. In a sense, such archetypal images of types of people also function as a baseline that critics of representation can use to compare individual depictions. To what extent, for instance, does the character of Catherine Tramell (Sharon Stone) in Paul Verhoeven's film *Basic Instinct* (1992) conform to or deviate from the classic template of the femme fatale? Further research is warranted to pinpoint how these various definitions and uses of baselines within critiques of representation might be affected by statistical models such as those presented in the present study. Third and finally, the perspective of the reader is lacking from *Character Constellations*. Due to a methodological choice to narrow down the focus on the social dynamics between characters at the level of the text (what has been referred to as 'character constellations' throughout the book), it has not been taken into account how readers perceive the interactions of characters present in the texts.

Given the importance scholars such as Liesbeth Korthals-Altes (1992), Vincent Jouve (2001), and Sven Vitse (2014) ascribe to the reader in any study of ideology in literature, it is worthwhile to assess which images of social groups readers construct from the text-based character constellations observed in this book. Further research might incorporate surveys, in-depth interviews, or focus groups to study how readers view the centrality, communities, and conflicts of characters in individual sample texts. Combining this book's text-centric approach to the representation of social groups with reader-response criticism might enable a fuller understanding of how narrative fiction contributes to the representation of groups of people in present-day society.

APPENDIX A

STATISTICAL TESTS

Education * Gender Crosstabulation

			Gender		
			Male	*Female*	*Total*
Education	High	Count	618ₐ	278ᵦ	896
		Expected Count	536.2	359.8	896.0
		%Within Education	69.0%	31.0%	100%
		%Within Gender	48.5%	32.5%	42.1%
		% of Total	29.0%	13.1%	42.1%
		Standardised Residual	3.5	-4.3	
	Low	Count	217ₐ	152ₐ	369
		Expected Count	220.8	148.2	369.0
		%Within Education	58.8%	41.2%	100.0%
		%Within Gender	17.0%	17.8%	17.3%
		% of Total	10.2%	7.1%	17.3%
		Standardised Residual	-0.3	0.3	
	99	Count	439ₐ	425ᵦ	864
		Expected Count	517.0	347.0	864.0
		%Within Education	50.8%	49.2%	100.0%
		%Within Gender	34,.5%	49.7%	40.6%
		% of Total	20.6%	20.0%	40.6%
		Standardised Residual	-3.4	4.2	
Total		Count	1274	855	2129
		Expected Count	1274.0	855.0	2129.0
		%Within Education	59.8%	40.2%	100.0%
		%Within Gender	100.0%	100.0%	100.0%
		% of Total	59.8%	40.2%	100.0%

Each subscript letter denotes a subset of Gender categories whose column proportions do not differ significantly from each other at the 0.05 level.

Age * Gender Crosstabulation

			Gender		
			Male	Female	Total
Age	<25	Count	245$_a$	246$_b$	491
		Expected Count	293.7	197.3	491.0
		%Within Education	49.9%	50.1%	100.0%
		%Within Gender	19.2%	28.7%	23.1%
		% of Total	11.5%	11.5%	23.1%
		Standardised Residual	-2.8	3.5	
	26-35	Count	106$_a$	100$_b$	206
		Expected Count	123.2	82.8	206.0
		%Within Education	51.5%	48.5%	100.0%
		%Within Gender	8.3%	11.7%	9.7%
		% of Total	5.0%	4.7%	9.7%
		Standardised Residual	-1.6	1.9	
	36-45	Count	99$_a$	96$_b$	195
		Expected Count	116.6	78.4	195.0
		%Within Education	50.8%	49.2%	100.0%
		%Within Gender	7.8%	11.2%	9.2%
		% of Total	4.6%	4.5%	9.2%
		Standardised Residual	-1.6	2.0	
	46-55	Count	111$_a$	40$_b$	151
		Expected Count	90.3	60.7	151.0
		%Within Education	73.5%	26.5%	100.0%
		%Within Gender	8.7%	4.7%	7.1%
		% of Total	5.2%	1.9%	7.1%
		Standardised Residual	2.2	-2.7	
	56-64	Count	59$_a$	32$_a$	91
		Expected Count	54.4	36.6	91.0
		%Within Education	64.8%	35.2%	100.0%
		%Within Gender	4.6%	3.7%	4.3%
		% of Total	2.8%	1.5%	4.3%
		Standardised Residual	.6	-.8	

			Gender		
			Male	*Female*	*Total*
	65+	Count	123$_a$	86$_a$	209
		Expected Count	125.0	84.0	209.0
		%Within Education	58.9%	41.1%	100.0%
		%Within Gender	9.7%	10.0%	9.8%
		% of Total	5.8%	4.0%	9.8%
		Standardised Residual	-.2	.2	
	99	Count	531a	256$_b$	787
		Expected Count	470.7	316.3	787.0
		%Within Education	67.5%	32.5%	100.0%
		%Within Gender	41.7%	29.9%	36.9%
		% of Total	24.9%	120%	36.9%
		Standardised Residual	2.8	-3.4	
Total		Count	1274	856	2130
		Expected Count	1274.0	856.0	2130.0
		%Within Education	59.8%	40.2%	100.0%
		%Within Gender	100.0%	100.0%	100.0%
		% of Total	59.8%	40.2%	100.0%

Each subscript letter denotes a subset of Gender categories whose column proportions do not differ significantly from each other at the 0.05 level.

Education * Descent_country Crosstabulation

Education		Dutch	Belgian	European	Western	Middle Eastern	Other
High	% within Education	64.8%	7.3%	13.0%	3.8%	3.7%	7.4%
	% within Descent Country	45.3%$_a$	29.8%$_b$	46.6%$_{a,c}$	52.6%$_{a,c}$	29.0%$_b$	32.4%$_{a,c}$
	% of Total	27.2%	3.0%	5.5%	1.6%	1.6%	3.1%
	Standardized Residual	1.7	-2.6	1.0	1.2	-2.0	-2.0
Low	% within Education	45.2%	13.0%	11.8%	1.2%	7.6%	21.2%
	% within Descent Country	13.3%$_a$	22.5%$_b$	17.8%$_{a,b}$	7.0%$_{a,b}$	25.0%$_{b,c}$	39.1%$_c$
	% of Total	8.0%	2.3%	2.1%	0.2%	1.3%	3.7%
	Standardized Residual	-3.5	1.6	0.1	-1.9	1.8	6.8
99	% within Education	61.7%	12.1%	10.3%	3.0%	6.1%	6.8%
	% within Descent Country	41.5%$_a$	47.6%$_a$	35.6%$_{a,b}$	40.4%$_{a,b}$	46.0%$_a$	28.5%$_b$
	% of Total	24.9%	4.9%	4.2%	1.2%	2.5%	2.7%
	Standardized Residual	0.6	1.6	-1.1	0.0	0.9	-2.5
Total	% within Education	60.1%	10.2%	11.7%	3.0%	5.3%	9.6%
	% within Descent Country	100.0%	100.0%	100.0%	100.0%	100.0%	100.0%
	% of Total	60.1%	10.2%	11.7%	3.0%	5.3%	9.6%

APPENDIX B
DISTRIBUTION OF RELATIONAL ROLES

Type of relation	Frequency	% of total	% male-male of type	% male-female of type	% female-female of type	% of all relations in books by male	% of all relations in books by female
collega	2226	25.49	55.80	33.02	10.83	28.68	16.80
vriend	1446	16.56	42.67	32.64	24.00	15.78	19.19
geliefde	853	9.77	6.10	92.38	0.94	9.82	10.53
vijand	512	5.86	62.30	28.13	9.57	6.61	2.84
collega_vriend	346	3.96	50.87	13.01	36.13	3.27	5.71
collega_vijand	308	3.53	57.47	23.05	18.83	3.50	2.99
moeder	262	3.00	1.91	47.71	50.38	2.74	3.70
dochter	239	2.74	2.09	43.10	54.39	2.05	4.41
zus	235	2.69	1.70	44.68	53.62	2.06	4.29
zoon	230	2.63	44.35	54.78	0.43	2.83	2.35
vader	210	2.40	49.52	49.52	0.95	2.29	2.91
broer	190	2.18	47.89	50.00	1.58	2.24	2.13
collega_geliefde	114	1.31	2.63	85.96	11.40	1.35	1.05
neef	88	1.01	62.50	37.50	0.00	1.35	0.41
geliefde_vijand	86	0.98	1.16	96.51	0.00	1.05	0.86
oom	76	0.87	56.58	43.42	0.00	0.96	0.75
geliefde_vriend	71	0.81	19.72	66.20	14.08	0.91	0.71
vriend_collega	67	0.77	77.61	17.91	4.48	0.96	0.37

Type of relation	Frequency	% of total	% male-male of type	% male-female of type	% female-female of type	% of all relations in books by male	% of all relations in books by female
nicht	66	0.76	0.00	56.06	43.94	0.58	1.16
vriend_vijand	63	0.72	57.14	26.98	15.87	0.68	0.90
schoonbroer	62	0.71	56.45	41.94	1.61	0.56	1.05
schoonzus	56	0.64	1.79	50.00	48.21	0.49	1.05
tante	50	0.57	2.00	54.00	44.00	0.54	0.67
grootmoeder	48	0.55	0.00	50.00	50.00	0.49	0.75
kleinzoon	44	0.50	45.45	54.55	0.00	0.51	0.56
kleindochter	39	0.45	0.00	38.46	61.54	0.31	0.78
vriend_geliefde	38	0.44	10.53	84.21	5.26	0.49	0.30
schoonmoeder	36	0.41	2.78	55.56	41.67	0.35	0.56
schoonzoon	36	0.41	47.22	52.78	0.00	0.33	0.60
grootvader	35	0.40	57.14	42.86	0.00	0.33	0.60
schoondochter	30	0.34	0.00	50.00	50.00	0.31	0.45
schoonvader	30	0.34	50.00	50.00	0.00	0.31	0.45
vijand_vriend	25	0.29	36.00	0.00	64.00	0.19	0.52
collega_vijand_vriend	23	0.26	65.22	0.00	26.09	0.26	0.30
achternicht	19	0.22	0.00	21.05	78.95	0.12	0.41
pleegmoeder	16	0.18	0.00	75.00	25.00	0.23	0.07
pleegzoon	16	0.18	6.25	81.25	12.50	0.26	0.00
stiefvader	14	0.16	71.43	28.57	0.00	0.14	0.22
stiefzoon	12	0.14	91.67	8.33	0.00	0.14	0.15
vader_vijand	12	0.14	58.33	41.67	0.00	0.12	0.19
oudtante	11	0.13	0.00	45.45	54.55	0.05	0.30
collega_geliefde_vijand	11	0.13	0.00	100.00	0.00	0.07	0.26
geliefde_vijand_vriend	11	0.13	36.36	63.64	0.00	0.19	0.00

Appendix B: Distribution of Relational Roles 211

Type of relation	Frequency	% of total	% male-male of type	% male-female of type	% female-female of type	% of all relations in books by male	% of all relations in books by female
familie_ongedefinieerd	11	0.13	27.27	54.55	18.18	0.19	0.00
achterneef	10	0.11	60.00	40.00	0.00	0.02	0.34
broer_vijand	10	0.11	20.00	70.00	10.00	0.05	0.26
dochter_vijand	10	0.11	0.00	50.00	50.00	0.10	0.15
collega_geliefde_vriend	9	0.10	0.00	77.78	22.22	0.16	0.00
pleegbroer	7	0.08	28.57	71.43	0.00	0.00	0.15
overgrootmoeder	7	0.08	0.00	57.14	42.86	0.02	0.22
zus_vijand	7	0.08	0.00	42.86	57.14	0.05	0.07
moeder_vijand	7	0.08	0.00	14.29	85.71	0.07	0.11
achterachternicht	6	0.07	0.00	0.00	100.00	0.00	0.22
schoonbroer_vijand	6	0.07	66.67	33.33	0.00	0.10	0.00
stiefdochter	6	0.07	0.00	66.67	33.33	0.02	0.19
broer_collega	6	0.07	66.67	33.33	0.00	0.07	0.07
stiefdochter_vijand	6	0.07	0.00	16.67	83.33	0.02	0.19
stiefmoeder_vijand	6	0.07	0.00	16.67	83.33	0.00	0.22
collega_zus	6	0.07	0.00	66.67	33.33	0.10	0.00
oudoom	5	0.06	40.00	60.00	0.00	0.05	0.07
achterkleindochter	5	0.06	0.00	40.00	60.00	0.00	0.19
achterkleinzoon	5	0.06	20.00	80.00	0.00	0.02	0.15
schoonzus_vijand	5	0.06	0.00	40.00	60.00	0.07	0.04
collega_vriend_vijand	4	0.05	50.00	0.00	0.00	0.07	0.00
geliefde_schoonzus	4	0.05	0.00	100.00	0.00	0.02	0.11
geliefde_schoonbroer	4	0.05	0.00	75.00	25.00	0.02	0.11
collega_vriend_geliefde	4	0.05	50.00	50.00	0.00	0.07	0.00
schoonbroer_vriend	4	0.05	50.00	50.00	0.00	0.07	0.00

Type of relation	Frequency	% of total	% male-male of type	% male-female of type	% female-female of type	% of all relations in books by male	% of all relations in books by female
geliefde_stiefvader_vijand	4	0.05	0.00	100.00	0.00	0.07	0.00
vijand_zoon	4	0.05	100.00	0.00	0.00	0.03	0.07
collega_neef	4	0.05	100.00	0.00	0.00	0.07	0.00
geliefde_vriend_collega	4	0.05	0.00	100.00	0.00	0.07	0.00
overgrootvader	3	0.03	33.33	66.67	0.00	0.00	0.11
schoonzus_vriend	3	0.03	33.33	66.67	0.00	0.00	0.11
stiefmoeder	3	0.03	0.00	33.33	66.67	0.02	0.07
stiefvader_vijand	3	0.03	66.67	33.33	0.00	0.03	0.04
verre_familie_ongedefinieerd	3	0.03	66.67	33.33	0.00	0.02	0.07
geliefde_collega	3	0.03	0.00	100.00	0.00	0.03	0.04
vriend_schoonbroer	3	0.03	100.00	0.00	0.00	0.00	0.11
achterachterneef	3	0.03	0.00	100.00	0.00	0.03	0.04
pleegbroer_vijand	3	0.03	66.67	33.33	0.00	0.03	0.00
neef_collega	3	0.03	100.00	0.00	0.00	0.05	0.00
nepvader	2	0.02	100.00	0.00	0.00	0.03	0.00
nepzoon	2	0.02	100.00	0.00	0.00	0.03	0.00
tweelingzus	2	0.02	0.00	0.00	100.00	0.03	0.00
oudoudtante	2	0.02	0.00	0.00	100.00	0.00	0.07
schoonbroer_collega	2	0.02	100.00	0.00	0.00	0.03	0.00
neef_vriend	2	0.02	100.00	0.00	0.00	0.03	0.00
geliefde_vader_vijand	2	0.02	0.00	100.00	0.00	0.00	0.07
pleegoom	2	0.02	50.00	50.00	0.00	0.03	0.00
collega_schoonzus	2	0.02	0.00	100.00	0.00	0.03	0.00
collega_schoonbroer	2	0.02	0.00	100.00	0.00	0.03	0.00

Appendix B: Distribution of Relational Roles   213

Type of relation	Frequency	% of total	% male-male of type	% male-female of type	% female-female of type	% of all relations in books by male	% of all relations in books by female
geliefde_vriend_vijand	2	0.02	0.00	100.00	0.00	0.00	0.07
zoon_vijand	2	0.02	50.00	50.00	0.00	0.00	0.07
vriend_geliefde_vijand	2	0.02	0.00	100.00	0.00	0.00	0.07
pleegvader	2	0.02	50.00	50.00	0.00	0.03	0.00
geliefde_stiefdochter_vijand	2	0.02	0.00	100.00	0.00	0.03	0.00
oudoudoudtante	2	0.02	0.00	50.00	50.00	0.00	0.07
neef_geliefde	2	0.02	0.00	100.00	0.00	0.00	0.07
pleegzus	2	0.02	0.00	50.00	50.00	0.00	0.00
pleegvader_vijand	2	0.02	100.00	0.00	0.00	0.00	0.00
pleegzoon_geliefde	2	0.02	100.00	0.00	0.00	0.00	0.00
collega_zoon	2	0.02	50.00	50.00	0.00	0.03	0.00
collega_schoondochter	2	0.02	0.00	50.00	50.00	0.03	0.00
halfbroer_collega	2	0.02	100.00	0.00	0.00	0.03	0.00
achteroudtante	2	0.02	0.00	100.00	0.00	0.03	0.00
vijand_collega_geliefde	2	0.02	0.00	100.00	0.00	0.03	0.00
stiefbroer	2	0.02	100.00	0.00	0.00	0.03	0.00
schoonzus_vijand_vriend	2	0.02	0.00	0.00	100.00	0.00	0.07
knecht	2	0.02	100.00	0.00	0.00	0.00	0.07
vijand_collega	2	0.02	100.00	0.00	0.00	0.03	0.00
nicht_vriend	2	0.02	0.00	0.00	100.00	0.00	0.07
achtertante	2	0.02	0.00	0.00	100.00	0.00	0.07
nepschoondochter_geliefde	1	0.01	0.00	100.00	0.00	0.02	0.00
nepschoonvader_geliefde	1	0.01	0.00	100.00	0.00	0.02	0.00
oom_vijand	1	0.01	0.00	0.00	100.00	0.02	0.00

Type of relation	Frequency	% of total	% male-male of type	% male-female of type	% female-female of type	% of all relations in books by male	% of all relations in books by female
nicht_geliefde	1	0.01	0.00	0.00	100.00	0.02	0.00
halfzus_geliefde	1	0.01	0.00	100.00	0.00	0.02	0.00
geliefde_nicht	1	0.01	0.00	100.00	0.00	0.02	0.00
halfbroer_geliefde	1	0.01	0.00	100.00	0.00	0.02	0.00
geliefde_oom	1	0.01	0.00	100.00	0.00	0.02	0.00
pleegvader_geliefde	1	0.01	0.00	100.00	0.00	0.00	0.04
overovergrootmoeder	1	0.01	0.00	0.00	100.00	0.00	0.04
pleegdochter	1	0.01	0.00	0.00	100.00	0.00	0.04
pleegdochter_geliefde	1	0.01	0.00	100.00	0.00	0.00	0.04
achterachterkleindochter	1	0.01	0.00	0.00	100.00	0.00	0.04
nichtje	1	0.01	0.00	0.00	100.00	0.00	0.04
dochter_peetkind	1	0.01	0.00	100.00	0.00	0.02	0.00
vader_peetvader	1	0.01	0.00	100.00	0.00	0.02	0.00
nepdochter	1	0.01	0.00	100.00	0.00	0.02	0.00
geliefde_vijand_zus	1	0.01	0.00	100.00	0.00	0.02	0.00
geliefde_vijand_broer	1	0.01	0.00	100.00	0.00	0.02	0.00
oom_vader	1	0.01	0.00	100.00	0.00	0.02	0.00
broer_geliefde	1	0.01	0.00	100.00	0.00	0.02	0.00
nicht_dochter	1	0.01	0.00	100.00	0.00	0.02	0.00
geliefde_zus	1	0.01	0.00	100.00	0.00	0.02	0.00
pleegnicht	1	0.01	0.00	100.00	0.00	0.02	0.00
pleegneef	1	0.01	100.00	0.00	0.00	0.02	0.00
vijand_geliefde	1	0.01	0.00	100.00	0.00	0.02	0.00
dochter_geliefde	1	0.01	0.00	100.00	0.00	0.00	0.04
geliefde_vader	1	0.01	0.00	100.00	0.00	0.00	0.04

Appendix B: Distribution of Relational Roles 215

Type of relation	Frequency	% of total	% male-male of type	% male-female of type	% female-female of type	% of all relations in books by male	% of all relations in books by female
geliefde_collega_vijand	1	0.01	0.00	100.00	0.00	0.00	0.04
vriend_oom	1	0.01	0.00	100.00	0.00	0.00	0.04
geliefde_neef_vriend	1	0.01	0.00	100.00	0.00	0.00	0.04
vriend_tante	1	0.01	0.00	0.00	100.00	0.00	0.04
geliefde_nicht_vriend	1	0.01	0.00	100.00	0.00	0.00	0.04
vriend_nicht	1	0.01	0.00	0.00	100.00	0.00	0.04
stiefzoon_vijand	1	0.01	100.00	0.00	0.00	0.00	0.04
broer_vriend	1	0.01	0.00	100.00	0.00	0.00	0.04
sabine	1	0.01	0.00	100.00	0.00	0.00	0.04
vriend_zus	1	0.01	0.00	100.00	0.00	0.00	0.04
achterachterachternicht	1	0.01	0.00	0.00	100.00	0.00	0.04
dochter_zus	1	0.01	0.00	0.00	100.00	0.00	0.04
collega_oom_vijand	1	0.01	100.00	0.00	0.00	0.00	0.04
dochter_geliefde_vijand	1	0.01	0.00	100.00	0.00	0.00	0.04
collega_neef_vijand	1	0.01	100.00	0.00	0.00	0.00	0.04
dochter_kleindochter	1	0.01	0.00	100.00	0.00	0.00	0.04
moeder_zus	1	0.01	0.00	0.00	100.00	0.00	0.04
grootvader_vader	1	0.01	0.00	100.00	0.00	0.00	0.04
vried	1	0.01	0.00	100.00	0.00	0.02	0.00
pleegtante_vijand	1	0.01	0.00	100.00	0.00	0.02	0.00
pleegneef_vijand	1	0.01	0.00	100.00	0.00	0.02	0.00
achtertante	1	0.01	0.00	0.00	100.00	0.00	0.00
pleegzus_vijand	1	0.01	0.00	100.00	0.00	0.00	0.00
collega_nicht_geliefde	1	0.01	0.00	100.00	0.00	0.00	0.04
collega_neef_geliefde	1	0.01	0.00	100.00	0.00	0.00	0.04

Type of relation	Frequency	% of total	% male-male of type	% male-female of type	% female-female of type	% of all relations in books by male	% of all relations in books by female
collega_vader	1	0.01	100.00	0.00	0.00	0.02	0.00
collega_moeder	1	0.01	0.00	100.00	0.00	0.02	0.00
collega_schoonvader	1	0.01	0.00	100.00	0.00	0.02	0.00
collega_schoonmoeder	1	0.01	0.00	0.00	100.00	0.02	0.00
collega_vijand_geliefde	1	0.01	0.00	0.00	100.00	0.00	0.04
oom_stiefvader	1	0.01	100.00	0.00	0.00	0.02	0.00
neef_stiefzoon	1	0.01	100.00	0.00	0.00	0.02	0.00
collega_vader_vijand	1	0.01	100.00	0.00	0.00	0.02	0.00
collega_vijand_zoon	1	0.01	100.00	0.00	0.00	0.02	0.00
vijand_zus	1	0.01	0.00	100.00	0.00	0.02	0.00
collega_vader_vijand_vriend	1	0.01	0.00	100.00	0.00	0.02	0.00
collega_dochter_vijand_vriend	1	0.01	0.00	100.00	0.00	0.02	0.00
schoonbroer_geliefde	1	0.01	0.00	100.00	0.00	0.02	0.00
schoonzus_geliefde	1	0.01	0.00	100.00	0.00	0.02	0.00
collega_schoonzoon_vriend	1	0.01	100.00	0.00	0.00	0.00	0.04
collega_schoonvader_vriend	1	0.01	100.00	0.00	0.00	0.00	0.04
schoonmoeder_vijand	1	0.01	0.00	0.00	100.00	0.02	0.00
schoondochter_vijand	1	0.01	0.00	0.00	100.00	0.02	0.00
schoonvader_vijand	1	0.01	100.00	0.00	0.00	0.02	0.00
schoonzoon_vijand	1	0.01	100.00	0.00	0.00	0.02	0.00
tante_vijand	1	0.01	0.00	100.00	0.00	0.02	0.00
geliefde_stiefvader	1	0.01	0.00	100.00	0.00	0.00	0.04
geliefde_stiefdochter	1	0.01	0.00	100.00	0.00	0.00	0.04
oom_collega	1	0.01	100.00	0.00	0.00	0.02	0.00

Appendix B: Distribution of Relational Roles 217

Type of relation	Frequency	% of total	% male-male of type	% male-female of type	% female-female of type	% of all relations in books by male	% of all relations in books by female
schoonbroer_vriend_vijand	1	0.01	100.00	0.00	0.00	0.00	0.04
stiefmoeder_vriend	1	0.01	0.00	100.00	0.00	0.02	0.00
stiefzoon_vriend	1	0.01	0.00	100.00	0.00	0.02	0.00
mogelijke_vader	1	0.01	100.00	0.00	0.00	0.02	0.00
mogelijke_grootvader	1	0.01	0.00	100.00	0.00	0.02	0.00
mogelijke_zoon	1	0.01	100.00	0.00	0.00	0.02	0.00
mogelijke_kleindochter	1	0.01	0.00	100.00	0.00	0.02	0.00
collega_geliefde_vriend	1	0.01	0.00	100.00	0.00	0.02	0.00
collega_petekind	1	0.01	0.00	100.00	0.00	0.00	0.00
collega_peetoom	1	0.01	0.00	100.00	0.00	0.00	0.00
collega_vijand_zus	1	0.01	0.00	100.00	0.00	0.00	0.00
broer_collega_vijand	1	0.01	0.00	100.00	0.00	0.00	0.00
vriend_collega_vijand	1	0.01	100.00	0.00	0.00	0.02	0.00
stiefkleindochter	1	0.01	0.00	100.00	0.00	0.00	0.04
stiefgrootvader	1	0.01	0.00	100.00	0.00	0.00	0.04
dochter	1	0.01	0.00	0.00	100.00	0.02	0.00
schoontante	1	0.01	0.00	0.00	100.00	0.02	0.00
collega_vriend_nicht	1	0.01	0.00	0.00	100.00	0.02	0.00
schoonnicht	1	0.01	0.00	0.00	100.00	0.02	0.00
collega_vriend_tante	1	0.01	0.00	0.00	100.00	0.02	0.00
collega_stiefvader	1	0.01	100.00	0.00	0.00	0.02	0.00
vriend_vijand_collega	1	0.01	100.00	0.00	0.00	0.02	0.00
collega_stiefzoon	1	0.01	100.00	0.00	0.00	0.02	0.00
collega_pleegzoon	1	0.01	100.00	0.00	0.00	0.02	0.00
collega_pleegvader	1	0.01	100.00	0.00	0.00	0.02	0.00

APPENDIX C

MAIN AND INTERACTION EFFECTS

Main effect gender: $F(1,169) = 47.83$, $p < 0.000$, partial $\eta2 = 0.22$ Main effect community: $F(1,169) = 200.090$, $p < 0.000$, partial $\eta2 = 0.54$ Interaction effect gender * community: No statistically significant effect of gender on community was found, $F(1, 169) = 1.002$, $p = 0.318$, partial $\eta2 = 0.006$.

Main effect descent: $F(1.584, 267.706) = 71.884$, $p < 0.0001$, $\varepsilon =0.792$, partial $\eta2 = 0.298$
Main effect community: $F(1,169) = 214.067$, $p < 0.0001$, $\varepsilon =1.000$, partial $\eta2 = 0.559$
Interaction effect descent * community: A statistically significant effect of descent on community was found, $F(1.595, 269.625) = 3.521$, $p = 0.041$, $\varepsilon =0.798$, but with a very small effect size (partial $\eta2 = 0.020$).

Main effect education: $F(1.921, 324.605) = 48.621$, $p < 0.0001$, $\varepsilon = 0.971$, partial $\eta2 = 0.223$
Main effect community: $F(1,169) = 209.229$, $p < 0.0001$, $\varepsilon = 1.000$, partial $\eta2 = 0.553$
Interaction effect education * community: No statistically significant effect of education on community was found, $F(1.776, 300.196) = 2.036$, $p = 0.138$, $\varepsilon = 0.897$, partial $\eta2 = 0.012$

Main effect age: $F(1.898, 320.731) = 23.249$, $p < 0.000$, $\varepsilon =0.949$, partial $\eta2 = 0.121$
Main effect community: $F(1,169) = 214.067$, $p < 0.000$, $\varepsilon =1.000$, partial $\eta2 = 0.559$
Interaction effect age * community: A statistically significant effect of age on community was found $F(1.905, 321.989) = 4.156$, $p = 0.018$, $\varepsilon=0.953$, again with a small effect size (partial $\eta2 = 0.024$)

APPENDIX D

PEARSON CORRELATIONS

		Token Count	Number of Nodes	Number of Edges	Density	Triadic Closure	Clustering Coefficient
Token Count	Pearson Correlation	1	0.559*	0.524**	-0.104	-0.023	-0.116
	Significance (2-tailed)		0.000	0.000	0.179	0.762	0.132
	N		170	170	170	170	170
Number of Nodes	Pearson Correlation		1	0.862**	-0.352**	-0.185*	-0.299**
	Significance (2-tailed)	0.000		0.000	0.000	0.016	0.000
	N	170		170	170	170	170
Number of Edges	Pearson Correlation	0.524**	0.862**	1	0.004	0.066	-0.145
	Significance (2-tailed)	0.000	0.000		0.954	0.395	0.059
	N	170	170		170	170	170
Density	Pearson Correlation	-0.104	-0.352**	0.004	1	0.713**	0.478**
	Significance (2-tailed)	0.179	0.000	0.954		0.000	0.000
	N	170	170	170		170	170
Triadic Closure	Pearson Correlation	-0.023	-0.185*	0.066	0.713**	1	0.507**
	Significance (2-tailed)	0.762	0.016	0.395	0.000		0.000
	N	170	170	170	170		170
Clustering Coefficient	Pearson Correlation	-0,116	-0.299**	-0.145	0.478**	0.507**	1
	Significance (2-tailed)	0.132	0.000	0.059	0.000	0.000	
	N	170	170	170	170	170	

**. Correlation is significant at the 0.01 level (2-tailed).
*. Correlation is significant at the 0.05 level (2-tailed).

NOTES

Chapter 1: Introduction

1. Several theoretical considerations presented in this chapter were published earlier in Smeets (2019).
2. In his early work, Walter Benjamin used the term 'constellation' as a metaphor for how ideas denote the relations between objects (1928). Although my use of the term 'character constellation' also emphasizes relationality, it bears a stronger resemblance to Eder, Jannidis, and Schneider's (2010) use of the term as a relational structure in which characters are embedded in narratives. In their view, a character constellation is 'more than the mere sum of all the characters', and 'is determined by all relationships between the characters: relations of importance, correspondences and contrasts of properties and functions, interaction and communication, conflict and agreement, mutual seeing and listening to, wishes and desires, power and value systems, narration and being narrated, perspective and participation' (p. 26).
3. For the sake of convenience, the terms 'migrant' and 'nonmigrant' will be used to refer to characters who either have or do not have a migration background. These terms are used in a loose sense. In the present study, migrant characters can also refer to characters whose parents migrated to the Netherlands or Belgium, but who were themselves born in the Netherlands or Belgium. In this broad definition, migrant characters are considered to have some sort of bond with a sociocultural tradition that is not the same as their current country of residence. The Netherlands and Belgium were chosen as a point of departure as the books in the corpus are either written by Dutch or Flemish authors who arguably operate in a shared literary field of Dutch literature.
4. An attempt to gather longitudinal data is made by the crowdsourced Personagebank database (http://personagebank.nl/), where people are asked to provide demographic data on characters in Dutch literature published after 1945.
5. Two literary prizes, De Gouden Uil (2009) and De Inktaap (2010), were granted to Vuijsje. No prizes were granted to Zwagerman for *De buitenvrouw*, but the novel received some positive reviews (but also as negative ones, see Brouwers, 2001, p. 12, for an overview of the novel's reception).
6. 'Wat voelt zij, wat streeft zij na, wat wil zij van haar leven maken, heeft zij een doel? We weten wel hoe ze ruikt (naar notenolie en bedauwde bosgrond) maar niet wat ze denkt' (Ramdas, 1997).

7   'De Nederlandse literatuur heeft een traditie op dit punt. Het blijkt heel moeilijk het over zwarte vrouwen te hebben en daar niet meteen de seksualiteit aan te koppelen. De zwarte vrouw met haar dikke billen en haar grote borsten is een dankbaar object van fascinatie. Dat literaire beeld werkt door in het imago van deze groep in de samenleving.' (Wekker, qtd. in Meershoek, 2009)

8   This is a central argument against ideological interpretations of texts, which is most obviously showcased within the recent discussions on cultural appropriation in which defenders of the unlimited freedom of the author refer to artistic autonomy (Shriver, 2016).

9   This blueprint is, obviously, only based on a cursory examination of the novels and not on the output of data-driven models combined with in-depth narratological analysis as is the case for the analyses presented in the subsequent chapters.

10 'Lire, c'est non seulement suivre une information linéarisée, mais c'est également la hiérarchiser, c'est redistribuer des éléments disjoints et successifs sous forme d'échelles et de systèmes de valeurs à vocation unitaire et spécifique, c'est reconstruire du global à partir du local' (Hamon [1984], p. 54, cited in Jouve [2001], p. 10).

11 For information on the corpus and dataset see section 1.4.2 'Corpus and Data' of this chapter, and see chapter 2 for an extensive overview of descriptive statistics related to the metadata on the characters.

12 This awareness is often described by the term 'wokeness' (being aware of biases and inequalities in society), which is increasingly used in the Dutch public debate as well (Van der Sanden, 2019).

13 It also does not aspire to settle debates on the extent to which literary texts function within an autonomous domain isolated from or within society. See, e.g., *The Autonomy of Literature at the Fins de Siècles (1900 and 2000)* (2007) by Gillis Dorleijn, Ralf Grüttemeier, and Liesbeth Korthals Altes for debates on the autonomy of literature.

14 Volker and Smeets (2019) presented a first exploration into this structural comparison. See section 1.4.3 'Preliminary Research on Dataset' for more information on this study.

15 The dataset contains more features than these four. See section 1.4.2, 'Corpus and Data'.

16 Most recently, Amanda Anderson, Rita Felski, and Toril Moi provide arguments in *Character: Three Inquiries in Literary Studies* (2019) to '[clear] the ground for new attempts to understand characters and the claims they make on their readers' (p. 3). They do so by disentangling the taboo on treating characters as real people (Moi), the modes of identification with characters (Felski), and the roles of characters in understanding moral experiences (Anderson).

17 Eder et al. (2010) distinguish four approaches to character studies: hermeneutic, psychoanalytic, structuralist and semiotic, and cognitive. This book primarily uses a hermeneutic approach, in which characters are viewed 'dominantly as representations of human beings' and in which 'the specific historical and cultural background of the characters and their creators' is taken into account (Eder et al., 2010, p. 5).

18 Animals, nonexistent animate creatures, and inanimate objects tend to be more frequently staged in texts outside the novelistic genre (although they also appear in novels, e.g., in Franz Kafka's *Die Verwandlung* [1915]), such as in fairy tales in which existing animals (e.g., wolves), nonexistent creatures (e.g. dragons), and inanimate objects (e.g., pancakes) can be found. See Karsdorp et al. (2012) for an approach to defining and detecting characters based on their degree of animacy.

19 There are exceptions to this rule: e.g., Sevillano and Fiske (2016) make a case for considering animals as social groups within the field of social psychology.

20 Vincent Jouve (2001, pp. 107–108) distinguishes four ways through which characters, and the values associated with them, take shape in the narrative: 1) explicitly, 2) through characterization, 3) through narration and focalization, and 4) through *mise-en-texte* (see 2.1 for more information on Jouve's narratological model).

21 This is not to say that flat (stereotypical) characters are necessarily negatively connoted. Protagonists from comic series such as Tintin or Asterix and Obelix are rather flat characters, but one can argue that their lack of complexity – their openness – enables a variety of identification possibilities, like a blank canvas on which readers can project their own preoccupations.

22 https://www.merriam-webster.com/words-at-play/the-history-origin-of-stereotype, last accessed November 25, 2019.

23 In *Latino Images in Film: Stereotypes, Subversion, Resistance* (2002), Charles Ramírez Berg emphasizes how cultural stereotypes (in film) are 'a graphic manifestation of the psychosocial process of stereotyping in society in general' (p. 4). He does so by studying the concrete sociohistorical contexts from which stereotypical imagery emerge, and more specifically by examining the role of cultural infrastructure ('the deep structure of Hollywood cinema'). In his view, stereotypes are co-constituted by 'standardized cinematic techniques, the accepted norms of "good" filmmaking (including the star system, casting, screenwriting, camera angles, shot selection, direction, production design, editing, acting conventions, lighting, framing, makeup, costuming, and mise-en-scene)' (p. 5). In parallel, it can be argued that similar 'accepted norms' of 'good' literature in the literary infrastructure (editors, publishers, critics, creative writing programs) co-shape stereotypical imagery in literary fiction.

24 Andrew Piper provides an argument confirming this using a large corpus of nineteenth-century novels written in the English language. Ranking character by their mentions, he shows that the highest ranked characters occur far more often than the vast majority of lower ranked, minor characters (Piper, 2018, p. 120).

25 In political theory, representation is commonly used to refer to things such as 'representative government', denoting a political entity representing the interests of a group of people (e.g. Pitkin, 1967). This meaning differs from its use in cultural studies, which is followed in this book.

26 'Representation implies a mediating activity: there is always someone who shaped the text, the image, the thought' (Meijer, 1996, p. 7). In Dutch: 'Representatie impliceert een bemiddelende activiteit: er is altijd iemand die de tekst, het beeld, de gedachte heeft gevormd'.

27 In order to explain the different functions of representation in the process of meaning making, Stuart Hall proposes 'the circuit of culture' model in which the interrelations between representation, identity, production, consumption, and regulation are described (1997, p. 1). According to Hall, 'meaning arises in relation to all the different moments or practices in our "cultural circuit" – in the construction of identity and the marking of difference, in production and consumption, as well as in the regulation of social conduct' (ibid., p. 4).

28 From a social sciences perspective, Jorge Larrain traces the historical origins of the concept from the sixteenth century up until the present. Although Machiavelli did not use the term, Larrain states that he is arguably one of the first authors to discuss issues related to ideological matters (1979, p. 17).

29 See Sven Vitse (2014) for a more detailed discussion of the various ways in which the term 'ideology' is defined in Marxist literary criticism, as well as in poststructuralist theory from the 1960s onwards.

30   For an overview of gender and ethnicity critiques of representation focusing on characters specifically, see Gymnich (2010) for gender and Florack (2010) for ethnicity.
31   Jouve defines the method proposed in his book as a combination of reception (in terms of the implied reader) and semiotics, focusing on how values within the implied reader's social world relate to (hierarchies between) values manifested in the text: 'L'approche sémiologique, avant de s'interroger sur le lien (indiscutable) entre l'idéologie de l'oeuvre et le contexte social, s'interroge sur la façon dont le texte peut présenter, mettre en scène et hiérarchiser des valeurs' (2001, p. 7).
32   Her formalistic, almost mathematical, approach climaxes in chapter 4, on the feature of redundancy in this genre of ideological novels, in which she ascribes a distinct code to a wide range of narrative elements such as characters, context, events, narration, focalization, and temporal organization. (Suleman, 1983, pp. 149–97).
33   Which is not to say that Said has a monopoly on the term. In modern French philosophy, ideas on otherness have a complex history, and the term obviously plays a crucial role in the writings of, e.g., Lacan and Levinas (see *Le Même et l'autre: Quarante-cinq ans de philosophie française* (1979) by Vincent Descombes for an overview of this history).
34   Joseph Conrad's *Heart of Darkness* (1899/2010) is commonly regarded as the classic example of othering in literature. The novel has received a wide variety of (academic) critiques for its depiction of the colonizer-characters on the one hand, and the colonized-characters on the other and is often used to illustrate how cultural imperialism and orientalism found their way into the literature produced in this period. In *Culture and Imperialism* (1993), Said interprets this novel as a product of its time and place. As European imperialism was still vivid at the end of the nineteenth century, he sees this reflected in the representational strategies through which a Western perspective on the non-Western 'dark continent' of Africa emerges via, among others, the attitudes of Conrad's white, European characters toward 'the non-European' as alien, strange, and thus as Other (Said, 1993, p. 26). While this example shows how the Other can be defined in terms of descent, ethnicity, or race, othering in literature obviously also takes shape with regard to gender, class, sexuality, age, or any other identity category.
35   Dutch: 'Nederlandse literatuur tegendraads gelezen'.
36   Dutch: 'wat minder frisse geurtjes'.
37   Dutch: 'een geur van heiligheid'.
38   E.g., Meijer, 1996a, 2011; Minnaard, 2010; Pattynama, 1994, 1998; Sintobin, 2006. Maaike Meijer's handbook *In tekst gevat* (1996) is explicitly introduced as an attempt to popularize (feminist) critiques of representation in Dutch literary studies (p. 9). A more recent example is provided by the special issue *in Nederlandse letterkunde* on representations of masculinity in Dutch literature edited by Saskia Pieterse and Sven Vitse (2019).
39   'Het beeld van een kolossale verwarring in de argumentatie van een vrijwel unanieme bewondering is al duidelijk genoeg, en de noodzaak om zich van de uitzonderlijke kwaliteiten die dit werk blijkbaar bezit, met enige zorgvuldigheid rekenschap te geven, is hiermee naar ik aanneem voldoende aangetoond, n'en déplaise à du Perron.' (Sötemann, 1966, p. 5)
40   See also Felski's *The Limits of Critique* (2015) and the collection of essays *Critique and Postcritique* (2017) edited by Felski and Elizabeth S. Anker.
41   As the statistical analyses are based on methods used in the social sciences, the book's methodology can also be seen as an attempt to contextualize, rather than to isolate or decontextualize, the literary works in a real-world setting. However, the object of focus in

42 In the article 'A Genealogy of Distant Reading', Ted Underwood warns against a conflation of distant reading with digital humanities. In tracing back the roots of distant reading to the social sciences, he emphasizes that 'distant reading is not a new trend, defined by digital technology or by contemporary obsession with the word *data*' (2017, p. 5; emphasis in the original text). In his view, the defining feature of distant reading is not digital technology but 'experimental inquiry' (p. 6).

43 On a more general level, Rens Bod disentangles (2019) the complex cross-fertilizations between the various strands of the humanities and the social and natural sciences in *Een wereld vol patronen*.

44 Babbage's Analytical Engine was a 'programmable mechanical calculator with a planned memory of 1,000 numbers and 50 digits' (Vanhoutte, 2013, p. 121).

45 Nowadays, the database of the *Index Thomisticus* can be consulted through the following URL: http://www.corpusthomisticum.org/it/index.age (accessed December 12, 2019).

46 'The difference between computing *for* the humanities (instrumental) and computing *in* the humanities (methodological) is exactly the lack (in the former case) of the importance (in the latter case) of modelling as the most essential analytical method of the many forms of computing. Whereas the latter is the realm of Humanities Computing, both exist side by side in Digital Humanities' (Vanhoutte, 2013, p. 140).

47 As of 2019, the debate has still not lost any of its fierceness, which is exemplified by the wide range of responses to Nan Z. Da's article 'The Computational Case against Computational Literary Studies' in *Critical Inquiry* (2019). For the responses, see: https://critinq.wordpress.com/2019/04/12/more-responses-to-the-computational-case-against-computational-literary-studies/ (last accessed December 13, 2019).

48 This building-epistemology is exemplified by a controversial statement made by Stephen Ramsay in a 2011 MLA panel: 'If you aren't building, you are not engaged in the "methodologization" of the humanities, which, to me, is the hallmark of the discipline that was already decades old when I came to it' (Ramsey, 2011a). Similar arguments are found in Ramsay (2011b) and Ramsay & Rockwell (2012).

49 This article appeared in a special issue on Digital Humanities of *Tijdschrift voor Nederlandse Taal- en Letterkunde*. Six years later, the same journal published a special issue on digital humanities and theory, to which I contributed an article containing some of the points made in this section (Smeets, 2019).

50 'De redactie van Merlyn zal uitgaan van het principe dat het behandelde object het einddoel dient te zijn voor de beschouwer, niet het toevallige startpunt van weinig ter zake doende betogen. Wat ons interesseert is wat een schrijver zegt, niet wat hij zou kunnen zeggen, of had moeten zeggen, of eigenlijk bedoeld heeft maar niet zegt. *Deze gerichtheid brengt de eis van controleerbaarheid der uitspraken met zich* mee' (Fens, Jessurun d'Oliveira, & Oversteegen, 1962, p. 2; emphasis added). The English translation of the last sentence is: 'This leads to a criterion of replicability' (my translation).

51 'Hoe integer en zorgvuldig de analyticus ook te werk gaat, het is een gegeven dat een dergelijke 'introspectieve methode' geen betrouwbare basis vormt voor oordelen over hoe vaak iets voorkomt in een tekst, of hoe algemeen gedeeld (generaliseerbaar) een bepaalde interpretatie is.' (Fagel et al., 2012, pp. 180–181).

52 'Het louter zoeken naar patronen, verbanden, en zelfs wetten is uiteindelijk onbevredigend. Ik zou daarom willen voorstellen om niet te lang stil te blijven staan bij Geesteswetenschappen 2.0 maar onmiddellijk door te stomen naar Geesteswetenschappen 3.0 – niet omdat alle goede dingen gedrieën komen, maar omdat Geesteswetenschappen 3.0 de Geesteswetenschappen 1.0 en 2.0 verenigt: *zowel de technologie als de reflectie, en zowel de patronen als de interpretatie*.' (Bod, 2013, p. 19; my emphasis)

53 'Ik ben uiteraard niet van mening dat waardering en kwaliteit uitsluitend worden bepaald door de tekstlengte en de gemiddelde hoofdstuklengte. [...] Het project concentreert zich op de tekstuele kant, maar zal de culturele context uiteraard ook niet uit het oog verliezen.' (Van Dalen-Oskam, 2012, pp. 2021)

54 In a blog post on computational hermeneutics, Andrew Piper provides an example of such a model focused on the genre of the conversional novel: https://txtlab.org/2015/01/modelling-plot-on-the-conversional-novel/ (accessed December 16, 2019).

55 Jesse Rosenthal makes a similar point: 'Literary criticism is not subject to the same factual negations that scientific criticism is' because it is 'talking about something fundamentally different' (2017, p. 8). Instead of factual negation, he contends, humanities scholar search for 'an ongoing relation with the past' (ibid).

56 Manovich's *Cultural Analytics Lab* represents scholarship 'using data science methods to analyze contemporary global culture – while critically interrogating these methods from the perspectives of humanities and media theory'. (http://lab.culturalanalytics.info/p/about.html (accessed December 16, 2019). Andrew Piper's *Journal of Cultural Analytics* aims to 'promote high quality scholarship that applies computational and quantitative methods to the study of cultural artifacts (text, image, sound) at significantly larger scales than traditional methods' and encourages 'theoretical sophistication, computational expertise, and grounding in a particular field toward the crafting of novel, thought-provoking arguments' (https://culturalanalytics.org/about/about-ca/ (accessed December 16, 2019).

57 Examples include Underwood et al. (2018), who study transformations in characterization of female and male characters throughout modern literary history, and So et al. (2019), who study racial difference in US novel from 1880 to 2000.

58 Symptomatic reading is often associated with scholarly work such as Fredric Jameson's *The Political Unconscious* (1981) and *Reading Capital* (1997) by Louis Althusser, Étienne Balibar, Roger Establet, Jacques Rancière, and Pierre Macherey. The modes of reading practiced in these works is akin to the resistant reading that Rita Felski characterizes as 'hermeneutics of suspicion' (see section 1.2.2).

59 In *Enumerations* (2019), Piper observes that 'the literary critic has traditionally been a purveyor of rarity, watching over the singular achievements of singular individuals' and proposes to instead focus on 'the meaning of literary quantity' (p. 2). In light of Best and Marcus's account of surface reading, it is salient that he thinks that quantitative, data-driven analysis can uncover the 'deep story' of literature, by which he means 'all of the ways that cultural practices manifest themselves in repetitive, often predictable, and sometimes excessive ways' (p. 3). In Piper's view, repetitions are part of the deep level rather than the surface level of the text as 'they are often invisible, because so common' (p. 3).

60 The information in this section is based on the official website of the Libris Literatuurprijs: https://www.librisprijs.nl/over-de-libris-literatuur-prijs, accessed December 20, 2019.

61 For those genres, other prizes exist in the Dutch language area. An example: the Gouden Strop is a Dutch prize for 'spannende boeken' ('exciting/thrilling books'), which is open to novels

from the genre of the (literary) thriller. The Flemish equivalent of this prize is the Diamanten Kogel.
62   Many thanks to Erik Vos for providing me with up-to-date information.
63   However, the list of books submitted to the Libris prize is not a random sample in the sense that all 170 novels are to a greater or lesser extent expected to be high-quality literature (and thus potential prize winners).
64   See https://github.com/dbamman/book-nlp (accessed December 20, 2019).
65   Evaluating the results of the gender predictions by BookNLP, Kraicer and Piper (2019) report a 'sensitivity of 83.75% / 78.57% for women in the top two / twenty characters respectively and a rate of 96% / 96.9% for men, suggesting that women characters are potentially being undercounted in our data'.
66   The data collection started as part of a tutorial guided by Saskia Pieterse in the first year of my Research Master in Dutch literature at Utrecht University (2014–2016).
67   People contributing to this phase of the data collection were, in addition to myself, Lucas van der Deijl, Saskia Pieterse, Marion Prinse, Obe Alkema, Nadine van Maanen, Evely Reijnders, David van Oeveren, Maria Dijkgraaf, Bram Galenkamp, Carmen Verhoeven, and Jetske Steenstra. The data for 100 of the 170 books resulting from this phase were stored in the online, crowd-sourced database De Personagebank as a point of departure for future data collection by the crowd (personagebank.nl).
68   See section 3.4 of chapter 3 for how characters are defined in the present research.
69   I am grateful for the precise work carried out by Lisa Rooijackers and Maartje Weenink, who were students of the Research Master in Historical, Literary, and Cultural Studies at Radboud University in this period.
70   https://github.com/roelsmeets/character-networks, accessed December 20, 2019.
71   Digital versions of these texts were acquired either by asking publishers or authors for ePubs, .txt, or PDF-files of the novels, or by purchasing the ePubs.
72   See chapter 2 for an overview of (missing) metadata.
73   Broadly speaking, this criticism came down to the general objections against the intellectual tradition of critiques of representation (see section 1.2.2). In the sixth, concluding chapter of this book, I will contextualize my findings in light of the points of criticism raised by, among others, Arjan Peters (2018) and Kees 't Hart (2019).
74   A study on this dataset not related to the topic of this book is H. van Uden & M van der Meulen, '"Fucking hoer, gore kankerpatiënt": Cursing in Modern Dutch Literature', *T.W.I.S.T. Conference*, Leiden, April 12–13, 2019.

Chapter 2: Data

1   The dataset can be accessed through the book's open-access GitHub repository (https://github.com/roelsmeets/character-networks).
2   I will be using the term 'Dutch literature' to refer to literature written by both Dutch and Flemish authors, which is not to say that Dutch and Flemish literature are indistinguishable or that the socioeconomic backgrounds of the Dutch and Flemish authors are the same. However, the literary fields of the Netherlands and Flanders are interconnected to such an extent that they are often referred to as one literary field, which is also what I will be doing in this book.

3   The same definition for '(non-)Western' is used as was done in the previous phases of data collection (see section 1.4.3 of the introductory chapter for previous studies on the present dataset): 'According to the definition of the Centraal Bureau voor de Statistiek (CBS), except for the fact that we do include Indonesian and Japanese people in this group. The CBS defines non-Western as 'originating from any country in Africa, Asia, Latin-America and Turkey, except for Indonesia and Japan', because the social-economical position of Japanese and Indonesian minorities equals the (Western) majorities. As we are interested in cultural and geographical diversity rather than socioeconomic diversity only, we decided to exclude Japan and Indonesia from the West. See: http://www.cbs.nl/nl-NL/menu/methoden/begrippen/default.htm?ConceptID=1013' (Van der Deijl, Pieterse, Prinse & Smeets, 2016, p. 29).

4   These numbers are based on the places of residences of the authors at the time of the data collection (see section 1.4.2 of the introductory chapter for more information on the data collection).

5   Brussels, Antwerp, Ghent, Bruges, Liège, Louvain, or Namur.

6   Contemporary Dutch literary fiction is defined here as books in the genre literary fiction (NUR code 301) from the past 10 years. From this period, 2012 is chosen as a random year of literary production. The 170 novels in the corpus represent 37% of all originally published books of literary fiction in the Dutch language in this year (see section 1.4.2 of the introductory chapter for more information on the corpus selection).

7   Volker and Smeets (2019) contains an extensive elaboration on this assumption. In this article, part of the present dataset is compared to data on real world social networks in the Netherlands (see section 1.4.3 of the introductory chapter for previous studies on the present dataset).

8   Findings from preliminary research support this hypothesis (Van der Deijl et al., 2016).

9   This hypothesis is tested in Volker and Smeets (2019), in which part of the present Libris-dataset is compared to a real-world dataset of people living in the Netherlands (see section 1.4.3 of the introductory chapter for previous studies on the present dataset). No effect of author gender was found on the extent of segregation between social groups in the fictional networks.

10 The statistical Pearson's chi-squared test ($\chi 2$) can be applied to so called categorical data (data falling in one or more categories) in order to check if a difference between the occurrences of data in one of the categories can be ascribed to chance. A goodness of fit test is a particular form of a chi-squared test that checks if an observed frequency distribution differs from an expected distribution.

11 A statistical test of independence is a particular form of a chi-squared test that tests the extent to which two variables are independent of one another.

12 See paragraph 1.1.3 in the introductory chapter on the delineation of the present study and the choice for these four categories.

13 The earlier dataset contained 1,297 characters; the present dataset contains 2,137 characters (see section 1.4.2 of the introductory chapter for more information on the various phases of data collection).

14 In Appendix B, the family roles are broken down by subcategories, such as father, mother, son, daughter, brother, sister, et cetera. The total percentage of family roles (42.39%) is calculated by the sum of all these subcategories. Appendix B also features combined labels such as colleague_friend and lover_friend.

15 Bechdel first introduced this test in her comic strip series *Dykes to Watch Out For* (1983-2008).
16 In cooperation with Maartje Weenink, a case study on opposite-sex relations in the corpus was carried out and presented at Digital Humanities Budapest 2018 (Smeets & Weenink, 2018). In general, opposite-sex relations appeared to be relatively balanced, although male characters were observed to be slightly more often higher educated and older.
17 See section 1.1.2 of the introductory chapter on the delineation of the present study, and paragraphs 1.2 and 1.3 for the theoretical motivations behind this text-centric approach.

Chapter 3: Centrality

1 Parts of this chapter have been published earlier in Smeets, Sanders, & van den Bosch (2019).
2 Social network theory or network theory is an application of the mathematical discipline of graph theory, in which graphs are viewed as mathematical structures of related objects. The foundation of graph theory can be ascribed to Leonhard Euler, who in 1736 solved the mathematical problem of the Seven Bridges of Köningsberg by using a network approach. Psychologist Jacob L. Moreno was one the first to use visual abstractions to study human interactions (Moreno, 1934).
3 https://scholar.google.nl/citations?user=OlKVqZ8AAAAJ&hl=en&oi=sra, last accessed Marc 3, 2018.
4 This by now popularized term can be traced back to *Everything Is Different* (1929), a collection of short stories by Hungarian writer Frigyes Karinthy, in which he alluded to the increasing connectedness between people in the modern age.
5 In case a network contains a variety of disconnected components, a convenient approach is to only compute closeness centrality for the largest component of the network.
6 Unipartite networks exclusively consist of elements from the same category, e.g. people connected to people. Bipartite networks consist of elements from different categories, e.g. people connected organizations. The number of elements in multipartite networks can be extended endlessly in theory, but in practice it is usually restricted to three different categories (tripartite).
7 Nodes with a very high degree centrality are called 'hubs'.
8 All translations of Dutch quotes are my own.
9 This is also suggested by Barthes in *S/Z*: "Lorsque des semes identiques traversent à plusieurs reprises le même nom propre et semblent […] il naît un personnage' (1970, p. 74).
10 Coreference resolution is defined by the Stanford Natural Language Processing Group as 'the task of finding all expressions that refer to the same entity in a text': https://nlp.stanford.edu/projects/coref.shtm, last accessed July 10, 2018.
11 An alternative approach to character detection is automatically classifying animacy in in texts (Karsdorp et al., 2012).
12 Furthermore, there are entities in a text that fall outside the scope of this formal definition but nevertheless do play a central role in a narrative. A good example is 'the hidden force' in Louis Couperus' *De stille kracht* (1900). This force cannot be traced back to a character, it is never present in the story but slumbers in the margins of the text. But this force is arguably one of the most governing and central entities in the novel. For a network approach, hidden forces as these cannot be taken into account, as one cannot measure what is not there.

13 Named Entity Recognition (NER) is a technique that recognizes names in texts, the most important categories being Persons, Places, and Organizations. There are several NER tools available but not all are suitable for the same task. NER tools have to be trained for specific languages, and their accuracy depends on the nature of the training data (e.g., a tool trained on newspaper articles performs badly on literary fiction). For the current research the Namescaptagger is used, which is trained on Dutch literary fiction and which is demonstrated to be the most accurate for the present purposes, although it is still not perfect as a F1-score of 0.72 was reported (Smeets, 2017).

14 All software and data are accessible through the following open access GitHub repository: https://github.com/roelsmeets/character-networks. This repository does not contain the corpora because of copyright limitations.

15 A similar approach is used by Grayson et al. (2016, p. 4), who replace character aliases with a character's name.

16 https://github.com/proycon/python-ucto, last accessed July 3, 2018.

17 As the plain texts of the novels in the corpus are unstructured, I could not rule out the possibility that characters co-occur in two sentence windows that transcend the boundaries of a paragraph or chapter. I am aware that this creates noise, as in those cases it could be argued that there is no meaningful interaction between characters.

18 I am grateful for the extensive and precise work which Research Master students Lisa Rooijackers and Maartje Weenink carried out in the period of 2017–2018. See the introductory chapter, section 1.4.2 'Corpus and Data' for more information on the different phases of data collection.

19 In some cases, two characters have a relational label such as family assigned to them while the weight of their relation is 0. This is possible as characters do not have to be adjacent in the text to have a family tie, just as people in real world networks can be family without being in each other's physical presence or without talking about them.

20 Many thanks to Research Master student Maartje Weenink for her precise annotations.

21 Exploratory experiments were conducted with different window units and sizes. As expected, it was reported that larger windows lead to more character interaction and thus higher weights between characters.

22 https://github.com/proycon/python-ucto, last accessed July 7, 2018.

23 https://networkx.github.io/, last accessed May 7, 2018.

24 In statistics, 'regression analysis' refers to models for computing the relation between predictor variables (independent variables) and outcome variables (dependent variables). A question suited for regression analysis is, for instance: does the sex of students predict the height of their exam results? The results of a regression analysis could demonstrate that gender does predict exam results, and that, more precisely, female students tend to score 0.8 higher.

25 Referring to characters who either have or do not have a migration background, the terms 'migrant' and 'nonmigrant' are used in a loose sense. In the present study, migrant characters can also refer to characters whose parents migrated to the Netherlands or Belgium, but who were themselves born in the Netherlands or Belgium. In this broad definition, migrant characters are considered to have some sort of bond with a sociocultural tradition that is not the same as their current country of residence. The Netherlands and Belgium were chosen as a point of departure as the books in the corpus are either written by Dutch or Flemish authors who arguably operate in a shared literary field of Dutch literature

26   In chapter 2, 'Data', chi-squared tests were conducted comparing the occurrence of characters with a certain demographic profile with hypothesized occurrences. In that chapter, a chi-squared goodness of fit test was calculated comparing the occurrence of male and female characters with the hypothesized occurrence of a 50–50 gender distribution. Significant deviation from the hypothesized values was found ($\chi2$ (1) = 82.030, $p < 0.001$). In the present chapter, descent of characters have been redefined as migrants and non-migrants (see footnote) above). A chi-squared goodness of fit test was calculated comparing the occurrence of characters with a Dutch/Belgian and other country of descent with the hypothesized occurrence of an equal distribution among those categories. Significant deviation from the hypothesized values was found ($\chi2$ (1) = 1350.773, $p < 0.001$). This means that the 40–60 gender divide and the 89.8–10.2 divide in descent are not due to chance, but is a statistically significant difference.

27   All translations from the novel are my own.

Chapter 4: Community

1   Aristotle writes in his *Nicomachean Ethics* that people 'love those who are like themselves'; Plato writes in his *Phaedrus* that 'similarity begets friendship' (cited in McPherson, Smith-Lovin, & Cook, 2001).
2   See chapter 1 'introduction', paragraph 1.4.3 for all previous studies on the dataset and corpus.
3   Building on Lacan's 'repudiation of the various ideals of unification of the personality or the mythic conquest of personal identity', Jameson sees problems for 'any narrative analysis which still works with naive, common-sense categories of "character", "protagonist", or "hero"' (Jameson, 1981, p. 139).
4   Scholars such as Joep Leerssen have studied the ways in which literature played a part in the formation of national communities during the emergence of the nation state in the nineteenth century (e.g., Leerssen, 2012). This does, however, not mean that only literary narratives of community contributed to the formation of national communities, as literary texts centering on the self might also have played a part in this.
5   Amongst many other examples, Zagarell uses Jewett's *The Country of the Pointed Firs* (1896) as a nineteenth-century example and Toni Morrison's *Song of Solomon* (1977) as a twentieth-century example. As Zagarell wrote the article in 1988, she obviously could not provide present-day examples. Zadie Smith's *White Teeth* (2000) is arguably a striking twenty-first-century example.
6   All translations from Dutch in this chapter are my own.
7   See chapter 1 'introduction', section 1.2.1.
8   Translated into English in *The Dialogic Imagination* (1935/2003b).
9   Parallel to Bakhtin's distinction between the monologic and the dialogic novel is the broader, historical distinction made by Julia Kristeva between the pre-novelistic and novelistic text. Kristeva distinguishes between the closed systems of earlier literary texts (epics, myths, fairy tales), texts of the symbol, and the heterogeneous, open-ended texts from the modern novelistic genre as emerging from the fifteenth century onwards, texts of the sign (Kristeva, 1970/1986, pp. 62–73). Whereas Bakhtin uses the term 'polyphony' to characterize the multiplicity and heterogeneity of voices in the dialogic novel, Kristeva uses the term 'ideologeme' to more broadly 'emphasize the fact that all forms of discourse are constructed by the social space in which they are enunciated' (Moi, 1986, p. 62). According to Kristeva, the

novelistic genre 'does not refer to a single unique reality, but evokes a collection of associated images and ideas' (Kristeva, 1970/1986, p. 72). While Bakhtin explicitly ascribes the notion of dialogism to particularly Dostoevskian novels, Kristeva sees the novelistic text in general as inherently dialogic as 'its meaning is the result of an interaction with other signs' (ibid).

10   The term 'social speech type' bears similarity to the term 'sociolect', which is defined by Greimas and Courtés as 'semiotic acts in relation to the social status' and as 'forming the foundation for social discourses' (1979/1987, p. 389)

11   The documentation of this algorithm can be found here: https://networkx.github.io/documentation/stable/reference/algorithms/generated/networkx.algorithms.community.kernighan_lin.kernighan_lin_bisection.html#networkx.algorithms.community.kernighan_lin.kernighan_lin_bisection, last accessed February 14,2020.

12   The software used for this analysis can be found in my open access GitHub repository: https://github.com/roelsmeets/character-networks/blob/master/communities_frequency_distributions.csv. The function detect_communities() in the file characternetworks.py is used to compute these distributions. The output is stored in the file communities_frequency_distributions.csv.

13   'ANOVA' stands for analysis of variance. The *repeated measures* ANOVA is used because the variance has to be tested on different levels: the levels for gender, for instance, are male, female, and gender unknown.

14   As the number of characters with gender unknown in the corpus is negligible (0.09%), only the difference scores for male and female characters were taken into account.

15   Three levels were taken into account: the difference scores for 1) higher educated characters, 2) lower educated characters, 3) characters with unknown education. Mauchly's Test of Sphericity indicated that the assumption of sphericity had been violated, $\chi 2(2) = 22.612$, $p < 0.0001$, and therefore, a Greenhouse-Geisser correction was used.

16   Three levels were taken into account: the difference scores for 1) nonmigrant characters (i.e., Dutch and Belgian characters), 2) migrant characters (i.e., all the characters with a non-Dutch or non-Belgian descent), and 3) characters with descent unknown. Mauchly's Test of Sphericity indicated that the assumption of sphericity had been violated, $\chi 2(2) = 49.137$, $p < 0.0001$, and therefore, a Greenhouse-Geisser correction was used.

17   Three levels were taken into account: the difference scores for 1) younger characters (i.e., characters below the age of 45), 2) older characters (i.e., characters above the age of 45), and 3) characters with age unknown. Mauchly's Test of Sphericity indicated that the assumption of sphericity had been violated, $\chi 2(2) = 8.569$, $p = 0.014$, and therefore, a Greenhouse-Geisser correction was used.

18   Dutch: 'Jongens waren we, maar aardige jongens'.

19   The term 'critical mimesis' is most often used in performance studies to denote processes of (artistic) imitation that call into question a phenomenon by imitating it in a specific way (e.g., Hughes, 2009) and also bears resemblance to Luce Irigaray's use of critical mimesis as a form of 'strategic essentialism' (1985).

20   For the documentation on the algorithm, see: https://networkx.github.io/documentation/stable/reference/algorithms/generated/networkx.algorithms.assortativity.attribute_assortativity_coefficient.html#networkx.algorithms.assortativity.attribute_assortativity_coefficient, last accessed September 16, 2019.

21   As described in chapter 2, 'Data', the dataset contains a relatively large portion of missing values, especially for education (40%) and age (37%). The percentage of missing values for

country of descent is far lower (12%), and for gender there are almost no missing values (0.09%). Other than in typical social sciences research, these missing values were not excluded from the analysis, as missing values are regarded in this dissertation as a meaningful marker of identity. For instance, it is insightful that education is significantly more often unknown for male than for female characters (see chapter 2, section 2.3, Figure 2). For that same reason, it is insightful to take into account characters for which e.g. education is unknown in the computation of the assortativity coefficient. As a result of this choice, a high assortativity coefficient for e.g. education in a network is also indicative of the extent to which characters with unknown education are connected.

[22] As in the analyses carried out in the previous chapter on centrality, descent has been redefined in a binary way in the present chapter (see chapter 2 for the original categorization of descent). Referring to characters who either have or do not have a migration background, the terms 'migrant' and 'nonmigrant' are used in a loose sense. In the present analysis, migrant characters can also refer to characters who are born in the Netherlands or Belgium but whose parents migrated to the Netherlands or Belgium. In this broad definition, migrant characters are considered to have some sort of bond with a sociocultural tradition that is not the same as their current country of residence. The Netherlands and Belgium were chosen as a point of departure as the books in the corpus are either written by Dutch or Flemish authors who operate in a shared literary field of Dutch literature.

[23] Permutation, or randomization, tests are defined by Ge, Yeo, and Winkler (2018) as a 'class of statistical tests that, under minimal assumptions, can provide exact control of false positives (i.e., type I error). The central assumption is simply that of exchangeability, that is, swapping data points keeps the data just as likely as the original' (https://www.ohbmbrainmappingblog.com/ blog/a-brief-overview-of-permutation-testing-with-examples, last accessed January 1, 2020).

[24] The software for this test can be found in the file permutation_test.py in the open-access GitHub repository (https://github.com/roelsmeets/character-networks), the output of the 1,000 permutations are stored in the folder 'permutations'.

[25] A one sample t-test is a statistical test to measure whether a mean of a variable in a sample (in this case: the mean assortativity coefficient for gender, descent, education, and age of the books in the corpus) statistically differs from another mean (in this case: the mean assortativity coefficient for gender, descent, education, and age of the 1,000 permutations).

[26] The permutation test has, furthermore, shown that this points at a relatively high amount age homophily, or segregation by age, as there is a significant difference between the actual mean age assortativity of -0.07 and the permutations' mean age assortativity of -0.15, i.e., what one would expect by chance (see section 4.5.1).

Chapter 5: Conflict

[1] Besides interpersonal and intergroup conflict, we distinguish *intra*personal conflict taking place within the psyche of a single character. A more extensive typology of conflict in narrative fiction is introduced in the section 5.3.

[2] See chapter 3 for more information on the databases.

[3] The software and data used in this section can be found in the following open access GitHub repository (see the file conflict.py for the Python code, and the file character-rankings_

4   conflictscore.csv for the output of the code): https://github.com/roelsmeets/character-networks.

4   The conflict score of a character was not normalized by dividing the resulting number through the number of enemies a character has, as this would level out relevant differences in conflict scores between characters with varying numbers of enemies. E.g., a character that has ten enemies and is higher ranked than eight of them, should have a higher conflict score than a character that has only one enemy to which he is higher ranked. When these scores are normalized, both of these characters would have a conflict score of 1, which does not do justice to the fact that one character is more often higher ranked than the other one.

5   Unless otherwise specified, all translations from Dutch to English are the author's own.

6   'Relations between two people have strictly specific characteristics – this is not only demonstrated by the fact that the relation changes fundamentally when a third one comes in, but even more by the following frequently stated fact: if the network is extended to four or more people, this will by no means change the essence of the network any further.' (Simmel, 1976, p. 92)

7   The software and data used in this section can be found in the following open access GitHub repository (see the file named 'conflict.py'): https://github.com/ roelsmeets/character-networks.

8   As mentioned before, characters can have multiple types of relations with the same character, e.g. colleague_friend. The analysis exclusively focused on the categories of friend and enemy, and ignored the other categories in case of double, triple, or more relational annotations.

9   Volker and Smeets (2019) compare the networks of people living in the Netherlands with the networks of characters in the Libris corpus. The research does not focus on social balance theory, but the dataset of actual personal networks does seem to conform to an overrepresentation of social balance as opposed to social imbalance. In this dataset (SSND) on personal networks of people in the Netherlands, networks were, however, delineated according to name generators that are likely to tap into structurally balanced network ties, such as the question 'with whom do you talk about important personal matters?'

10   In Dutch: 'kazerne'.

11   In a review in *De Reactor*, Jan-Willem Anker underscores this: 'In this black-and-white world it is necessary to keep the losers under control and to eliminate them. It should not be a surprise by now, but the Muslims and Arabs in *VSV* are evil without any exceptions.' (2012; my translation.)

12   Of the five Moroccan characters in the novel, this scheme does not apply to Kichie, who is the only nonextremist in the group. In a sense, Kichie can in a sense better be classified as belonging to the group of non-Moroccans, as he, together with Kohn, is commissioned by the Dutch government to take down the terrorist attack caused by Sallie, Frits, Karel, and others.

Chapter 6: Conclusion

1   See section 1.2 of the introductory chapter for how this book is situated within this academic tradition.

2   See section 1.2.1 of the introductory chapter for perspectives on the mediatedness of representation.

3   While it responds to these existing methodological issues, the book has also invoked new methodological issues, which are discussed in section 6.3 of this chapter.
4   'Instead of measuring things, finding patterns, and then finally asking what they mean, we need to start with an interpretive hypothesis (a "meaning" to investigate) and invent a way to test it' (Underwood, 2019, p. 17). See section 1.3.2 in the introductory chapter for a discussion on modeling within cultural analytics.
5   See section 1.4.2 of the introductory chapter for more information on the corpus and the dataset.
6   Although the dimension of the author has not systematically been taken into account in this book, this finding invokes the question whether or not this is a result of a specific group of authors – female or with a migration background who thematize the female gender and/or a migration background. However a comparative analysis of the present dataset with real personal networks of the Dutch population suggests that at least author gender has *no* effect on the structure of fictional networks (Volker & Smeets, 2019). See section 1.4.3 of the introductory chapter for more information previous research on the present corpus and dataset.
7   For the emancipation of women, this has most recently been exemplified by, for instance, the #MeToo discussions from 2017 onward, which raised awareness of the subordination and biases women are facing today. For the emancipation of migrants, this is highlighted by, for instance, recent anti-immigration sentiments voiced by extreme right-wing parties all over Europe.
8   See section 1.4.3 of the introductory chapter for more information on previous studies on the corpus and dataset.
9   The first article is one of the previous studies on a part of the present dataset (see section 1.4.3 of the introductory chapter for more information on previous studies on the corpus and dataset): 'Mapping the Demographic Landscape of Characters in Recent Dutch Prose: A Quantitative Approach to Literary Representation' by Lucas van der Deijl, Saskia Pieterse, Marion Prinse, and me, published in *Journal of Dutch Literature* (2016). The second article is 'Tussen close en distant. Personage-hiërarchieën in Peter Buwalda's *Bonita Avenue*' by Lucas van der Deijl and me, published in *Tijdschrift voor Nederlandse Taal- en Letterkunde* (2018).
10 'Classifying human characters based on social features? Isn't that a little bit weird, didn't they do that back in the days as well, during the war, I guess, I read something about that. Excuse me, I'm just saying. Or are they real? But they are not real, right? You know. Or am I wrong? And what exactly are we going to do with this information, sorry, data? (Translated from Dutch). Original quote: 'Mensfiguren indelen naar eigenschappen? Is dat niet een heel klein beetje raar, deden ze dat vroeger ook niet, in de oorlog, of zo, daar las ik iets over. Sorry, ik zeg maar wat. Of zijn ze echt? Maar ze zijn toch niet echt? Weet je wel. Of niet dan? En wat gaan we met deze gegevens, sorry data, precies doen?' ('t Hart, 2019).
11 'Characters function in novels as rhetoric constructs, not as substitutes of reality. They are vehicles of opinions, they inhabit contrasts, interrelations, oppositions, misunderstandings, contradictions, they are the accomplices of writers, messengers, they are symbols of writers' illusions. [...] They are elements in a rhetoric system called literature, they constitute its matter' (Translated from Dutch). Original quote: 'Personages functioneren in romans als retorische constructies, niet als werkelijkheidsvervangers. Het zijn vervoermiddelen van opinies, ze leven van contrasten, onderlinge verhoudingen, tegenstellingen, misverstanden, tegenspraken, ze zijn handlangers van schrijvers, boodschappenjongens, ze zijn symbolen van

de illusies van schrijvers. [...] Het zijn zetstukken in een retorisch systeem dat literatuur heet, ze vormen de materie ervan' ('t Hart, 2019)

12 See section 1.1.2 of the introductory chapter for more information on this debate.

13 Dat is wat Saskia Pieterse doet: de literatuur met shaky politieke argumenten duidelijk maken dat ze zich meer met allochtonen en emigranten bezig moet houden. Romans mogen niet iets op zichzelf zijn. Pieterse noemt het 'monologen', 'zuivere fictie'. Het moeten 'dialogische teksten' worden waarin rekening wordt gehouden met de politieke gezindheid van die geëmancipeerde lezer. Maar welke politieke gezindheid van welke lezer dan? Van de politiek correcte lezer? Of ook van een politiek incorrecte, rechtse lezer?' (Peeters, 2014)

14 This term was used by Saskia Pieterse to characterize the type of research we published in *Journal of Dutch Literature* (2016). Also see Lucas van der Deijl's research master's thesis 'Towards a Sociology of Imagination' (2016), in which he presented the crowdsourced database De Personagebank (personagebank.nl).

15 'Wat ik wel weet: een roman wordt plat als je hem voor een turftabel gebruikt; hij dient bovendien met openheid en aandacht te worden gelezen' (Huff, 2018). In the same piece, Huff also responds to a wrongfully paraphrased quote by me on the characterization of female characters in his novel *Niemand in de stad* (2012), which is part of this book's research corpus. See chapter 4 for an in-depth close reading of this novel in light of the observed statistical patterns of segregation in the corpus as a whole.

16 Developed by Lucas van der Deijl, De Personagebank (personagebank.nl) aims to collect demographic information on characters in books of fiction written in the Dutch language from 1945 onwards. As of February 24, 2020, the database contains information on 1,392 characters in 304 books. Part of the present dataset is stored in this database (see section 1.4.2 of the introductory chapter for more information on the different phases of data collection).

REFERENCES

Aalten, T. van. (2009). Weten we nog wel wat een roman is? Retrieved from Sargasso.nl website: https://sargasso.nl/ weten-we-nog-wel-wat-een-roman-is/.

Akyol, Ö. (2012). *Eus*. Amsterdam: Promentheus.

Alberich, R., Miro-Julia, J., & Rossello, F. (2002). Marvel Universe looks almost like a real social network. *Elsevier Preprint*. Retrieved from http://arxiv.org/abs/cond-mat/0202174.

Almack, J. C. (1922). The influence of intelligence on the selection of associates. *School and Society, 16*, 529–530.

Althusser, L. (1969). Marxism and humanism. In *For Marx*. New York: Pantheon Books.

Althusser, L. (1971). Ideology and ideological state apparatuses. In *Lenin and philosophy and other essays*. New York: Monthly Review Press.

Althusser, L., & Balibar, E. (1997). *Reading capital*. New York: Verso.

Anderson, A., Felski, R., & Mori, T. (2020). *Character: Three inquiries in literary studies*. Chicago: University of Chicago Press.

Anker, J.W. (2012, August). Een boek om gisteren al vergeten te zijn. *De Reactor*. Retrieved from http://www.dereactor.org/ home/detail/een_boek_om_gisteren_al_vergeten_te_zijn/.

Anker, A. S., & Felski, R. (2017). *Critique and postcritique*. Durham: Duke University Press.

Aristotle. (1999). *Metaphysics* (J. Sachs, Trans.). Santa Fe: Green Lion Press. (Original work published 350 BC).

Aristotle. (2013). *Poetics*. Oxford: Oxford University Press. (Original work published 335 BC).

Auerbach, E. (2003). *Mimesis: The representation of reality in Western literature*. Princeton: Princeton University Press. (Original work published 1946).

Bakhtin, M. (2003a). Problems of Dostoevsky's poetics. In Pam Morris (Ed.), *The Bakhtin reader: Selected writings of Bakhtin, Medvedev, Voloshinov*. London: Hodder Arnold Publication. (Original work published 1929).

Bakhtin, M. (2003b). The dialogic imagination. In Pam Morris (Ed.), *The Bakhtin reader: Selected writings of Bakhtin, Medvedev, Voloshinov*. London: Hodder Arnold Publication. (Original work published 1935).

Bal, M. (1977). *Narratologie: Essais sur la signification narrative dans quatre romans modernes*. Paris: Klincksieck.

Bal, M. (2009). *Narratology: Introduction to the theory of narrative* (3rd ed.). Toronto: University of Toronto Press.

Bamman, D., Underwood, T., & Smith, N. A. (2014). A bayesian mixed effects model of literary character. *Proceedings of the 52nd Annual Meeting of the Association for Computational Linguistics*, 370–379.

Barrat, A., Barthélemy, M., Pastor-Satorras, R., & Vespignani, A. (2004). The architecture of complex weighted networks. *Proceedings of the National Academy of Sciences*, *101*(11), 3747–3752. https://doi.org/10.1073/PNAS.0400087101.

Barrera, F., & Ibáñez, A. M. (2004). Does violence reduce investment in education?: A theoretical and empirical approach. *Universidad de Los Andes, Documentos CEDE 002382*.

Barthes, R. (1970). *S/Z. Essai. Collection "Tel Quel."* Paris: Seuil.

Barthes, R. (2006). The structuralist activity. In J. Culler (Ed.), *Structuralism. Critical concepts in literary and cultural studies* (pp. 25–30). London: Routledge.

Becker, S. (2018, July 20). 'De hoogopgeleide witte man domineert de literatuur. Hoe erg is dat? *Trouw*.

Benjamin, W. (1928). *Ursprung des deutschen Trauerspiels*. Berlin: Suhrkamp Verlag Gmbh.

Berg, C. R. (2002). *Latino images in film. Stereotypes, subversion, resistance*. Austin: University of Texas Press.

Berry, D. (2011). The computational turn: Thinking about the digital humanities. *Culture Machine*, 12.

Besser, S., & Vaessens, T. (2013). Digital humanities: The next big thing? *Tijdschrift voor Nederlandse Taal- en Letterkunde*, 4, 191–204.

Best, S., & Marcus, S. (2009). Surface reading: An introduction. *Representations*, 108 (209), 1–21.

Blau, P. M. (1977). *Inequality and heterogeneity: A primitive theory of social structure*. Vol. 7. New York: Free Press.

Blühdorn, H. (2010). A semantic typology of sentence connectives. In T. Harden & E. Hentschel (Eds.), *40 Jahre Partikelforschung* (pp. 215–231). Tübingen/Stauffenburg: Stauffenburg Linguistik.

Bod, R. (2013). *Het einde van de geesteswetenschappen 1.0* (Oratiereeks; Vol. 475). Amsterdam: Vossiuspers UvA.

Bod, R. (2019). *Een wereld vol patronen: de geschiedenis van kennis*. Amsterdam: Promentheus.

Bohn, A., Buchta, C., Hornik, K., & Mair, P. (2014). Making friends and communicating on Facebook: implications for the access to social capital. *Social Networks*, 37, 29–41.

Bott, H. (1928). Observation of play activities a nursery school. *Genetic Psychology Monographs*, 4, 44–88.

Box-Steffensmeier, J. M., & Christenson, D. P. (2014). Making friends and communicating on Facebook: implications for the access to social capital. *Social Networks*, 36, 82–96.

Brandes, U. (2001). A faster algorithm for betweenness centrality. *Journal of Mathematical Sociology*, 25(2), 163–177. https://doi.org/10.1080/0022250X.2001.9990249.

Brouwers, T. (2001). Joost Zwagerman. *Lexicon van literaire werken*. Groningen: Wolters-Noordhoff / Antwerpen: Garant-Uitgevers.

Bucur, D. (2019). Gender homophily in online book networks. *Information Sciences*, 481, 229–243.

Butler, J. (1990). *Gender trouble*. New York: Routledge.

Campbell, D. T. (1965). *Ethnocentric and other altruistic motives*. Lincoln: University of Nebraska Press.

Campbell, J. (1949). *The hero with a thousand faces*. Princeton: Princeton University Press.

Cartwright, D., & Harary, F. (1956). Structural balance: A generalization of Heider's theory. *Psychological Review*, 63.

Cassin, B. (1994). Nos Grecs et leurs modernes. In *L'antiquité classique* (pp. 151–276).

Cecire, N. (2011). Introduction: Theory and the virtues of digital humanities. *Journal of Digital Humanities*, 1.

Clark, K., & Manning, C. D. (2016). Improving coreference resolution by learning entity-level distributed representations. *54th Annual Meeting of the Association for Computational Linguistics, ACL 2016 - Long Papers*, 2, 643–653. https://doi.org/10.18653/v1/p16-1061.

Clauset, A., Newman, M. E., & Moore, C. (2004). Finding community structure in very large networks. *Physical Review E*, 70(6).

Conference resolution. (n.d.). Retrieved July 10, 2018, from The Stanford Natural Language Processing Group website: https://nlp.stanford.edu/projects/coref.shtml

Conrad, J. (2010) *Heart of darkness*. New York: HarperCollins Publishers. (Original work published 1899).

Couperus, L. (1900). *De stille kracht*. Amsterdam: L.J. Veen.

Culler, J. (1983). *On deconstruction. Theory and criticism after structuralism*. London: Routledge.

Culpeper, J. (2000). A cognitive approach to characterization: Katherina in Shakespeare's the taming of the shrew. *Language and Literature*, 9(4), 291–316.

Culpeper, J. (2001). *Language and characterization: People in plays and other texts*. Harlow: Longman.

Da, N. Z. (2019). The computational case against computational literary studies. *Critical Inquiry*, 45(3), 601–639.

Davis, J. (1967). Clustering and structural balance in graphs. *Human Relations*, 20.

Davis, L. J. (1987). *Resisting novels: Ideology and fiction*. New York: Methuen.

de Winter, L. (2012). *VSV, of daden van onbaatzuchtigheid*. Amsterdam: De Bezige Bij.

Descombes, V. (1979). *Le même et l'Autre quarante-cinq ans de philosophie Française*. Paris: Editions de Minuit.

Destutt de Tracy, A. L. (2015). Éléments d'idéologie. Ligaran. (Original work published 1827).

Dijkstra, E. W. (1959). A note on two problems in connexion with graphs. *Numerische Mathematik*, *1*(1), 269–271. https://doi. org/10.1007/BF01386390

Doreian, P. (2011). Signed networks. In G. A. Barnett (Ed.), *Encyclopedia of social networks*. Thousand Oaks, CA: SAGE Publications.

Dorleijn, G. J., Grüttemeier, R., & Korthals Altes, E. J. (2007). *The autonomy of literature at the Fins de Siècles (1900 and 2000). A critical assessment.* (XXXII ed.). Leuven: Peeters.

Durkheim, E. (2013). *The division of labour in society*. London: Palgrave Macmillan. Original work published 1893.

Dyer, R. (1999). The role of stereotypes. In P. Marris & S. Thornham (Eds.), *Media studies: A reader* (2nd ed.). Edinburgh: Edinburgh University Press.

Eagleton, T. (1991). *Ideology*. London: Verso.

Easley, D., & Kleinberg, J. (2010). *Networks, crowds, and markets: Reasoning about a highly connected world*. Cambridge: Cambridge University Press.

Eder, J. (2008). *Die Figur im Film. Grundlagen der Figurenanalyse*. Marburg: Schüren Verlag.

Eder, J., Jannidis, F., & Schneider, R. (2010). Characters in fictional worlds: An introduction. In J. Eder, F. Jannidis, & R. Schneider (Eds.), *Characters in fictional worlds: understanding imaginary beings in literature, film, and other media* (pp. 3–64). Berlin: de Gruyter.

Elson, D. K., Dames, N., & McKeown, K. R. (2010). Extracting social networks from literary fiction. *Proceedings of the 48th Annual Meeting of the Association for Computational Linguistics, Proceedings of the Conference*, 138–147. Uppsala, Sweden.

Everett, M. G., & Borgatti, S. P. (2014). Networks containing negative ties. *Social Networks*, *38*(1), 111–120.

Eyers, T. (2017). *Speculative formalism: Literature, theory, and the critical present*. Evanston: Northwestern University Press.

Fagel, S. (2015). *De stijl van gewoon proza* (Doctoral thesis). Leiden: Leiden University Centre for the Arts in Society. Retrieved from: https://openaccess.leidenuniv.nl/handle/1887/31606

Fagel, S., Stukker, N., & van Andel, L. (2012). Hoe telbaar is stijl? Een kwantitatieve analyse van observatie en participatie in de stijl van Arnon Grunberg. *Nederlandse Letterkunde*, *17*(3), 178–203.

Felski, R. (2009). After suspicion. *Profession*, 28–35.

Felski, R. (2015). *The limits of critique*. Chicago: University of Chicago Press.

Fens, K., Jessurun d'Oliveira, H. U., & Oversteegen, J. J. (1962). Ter inleiding. *Merlyn*, *1*, 1–2.

Fleming, P. (2017). Tragedy, for example: Distant reading and exemplary reading (Moretti). *New Literary History*, *48*(3), 437–455.

Florack, R. (2010). Ethnic stereotypes as elements of character formation. In J. Eder, F. Jannidis, & R. Schneider (Eds.), *Characters in fictional worlds: understanding imaginary beings in literature, film, and other media* (pp. 478–505). Berlin: de Gruyter.

Forster, E. M. (1927). *Aspects of the novel*. New York: Harcourt, Brace and Company.

Fortunato, S., & Barthélemy, M. (2007). Resolution limit in community detection. *Proceedings of the National Academy of Sciences*, *104*, 36–41.

Freeman, L. C. (1978). Centrality in social networks conceptual clarification. *Social Networks*, *1*(3), 215–239. https://doi.org/10.1016/0378-8733(78)90021-7

Frow, J. (2014). *Character and person*. Oxford: Oxford University Press.

Galtung, J. (2010). Breaking the Cycle of Violent Conflict. Retrieved September 26, 2018, from Public Speech at University of California Television website: https://www.youtube.com/watch?v=16YiLqftppo

Gans, H. (1968). *People and plans: essays on urban problems and solutions*. New York: Basic.

Ge, T., Yeo, B. T. T., & Winkler, A. M. (2018). A brief overview of permutation testing with examples. Retrieved from Organization for Human Brain Mapping website: https://www.ohbmbrainmap-pingblog.com/blog/a-brief-overview-of-permutation-testing-with-examples

Genette, G. (1980). *Narrative discourse. An essay in method*. New York: Cornell University Press.

Girvan, M., & Newman, M. E. J. (2002). Community structure in social and biological networks. *Proceedings of the National Academy of Sciences*, *99*, 7821–7826.

Giuffre, K. (2013). *Communities and networks: Using social network analysis to rethink urban and community studies*. Cambridge: Polity Press.

Granovetter, M. S. (1973). The strength of weak ties. *American Journal of Sociology*, *78*(6), 1360–1380.

Greimas, A. J. (1966). *Sémantique structurale*. Paris: Presse universitaires de France.

Greimas, A. J., & Courtés, J. (1987). *Analytisch woordenboek van de semiotiek*. (K. Joosse & P. de Maat, Trans.) Tilburg: Tilburg University. (Original work published 1979).

Grayson, S., Wade, K., Meaney, G., & Greene, D. (2016). *The sense and sensibility of different sliding windows in constructing co-occurrence networks from literature BT - Computational history and data-driven humanities*. Cham: Springer International Publishing.

Gymnich, M. (2010). The gendering of fictional characters. In J. Eder, F. Jannidis, & R. Schneider (Eds.), *Characters in fictional worlds: understanding imaginary beings in literature, film, and other media* (pp. 506–524). Berlin: de Gruyter.

Hall, S. (1997). *Representation*. London: SAGE Publications.

Hamon, P. (1984). *Texte et idéologie: Valeurs, hiérarchies et évaluations dans l'œuvre littéraire.* Paris: PUF.

Heider, F. (1946). Attitudes and cognitive organization. *The Journal of Psychology, 21,* 107–112.

Hegel, G. W. F. (1832). *Phänomenologie des Geistes.* Berlin: Verlag von Duncker und Humblot. (Original work published 1807).

Heidbrink, H. (2010). Fictional characters in literary and media studies. In J. Eder, F. Jannidis, & R. Schneider (Eds.), *Characters in fictional worlds: understanding imaginary beings in literature, film, and other media* (pp. 67–110). Berlin: de Gruyter.

Herman, L., & Vervaeck, B. (2013). Ideology and narrative fiction. In P. Hühn et al. (Ed.), *The living handbook of narratology.* Retrieved from http://www.lhn.uni-hamburg.de/article/ideology-and-narrative-fiction

Hoggart, R. (1966). Literature and society. *The American Scholar, 35*(2), 277–289.

Homans, G. C. (1950). *The human group.* Harcourt: Brace.

Huff, P. (2012). *Niemand in de stad.* Amsterdam: De Bezige Bij.

Huff, P. (2018, July 25). Inderdaad, ik schreef een boek over het corps. Over jongens dus. *Trouw.*

Hughes, J. S. (2009). *Performance in a time of terror: Critical mimesis and the age of uncertainty* (Doctoral dissertation, The University of Manchester).

Irigaray, L. (1985). *This Sex Which Is Not One.* (C. Porter, Trans.) New York: Cornell University Press.

Jahn, M. (1996). Windows of focalization: Deconstructing and reconstructing a narratological concept. *Style, 30*(2), 241–267.

Jameson, F. (1981). *The political unconscious.* New York: Cornell University Press.

Jannidis, F. (2004). *Figur und person. Beitrag zu einer historischen narratologie.* Berlin: de Gruyter.

Jannidis, F. (2013). Character. In P. Hühn et al. (Ed.), *The living handbook of narratology.* Retrieved from http://www.lhn.uni-hamburg.de/article/character

Jayannavar, P., Agarwal, A., Ju, M., & Rambow, O. (2015). Validating literary theories using automatic social network extraction. *Proceedings of NAACL-HLT Fourth Workshop of Computational Linguistics for Literature,* 32–41. https://doi.org/10.3115/v1/w15-0704

Jockers, M., & Kirilloff, G. (2016). Understanding gender and character agency in the 19th Century novel. *Journal of Cultural Analytics.* DOI: 10.31235/osf.io/sw85m

Jockers, M. L. (2013). *Macroanalysis: Digital methods and literary history.* Illinois: University of Illinois Press.

Johnson, L. B. (1965). Speech at Howard University. Retrieved May 7, 2018, from https://www.apprenticeshipofbeinghuman.com/family-as-the-cornerstone-of-society/

Johnson, S. C. (1967). Hierarchical clustering schemes. *Psychometrica, 32,* 241–254.

Jouve, V. (2001). Poétique des valeurs. *Presses Universitaires de France,* 239–242.

Karinthy, F. (1929). *Everything is different*. Budapest: Atheneum Press.

Karsdorp, F. B., van Kranenburg, P., Meder, T., & van den Bosch, A. (2012). Casting a spell: Identification and ranking of actors in folktales. In F. Mambrini, M. Passarotti, & C. Sporleder (Eds.), *Proceedings of the Second Workshop on Annotation of Corpora for Research in het Humanities (ACRH-2)* (pp. 39–50). Lisbon: Edicoes Cilibri.

Kavanagh, J. H. (1995). Ideology. In F. Lentricchia & T. McLaughlin (Eds.), *Critical Terms for Literary Study* (2nd ed.). Chicago: University of Chicago Press.

Katz, T. (1995). Modernism, subjectivity, and narrative Form: Abstraction in "The Waves." *Narrative*, *3*(3), 232–251.

Kaur, M., & Singh, S. (2015). Analyzing negative ties in social networks: A survey. *Egyptian Informatics Journal*, *17*(1), 21–43.

Kernighan, B. W., & Lin, S. (1970). An efficient heuristic procedure for partitioning graphs. *The Bell System Technical Journal*, *49*(2), 291–307. https://doi.org/10.1002/j.1538-7305.1970.tb01770

Koch, T. (1991). *Literarische Menschendarstellung, Studien zu ihrer Theorie und Praxis*. Tübingen: Stauffenburg Verlag.

Korthals Altes, L. (1992). *Le salut par la fiction? Sens, valeurs et narrativité dans 'Le Roi des Aulnes' de Michel Tournier*. Amsterdam: Rodopi.

Koubaa, B. (2012). *De Brooklynclub*. Amsterdam: Singel Uitgeverijen.

Kraicer, E., & Piper, A. (2019). Social characters: The hierarchy of gender in contemporary English-language Fiction. *Journal of Cultural Analytics*. https://doi.org/10.31235/osf.io/4kwrg

Kristeva, J. (1969). *Séméiôtiké: recherches pour une sémanalyse*. Paris: Edition du Seuil.

Kristeva, J. (1986). From symbol to sign. In T. Moi (Ed.), *The Kristeva reader* (pp. 34–61). Oxford: Blackwell Publishing Ltd. Original work published 1970.

Lanser, S. (2013). Gender and narrative. In P. Hühn et al. (Ed.), *The living handbook of narratology*. Retrieved from http://www.lhn.uni-hamburg.de/article/character.

Larrain, J. (1979). *The concept of ideology*. London: Hutchinson of London.

Lazarsfeld, P. F., & Merton, R. K. (1954). Friendship as social process: A substantive and methodological analysis. In M. Berger (Ed.), *Freedom and control in modern society*. New York: Van Nostrand.

Lee, J. S., & Wong, T. S. (2016). Hierarchy of characters in the Chinese buddhist canon. *Proceedings of the Twenty-Ninth International Florida Artificial Intelligence Research Society Conference*.

Lee, J. S., & Yeung, C. Y. (2012). Extracting Networks of People and Places from Literary Texts. *Proceedings of the 26th Pacific Asia Conference on Language, Information, and Computation*.

Leerssen, J. (2012). Oral epic: the nation finds a voice. In T. Baycroft & D. Hopkin (Eds.), *Folklore and nationalism in Europe during the long nineteenth century* (pp. 11–26). Leiden.

Leinhardt, S. (1977). *Social networks: A developing paradigm*. New York: Academic Press.

Lippmann, W. (1922). *Public opinion*. Project Gutenberg eBook.

Lochner, L., & Moretti, E. (2004). The effect of education on crime: Evidence from prison inmates, arrests and self-reports. *American Economic Review, 94*, 155–189.

Luce, R. D., & Perry, A. D. (1949). A method of matrix analysis of group structure. *Psychometrika, 14*(2), 95–116.

Maccoby, E. (1998). *The two sexes: Growing up apart, coming together*. Cambridge: Harvard University Press.

Manovich, L. (n.d.). Cultural analytics lab. Retrieved from http:// lab.culturalanalytics.info/p/about.html

Mann, William, C., & Thompson, Sandra, A. (1988). Rhetorical structure theory: Toward a functional theory of text organization. *Text - Interdisciplinary Journal for the Study of Discourse, 8*(3), 243–281.

Marche, S. (2012). Literature is not data: Against digital humanities. *LA Review of Books, 28*.

Margolin, U. (1983). Characterization in narrative: Some theoretical prolegomena. *Neophilologus, 67*, 1–14.

Marsden, P. V. (1987). Core discussion networks of Americans. *American Sociological Review, 52*, 122–313.

Marsden, P. V. (1988). Homogeneity in confiding relations. *Social Networks, 10*, 57–76.

Marsden, P. V. (2011). Network clusters and communities. In G.A. Barnett (Ed.), *Encyclopedia of social networks*.

McPherson, M., Smith-Lovin, L., & Cook, J. M. (2001). Birds of a feather: Homophily in social networks. *Annual Review of Sociology, 27*(1), 415–444.

Meershoek, P. (2009, May 14). Zwarte vrouwen furieus over boek Vuijsje. *Het Parool*.

Meijer, M. (1996a). De verschrikkelijke sneeuwman: projectie, geweld en nieuwe mannelijkheid in het werk van Jan Wolkers. In R. Romkens & S. Dijkstra (Eds.), *Het omstreden slachtoffer: geweld van vrouwen en mannen* (pp. 39–58). Baarn: Ambo.

Meijer, M. (1996b). *In tekst gevat. Inleiding tot de kritiek van de representatie*. Amsterdam: Amsterdam University Press.

Meijer, M. (2011). Zwartheid in de witte verbeelding. In *Diversiteit* (pp. 47–74). Boedapest: Printart Press Kft.

Meijer, M., & van Alphen, E. (1991). *De canon onder vuur*. Amster
dam: Van Gennep.

Meister, J. C. (2011). Narratology. In P. Hühn et al. (Ed.), *The living handbook of narratology*. Retrieved from http://www.lhn. uni-hamburg.de/article/narratology

Milgram, S. (1967). The Small-World Problem. *Psychology Today, 1*(1), 61–67.

Minnaard, L. (2010). The spectacle of an intercultural love affair. Exoticm in Van Deyssel's Blank en Geel. *Journal of Dutch Literature, 1*(1), 74–90.

Mitchell, W. (1995). Representation. In F. Lentricchia & T. McLaughlin (Eds.), *Critical terms for literary study* (2nd ed.). Chicago: University of Chicago Press.

Moi, T. (2019). Character: three inquiries in literary studies. In T. Moi, R. Felski, & A. Anderson (Eds.), *Character: three inquiries in literary studies*. Chicago: University of Chicago Press.

Moreno, J. L. (1934). *Who shall survive: A new approach to the problem of human interrelations*. Washington: Nervous and Mental Disease Publishing Co.

Moretti, F. (2005). *Graphs, maps, trees: Abstract models of literary history*. London: Verso.

Moretti, F. (2013). *Distant reading*. London: Verso.

Moretti, F. (2017). Patterns and interpretation. *Pamphlets of the Stanford Literary Lab, 15*.

Morris, P. (2003). *The Bakhtin reader: Selected writings of Bakhtin, Medvedev, Voloshinov*. London: Hodder Arnold Publication.

Nelles, W. (1990). Getting focalization into focus. *Poetics Today, 11*(2), 365–382.

Nescio. (2018). *De Uitvreter, Titaantjes, Dichtertje*. Amsterdam: Nijgh & van Ditmar. Original work published 1911.

Newman, M. E. J. (2001). Scientific collaboration networks. II. Shortest paths, weighted networks, and centrality. *Physical Review E, 64*(1). https://doi.org/10.1103/PhysRevE.64.016132

Nyhan, J., Terras, M., & Vanhoutte, E. (2013). Introduction. In M. Terras, J. Nyhan, & E. Vanhoutte (Eds.), *Defining Digital Humanities. A Reader* (pp. 1–10). Surrey: Ashgate.

Opsahl, T., Agneessens, F., & Skvoretz, J. (2010). Node centrality in weighted networks: Generalizing degree and shortest paths. *Social Networks, 32*(3), 245–251. https://doi.org/10.1016/j.socnet.2010.03.006

Oversteegen, J. J. (1968). Analyse en oordeel. *Merlyn, 3*, 161–180.

Page, L., Brin, S., Motwani, R., & Winograd, T. (1999). *The PageRank Citation Ranking: Bringing Order to the Web*. Retrieved from http://ilpubs.stanford.edu:8090/422/

Palmer, A. (2004). *Fictional minds*. Lincoln: University of Nebraska Press.

Pattynama, P. (1994). Oorden en woorden. Over rassenvermenging, interetniciteit, en een Indisch meisje. *Tijdschrift Voor Vrouwenstudies, 15*(1), 30–45.

Pattynama, P. (1998). Secrets and danger: Interracial sexuality in Louis Couperus's the hidden force and Dutch colonial culture around 1900'. In J. Clancy-Smith & F. Gouda (Eds.), *Domesticating the empire. Race, gender, and family life in French and Dutch colonialism* (pp. 84–107). London: University Press of Virginia.

Pavis, P. (2004). *Dictionnaire du théâtre*. Paris: Armand Colin.

Peeters, C. (2014, July 28). Waarom jij, lezer, echt geen lege huls bent. *Vrij Nederland*.

Peters, A. (2018, October 12). Goed & slecht: Drabbige drek. *De Volkskrant*.

Phelan, J. (1989). *Reading people, reading plots: Character, progression, and the interpretation of narrative*. Chicago: University of Chicago Press.

Pieterse, S. (2014, July 9). De emancipatie van de lezer. *NY*.

Pieterse, S., & Vitse, S. (2019). Mannelijkheid in de Nederlandse literatuur. *Nederlandse Letterkunde, 24*(2), 155–162.

Piper, A. (2016). There will be numbers. *Journal of Cultural Analytics*.

Piper, A. (2018). *Enumerations*. Chicago: University of Chicago Press.

Pitkin, H. F. (1967). *The concept of representation*. Berkeley, CA: University of California Press.

Plato. (1943). *The republic*. New York: Books, Inc. (Original work published c. 375 BC).

Porter, M. A., Onnela, J.-P., & Mucha, P. J. (2009). Communities in Networks. *Notices of the American Mathematical Society, 56*(9), 1082–1097.

Prince, G. (2005). On a postcolonial narratology. In J. Phelan & P. Rabinowitz (Eds.), *A companion to carrative theory* (pp. 372–381). Oxford: Blackwell Publishing Inc.

Prokhorenkova, O. L., Prałat, P., & Raigorodskii, A. (2016). Modularity of complex networks models. In A. Bonato, F. C. Graham, & P. Prałat (Eds.), *Algorithms and Models for the Web Graph: 13th International Workshop* (pp. 115–126). Montreal: Springer International Publishing.

Propp, V. (1968). *Morphology of the folktale* (2nd, Ed.; L. Scott, Trans.). Austin: University of Texas Press. (Original work published 1928).

Ramdas, A. (1997, March 14). Moedwil en kwade trouw bij blanke schrijvers. Niemand heeft oog voor het vreemde. *NRC Handelsblad*. Retrieved from https://www.nrc.nl/nieuws/1997/03/14/ moedwil-en-kwade-trouw-bij-blanke-schrijvers-niemand-7346072-a1345038

Ramsay, S. (2016). *Who's in and who's out* (pp. 255-258). Routledge.

Ramsay, S. (2011b). *Reading machines. Towards an algorithmic criticism*. Urbana: University of Illinois Press.

Ramsay, S. (2011c). Who's In and Who's Out. Retrieved from http://lenz.unl.edu/papers/2011/01/08/%0Awhos-in-and-whos-out.html

Ramsay, S., & Rockwell, G. (2012). Developing things: Notes toward an epistemology of building in the digital humanities. In M. K. Gold (Ed.), Debates in the Digital Humanities. Minneapolis, MN: University of Minnesota Press.

Reicher, M. E. (2010). The ontology of fictional character. In J. Eder, F. Jannidis, & R. Schneider (Eds.), Characters in fictional worlds: understanding imaginary beings in literature, film, and other media (pp. 111–133). Berlin: de Gruyter.

Rice, S. A. (1927). The identification of blocs in small political bodies. American Political Science Review, 21, 619–627.

Ricoeur, P. (1979). Freud and philosophy: An essay on interpretation. New Haven: Yale University Press.

Rimmon-Kenan, S. (1983). Narrative fiction: Contemporary poetics. London: Routledge.

Rombout, R. (2012). Kunstroof. Antwerpen: van Halewyck. Rosenthal, J. (2017). Introduction: Narrative against data. Genre, 50(1), 1–18.

Ross, S. (2014). In praise of overstating the case: A review of Franco Moretti, distant reading. Digital Humanities Quarterly, 8(1).

Said, E. (1978). Orientalism. New York: Pantheon Books.

Said, E. (1993). Culture and imperialism. London: Chatto & Windus.

Scheinfeldt, T. (2010). Why digital humanities is "Nice." Retrieved from Found History website: https://foundhistory.org/2010/05/ why-digital-humanities-is-nice/

Schneider, R. (2000). *Grundriß zur kognitiven Theorie der Figurenrezeption am Beispiel des viktorianischen Romans*.Tübingen: Stauffenburg Verlag.

Schriver, L. (2016, September 13). Lionel Shriver's full speech:'I hope the concept of cultural appropriation is a passing fad. *The Guardian*.

Schweinitz, J. (2010). Stereotypes and the narratological analysis of film characters. In J. Eder, F. Jannidis, & R. Schneider (Eds.), *Characters in fictional worlds: understanding imaginary beings in literature, film, and other media* (pp. 276–289). Berlin: de Gruyter.

Scott, J. (2000). *Social network analysis: A handbook*. London: SAGE Publications.

Seidel, M.-D. L. (2011). Network clusters and communities. In *Encyclopedia of social networks* (pp. 598–599). London: SAGE Publications.

Sevillano, V., & Fiske, S. (2016). Animals as social objects: Groups, stereotypes, and intergroup threats. *European Psychologist, 21*.

Simmel, G. (1967). *Een keuze uit het werk van George Simmel* (H. Israëls, Trans.). Deventer: Van Loghum Slaterus.

Simmel, G. (1971). Group expansion and the development of individuality. In *On individuality and social forms*. Chicago: The University of Chicago Press. (Original work published 1908).

Sintobin, T. (2006). 'Schamel stuk mens'? Handicap in regionale literatuur uit de eerste helft van de twintigste eeuw. *Tijdschrift voor Nederlandse Taal- en Letterkunde, 122*(1), 309-327.

Situngkir, H., & Khanafiah, D. (2004). *Social balance theory: Revisiting Heider's balance theory for many agents*. Retrieved from http://www.au.af.mil/au/awc/awcgate/lanl/ social_balance_0405041.pdf

Smeets, R. (2017). Finding characters: An evaluation of named entity recognition tools for Dutch literary fiction. *European Alliance for Digital Humanities (EADH) Day*. Rome, Italy.

Smeets, R. (2019). Tussen de regels. Representatie-kritiek in de Digital Humanities. *Tijdschrift voor Nederlandse Taal- en Letterkunde, 135*(4), 373–383.

Smeets, R., & Sanders, E. (2018). Character centrality in present-day Dutch literary fiction. *Digital Humanities Benelux*. Amsterdam, The Netherlands.

Smeets, R., & Weenink, M. (2018). Opposite-sex relations in present-day Dutch literature. A quantitative approach to character representations. *Digital Humanities Budapest*. Budapest (Hungary).

Smeets, R., Sanders, E., & van den Bosch, A. (2019). Character centrality in present-day Dutch literary fiction. *Digital Humanities Benelux*, *1*, 71–90.

Smits, J., Ultee, W., & Lammers, J. (2000). More or less educational homogamy? A test of different versions of modernization theory using cross-temporal evidence for 60 countries. *American Sociological Review*, *65*, 781–788.

So, R. J., Long, H., & Zhu, Y. (2019). Race, Writing, and Computation: Racial Difference and the US Novel, 1880-2000. *Journal of Cultural Analytics*.

Sötemann, A. L. (1966). *De structuur van Max Havelaar. Bijdrage tot het onderzoek naar de interpretatie en evaluatie van de roman*. Groningen: Wolters-Noordhoff.

Stiller, J., Nettle, D., & Dunbar, R. I. M. (2003). The small world of Shakespeare's plays. *Human Nature*, *14*(4), 397–408.

Stronks, E. (2013). De afstand tussen close en distant. Methoden en vraagstellingen in computationeel letterkundig onderzoek. *Tijdschrift voor Nederlandse Taal- en Letterkunde*, *129*(4), 17–26.

Suleiman, S. R. (1983). *Authoritarian fictions: The ideological novel as a literary genre*. Princeton: Princeton University Press.

't Hart, K. (2019). Lezen met een zaklantaarn. *De Gids*, *2*, 24–27.

Tajfel, H., & Turner, J. C. (1979). An integrative theory of intergroup conflict. In W. G. Austin & S. Worchel (Eds.), *The social psychology of intergroup relations. Monterey* (pp. 33–47). Monterey: Brooks/Cole.

Tönnies, F. (2005). *Gemeinschaft und gesellschaft*. Darmstadt: Wissenschaftliche Buchgesellschaft. Original work published 1887.

Underwood, T. (2017). A genealogy of distant reading. *Digital Humanities Quarterly*, *11*(2).

Underwood, T. (2019). *Distant horizons: Digital evidence and literary change*. Chicago: University of Chicago Press.

Underwood, T., Bamman, D., & Lee, S. (2018). The transformation of gender in English language fiction. *Journal of Cultural Analytics*. DOI: 10.31235/osf.io/fr9bk

Vala, H., Jurgens, D., Piper, A., & Ruths, D. (2015). Mr. Bennet, his coachman, and the Archbishop walk into a bar but only one of them gets recognized: On the Difficulty of detecting characters in literary texts. *Proceedings of the 2015 Conference on Empirical Methods in Natural Language Processing*, 769–774. Lisbon, Portugal: Association for Computational Linguistics.

van Boven, E., & Dorleijn, G. (2013). *Literair mechaniek*. Bussum: Coutinho.

van Dalen-Oskam, K. (2012). *De stijl van R*. Amsterdam: Huygens ING.

van Keulen, M. (2012). *Liefde heeft geen hersens*. Amsterdam: Atlas.

van der Aa, I. (2012). *De lichtekooi van loven*. Amsterdam: De Geus.

van de Camp, M., & van den Bosch, A. (2012). The socialist network. *Decision Support Systems*, *53*(4), 761–769.

van der Deijl, L. (2015). De semiotiek van het algoritme. *Vooys, 33*(2).

van der Deijl, L. (2016). *Naar een sociologie van de verbeelding. Crowdsourcing als hermeneutisch experiment.* (Master Thesis). Utrecht: Utrecht University.

van der Deijl, L., Pieterse, S., Prinse, M., & Smeets, R. (2016). Mapping the demographic landscape of characters in recent Dutch prose: A quantitative approach to literary representation. *Journal of Dutch Literature, 7*(1), 20–42.

van der Deijl, L., & Smeets, R. (2018). Tussen close en distant. Personage-hiërarchieën in Peter Buwalda's Bonita Avenue. *Tijdschrift voor Nederlandse Taal- en Letterkunde, 134*(2), 123–145.

van der Sanden, G. (2019, June 27). Woke, woker, wokest – het is geen wedstrijd. *Vrij Nederland.*

van Uden, H., & van der Meulen, M. (2019). "Fucking hoer, gore kankerpatiënt": cursing in modern Dutch literature.*T.W.I.S.T. Conference.* Leiden.

van Rooden, A. (2019). *Literature, autonomy and commitment.* London: Bloomsbury Academic.

Vanhoutte, E. (2013). The gates of hell: History and definition of Digital | Humanities | Computing. In M. Terras, J. Nyhan, & E. Vanhoutte (Eds.), *Defining digital humanities. A reader.* Surrey: Ashgate.

Verbrugge, L. M. (1977). The structure of adult friendship choices. *Social Forces, 56,* 576–597.

Vitse, S. (2014). Ideologiekritiek na het postmodernisme. *Cahier Voor Literatuurwetenschap, 6,* 147–165.

Volker, B., & Smeets, R. (2019). Imagined social structures: Mirrors or alternatives? A comparison between networks of characters in contemporary Dutch literature and networks of the population in the Netherlands. *Poetics,* (July), 101379. https://doi.org/10.1016/j.poetic.2019.101379

Voloshinov, V. (2003). Marxism and the philosophy of language. In Pam Morris (Ed.), *The Bakhtin reader: Selected writings of Bakhtin, Medvedev, Voloshinov.* London: Hodder Arnold Publication. Original work published 1929.

Vuijsje, R. (2008). *Alleen maar nette mensen.* Amsterdam: Nijgh & Van Ditmar.

Wade, K., & Grayson, S. (2016). Windows on Waverley: exploring the effect of variations in the construction of literary social networks. *Digital Humanities Congress.* Sheffield, United Kingdom.

Weiss, R. S., & Jacobsen, E. (1955). A method for the analysis of the structure of complex organizations. *American Sociological Review, 20,* 661–668.

Wieringa, T. (2012). *Dit zijn de namen.* Amsterdam: De Bezige Bij.

Wieringa, T. (2017). *De heilige Rita.* Amsterdam: De Bezige Bij.

Williams, R. (1977). *Marxism and literature.* Oxford: Oxford University Press.

Woloch, A. (2003). *The one vs. the many: Minor characters and the space of the protagonist in the novel.* Princeton: Princeton University Press.

Woolf, V. (1929). *A room of one's own*. Retrieved from http://gutenberg.net.au/ebooks02/0200791.txt

Zadeh, B. Q., & Handschuh, S. (2014). Evaluation of technology term recognition with random indexing. *Proceedings of 9th International Conference on Language Resources and Evaluation*, 4027–4032. Reykjavik, Iceland: European Language Resources Association.

Zagarell, S. (1988). Narrative of community: The identification of a genre. *Signs*, *13*(3), 498–527.

Zwagerman, J. (1994). *De buitenvrouw*. Amsterdam: Arbeiderspers. Zwagerman, J. (1997, March 28). Literatuur als inloopcentrum. *NRC Handelsblad*.